POPULATION PUZZLE

Boom or Bust?

POPULATION PUZZLE

Boom or Bust?

Edited by
Laura E. Huggins
and
Hanna Skandera

HOOVER INSTITUTION PRESS

Stanford University   Stanford, California

www.hoover.org

Hoover Institution Press Publication No. 529

First printing, 2004
11 10 09 08 07 06 05 04   9 8 7 6 5 4 3 2 1

Manufactured in the United States of America
The paper used in this publication meets the minimum requirements of the American National Standard for Information Sciences—Permanence of Paper for Printed Library Materials, ANSI Z39.48–1992.

Library of Congress Cataloging-in-Publication Data
Population puzzle : boom or bust? / edited by Laura E. Huggins and Hanna Skandera.
       p. cm. — (Hoover Institution Press publication ; no. 529)
    Includes bibliographical references and index.
    ISBN 0-8179-4532-6 (alk. paper)
    1.   Overpopulation. 2. Population. 3. Quality of life. I. Huggins, Laura E., 1976– II. Skandera, Hanna, 1973– III. Series.
HB871.P654 2004
304.6′2 — dc22   2004004532

Contents

Figures and Tables

PART IV

PART VI

Foreword

At least since Malthus's population essay in 1798, there has been great interest and concern among many about population growth and its economic, social, and environmental effects. Some scholars have argued over the decades that the world would experience widespread disaster and starvation because of rising population rates.

Yet much of the world has quietly undergone a demographic transition. Almost half the countries of the world have population birthrates that are below replacement. Although families are having fewer and fewer children, average life expectancy is growing. Thus young working adults make up a declining share of the total population, and senior citizens account for a growing share. This transition raises major questions relating to intergenerational transfer burdens, such as a "pay as you go" social security system. This leads to policy questions relating to whether a decline in birthrates will make it easier for people to turn their attention from the numbers to the qualities of humankind.

Such questions have inspired several fellows at the Hoover Institution, notably, Gary Becker, Milton Friedman, and George Shultz, to advocate a research initiative on a topic of such prominent importance. The goal of this effort is to present pertinent facts surrounding the population debate that will add to the debate a constructive voice, with positive policy messages for societal consideration.

Population Puzzle: Boom or Bust? provides an overview of the principal issues surrounding world population growth and conveys the various viewpoints of the population debate with the goal of giving those not familiar with the prevailing literature an idea of the differing views. After exploring the many perspectives of the debate, the reader is left to evaluate the population bomb hypothesis and what it might mean for the future of humanity.

I hasten to thank Bill Draper for his support of this project, in addition to his wise counsel as a longtime member of Hoover's Board of Overseers. We could not have launched this project without his generous backing. I also acknowledge another overseer and supporter, Bill Edwards, who for a long time has encouraged me to think about population as an important topic for the Institution to investigate.

Population Puzzle: Boom or Bust? has allowed us to get our own arms around this issue in terms of yielding a first step forward in shaping our future efforts. We hope that this book will provide others with a basis for assessing the population conundrum.

> John Raisian
> Director
> Hoover Institution

Acknowledgments

For his idea entrepreneurship and encouragement along the way, we owe a debt of thanks to John Raisian, director of the Hoover Institution. In addition, many scholars have helped us grapple with the immense and often complex issues surrounding the population debate. Two scholars stand out: Gary S. Becker encouraged us to look at the bigger picture while staying focused; Nicholas Eberstadt was kind enough to allow us to tap into his endless store of knowledge. Thanks also to Douglass C. North and Bjørn Lomborg for their academic input. We also wish to extend appreciation to the Hoover Press, Lolita Guevarra, and Matt Reed for their assistance. We are fortunate to have had the opportunity to have worked with such exceptional individuals. Finally we wish to thank Matt and Elizabeth Huggins and Carol and Harry Skandera for providing their love and encouragement.

Introduction

According to pollsters, the belief that the earth is overpopulated pervades American thought. This mind-set often assumes the following: the earth has reached or has exceeded its carrying capacity; we are running out of resources; the standard of living is dropping over time; and if population remains unchecked, the earth and its inhabitants are on a collision course. Others assert a seemingly opposing view: quality of life is improving over time; the prices of resources are dropping; the standard of living is rising; average life expectancy is higher than in any previous era; and mortality rates are lower than ever before. These differing views are the basis for the population conundrum and the catalyst for producing this collection of readings, which explore the various angles of the population debate.

The purpose of this primer is to provide an overview of the issues surrounding world population growth. We highlight that our intent is not to cover all the intricacies of the subject but rather to give nonexperts an idea of what the population debate is all about. Some of the questions we address are as follows: Who are the "experts" who have framed the debate? What are the ethical issues related to population policy? What has happened to our resources and quality of life over time? Who should decide what is best when it comes to population policy? And, how accurate have our historical predictions been?

The issue of world population frequently grabs front-page headlines, but the articles often convey differing conclusions. One account may address the fears of overpopulation while another may point to the recent dearth in births. To date, changes in population have been most significant in the twentieth century. Since 1900, world population has more than tripled in size, owing in part to a significant increase in average life expectancy. At the same time, the dramatic decline in birthrates and significant shifts in population distribution are more striking than in any other era. Moreover, the world has experienced extraordinary improvements in technology, health, education, and agriculture. But what do these changes mean for the future of humanity?

Differing views on population growth and its effect have surfaced throughout the ages. In the sixth century B.C., Confucius argued that population growth might reduce output per worker and lower the living standards of the masses. Aristotle (384–322 B.C.) cautioned that populations could strip their resource base and that poverty and social unrest would follow. The Romans (63 B.C.–A.D. 14) instituted laws encouraging people to marry early and produce offspring, offering tax relief for those who went along. In the late eighteenth century, Thomas Malthus became renowned for his pessimistic view of humanity, arguing that unless family size were regulated, famine would become a global epidemic and eventually lead to humankind's demise.

Even in the past century, the pendulum of opinion on population has swung back and forth several times. In the 1930s, for example, the threat of underpopulation was of primary concern for those writing on the issue. By the 1940s, it became fashionable to emphasize the negative consequences of overpopulation. In 1945 Kingsley Davis wrote, "Viewed in the long-run, earth's population has been like a long, thin powder fuse that burns slowly and haltingly until it finally reaches the charge and explodes."

The age-old debate of population once again became front-page news in 1968 when Paul R. Ehrlich, Bing Professor of Population Studies at Stanford University, published his environmental best-seller *The Population Bomb*. Simultaneously, a group of international scientists, referred to as the Club of Rome, called for extraordinary political measures in relation to population. In 1972, these scientists released their "Limits to Growth" study, declaring that in a world of finite resources, unlimited economic expansion and prosperity are impossible to pursue. *The Population Bomb* and the "Limits to Growth" report proved successful in drawing worldwide attention to the "inevitable crisis" of overpopulation.

The catalyst of the current population debate began in the early 1980s and extends in varying degrees to the present day. The design of *Population Puzzle: Boom or Bust?* stems from what is considered by many to be the most heated discussion of the twentieth century: the Simon-Ehrlich debate—a continual clash between ecological and economic points of view, which will be repeatedly visited throughout this book.

In 1980, Paul Ehrlich and Julian Simon (an economist and professor of business administration at the University of Maryland) made a public wager regarding population and its impact. Simon, feeling the need to respond to what he considered false predictions, penned his own view of the population dilemma, "Resources, Population, Environment: An Oversupply of False Bad News" in *Science* (June 27, 1980). Ehrlich replied to Simon, claiming that his work was error-laden. Soon after, Simon challenged Ehrlich to put his money where his mouth was. Simon, nicknamed "the doomslayer," told Ehrlich and all other "doomsayers and catastrophists" that they could name their own terms, select any raw materials they wanted, and pick any date in the future (more than a year away), and he would bet that the commodity's price would be lower than what it was at the time of the wager. Ehrlich responded to the challenge.

Ehrlich and his colleagues chose five metals (chrome, copper, nickel, tin, and tungsten) and hypothetically purchased $200 worth of each at the 1980 price for a total of $1,000. September 29, 1990, was designated the payoff day. If the inflation-adjusted combined prices of the metals increased, Simon would pay Ehrlich the combined difference; if the prices decreased, Ehrlich would pay Simon.

Over the next ten years, the world's population grew by more than 800 million, the largest increase in one decade to that date. But the combined prices of the metals fell in constant 1980 dollars. According to Ehrlich, the combined prices of the metals decreased in part because of the doubling of world oil prices in 1979 and a recession in the first half of the decade that slowed demand for industrial metals. (For more on Ehrlich's explanation of why the bet was flawed, see www.Stanford.edu/group/CCB/Staff/paul.htm.) Nevertheless, in 1990, Paul Ehrlich mailed Julian Simon a check in the amount of $576.07, based on a panel verdict by scientists chosen by the president of the National Academy of Sciences.

Despite these seemingly suggestive results, the larger population debate continues. In October 1999, world population reached the 6 billion mark—once again making front-page news. A few of the headlines read as follows: "Six Billion Strong: World Population Growing Astronomically"

(*ABC News*), "Six Billion and Counting—but Slower" (*Washington Post*), and "Six Billion of Us: Boo? Hooray?" ("The Global Citizen," a weekly column of the Sustainability Institute). More specifically, recent stories have focused on the below-replacement birthrates in developed nations and the global epidemic of AIDS.

Not surprisingly, the essence of the population debate has not changed. At its foundation, the debate is about the race between human population and human ingenuity. The seemingly pessimistic view (often referred to as neo-Malthusian) argues the merits of government intervention—progress by design. The optimistic countermovement (neoinstitutionalist) often places its faith in free market principles and the rule of law—progress "laissez faire" style. This book explores these differing views and allows the reader to put together the pieces of the population puzzle.

Overview

*P*opulation Puzzle: Boom or Bust? is a primer of collected readings that provides an overview of the major issues concerning world population growth, with special consideration given to the impact of population growth on the United States. Excerpts from magazines, scholarly journals, newspapers, government reports, think tank studies, and books offer the reader a chance to learn about the contrasting viewpoints and policy perspectives surrounding population issues. Each part is prefaced with a brief overview and introduction. General facts and figures are incorporated throughout the chapters to give the reader a greater understanding of the larger picture. Moreover, we have often included a supplementary snapshot—a specific example that captures the issue at hand. Because of the nature of this book, which consists of excerpts from an array of sources, we suggest that the reader visit the original article for a full listing of reference information.

Part 1 provides the evolution of the "neo-Malthusian" and "neoinstitutional" arguments. The popular debate between Paul Ehrlich and Julian Simon is highlighted and used as a foundation for present-day population debates that unfold in the chapters that follow. The fundamental ethical issues and dividing lines relating to population are also examined.

Providing both the neo-Malthusian and neoinstitutional perspectives, parts 2 and 3 address the effect of population growth on water, food, pollution and climate change, energy, and land; and the differing views on the relationship between population and fertility and mortality rates, public health, migration, and war and violence.

Part 4, "Population and Prosperity," explores the arguments of prosperity by "design" and prosperity "laissez faire" style. The prosperity by design argument prescribes consistent government intervention to assist in managing overpopulation. The government-imposed "solutions" address the relationship between women and fertility, education, poverty, and population. The laissez faire perspective emphasizes the effect of institutional structures on population. Institutions, such as secure property rights and the rule of law, help determine what opportunities individuals have to sustain themselves and their families, and therefore affect population size and sustainability. This section also examines how technological change and globalization can promote economic growth and advance human welfare.

Part 5 discusses important jurisdictional questions that arise regarding reproduction: Do governments have the right or the duty to preside over the reproductive process and, if so, for what purposes, to what extent, and at what price? Are direct controls on population growth effective? Should the U.S. government provide funds for family planning in the United States and abroad? Or, are reproductive decisions personal and therefore a private and protected right? Who should decide?

Part 6 tackles the pitfalls of predictions and raises important questions: Do demographers fail to make clear the uncertainty about the demographic future, have estimates been formed without adequate consideration of all of the data, and can population projections be improved?

Finally, the book concludes with a piece that addresses three primary factors behind recent changes in academic arguments today: (1) the influence of new statistical data on population growth, (2) human rights abuses committed in the name of population control, and (3) theoretical and empirical research on the actual results of population growth. After exploring the many pieces of the population debate, we hope the reader is left with a clearer picture of the population puzzle.

Man's March to "The Summit"

The Conservationist's Lament

The world is finite
Resources are scarce
Things are bad
And will be worse
Coal is burnt
And gas exploded
Forests cut
And soils eroded
Wells are drying
Air's polluted
Dust is blowing
Trees uprooted
Oil is going
Ores depleted
Drains receive
What is excreted
Land is sinking
Seas are rising
Man is far
Too enterprising
Fire will rage
With man to fan it
Soon we'll have
A plundered planet
People breed
Like fertile rabbits
People have
Disgusting habits

moral

The evolutionary plan
Went astray
By evolving Man

The Technologist's Reply

Man's potential
Is quite terrific
You can't go back
To the Neolithic
The cream is there
For us to skim it
Knowledge is power
And the sky's the limit
Every mouth
Has hands to feed it
Food is found
When people need it
All we need
Is found in granite
Once we have
The men to plan it
Yeast and algae
Give us meat
Soil is almost
Obsolete
Man can grow
To pastures greener
Till all the earth
Is Pasadena

moral

Man's a nuisance
Man's a crackpot
But only man
Can hit the jackpot

Kenneth Boulding
Population Bulletin (1955)

BEGINNINGS

PART I: QUICK FACTS

"Everybody understands that the population explosion is going to come to an end. What they don't know is whether it's going to come to an end primarily because we humanely limit births or because we let nature have her way and the death rate goes way up."

Paul R. Ehrlich, *The Population Bomb* (1968)

"The material conditions of life will continue to get better for most people, in most countries, most of the time, indefinitely. Within a century or two, all nations and most of humanity will be at or above today's Western living standards."

Julian Simon, *Hoodwinking the Nation* (1999)

- In 2003, world population was more than 6.3 billion, increasing more than 150 percent over the last fifty years. The population of the United States totaled more than 291 million, having increased nearly 100 percent over the last fifty years.

  U.S. Bureau of the Census (2003; see figure 1.1).

- The global rate of population growth has decreased over the last three decades. In 1970, the global rate of growth was 2.1 percent a year; in 2002, it was approximately 1.3 percent (roughly 78 million people annually).

  U.S. Bureau of the Census (2003)

- In 2001, 29.8 percent of the world's population was under the age of fifteen and 7.0 percent of the world's population was age sixty-five and above. In the United States, 21.7 percent of the population was under the age of fifteen and 12.3 percent was age sixty-five and above.

  United Nations Development Programme (2003)

- In 2002, worldwide life expectancy at birth was sixty-seven years, having increased by twenty-two years since 1950.

  Population Reference Bureau (2002)

- In 2003, the United States had the third largest population in the world with 292 million; China was ranked first with nearly 1.3 billion, and India was ranked second with more than one billion.

  Population Reference Bureau (2003; see table 1.1).

FIGURE 1.1.　World Population

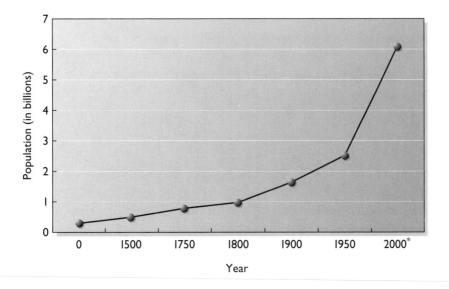

Source: Population Division of the Department of Economic and Social Affairs of the United Nations Secretariat (1999). *The World at Six Billion.* New York: United Nations. Available via the Internet: http://www.un.org/esa/population/publications/sixbillion/sixbilpart1.pdf.

*Time series not drawn to scale.

TABLE 1.1.   World's Largest Countries

World's Largest Countries in 2003			World's Largest Countries in 2050		
Rank	*Country*	*Population (Millions)*	*Rank*	*Country*	*Population (Millions)*
1	China	1,289	1	India	1,628
2	India	1,069	2	China	1,394
3	United States	292	3	United States	422
4	Indonesia	220	4	Pakistan	349
5	Brazil	176	5	Indonesia	316
6	Pakistan	149	6	Nigeria	307
7	Bangladesh	147	7	Bangladesh	255
8	Russia	146	8	Brazil	221
9	Nigeria	134	9	Congo, Dem. Rep. of	181
10	Japan	128	10	Ethiopia	173
11	Mexico	105	11	Mexico	153
12	Germany	83	12	Philippines	133
13	Philippines	82	13	Egypt	127
14	Vietnam	81	14	Russia	119
15	Egypt	72	15	Vietnam	117
16	Turkey	71	16	Japan	101
17	Ethiopia	71	17	Turkey	98
18	Iran	67	18	Iran	96
19	Thailand	63	19	Sudan	84
20	France	60	20	Uganda	82

Source: Copyright ©2003 Population Reference Bureau. Available via the Internet: http://www.prb.org/Template.cfm?Section...ts/2003_World_Population_Data_Sheet.htm.

INTRODUCTION

Beginnings

As in most cases, context is everything. According to a September 1998 public opinion survey by RAND, the vast majority of Americans (72 percent) think that population is a critical issue. It is apparent, however, that the knowledge base of the general populace is limited. For example, while most know that total world population has grown over time, few have a sense of population size or rates of growth. In 1998, for instance, only 14 percent of those surveyed were able to identify population as being in the 5 to 6 billion range (in 1998, population was estimated at 5.9 billion). Moreover, 29 percent of those surveyed believed the world's population would double in ten years or less; another 19 percent believed it would double in eleven to twenty years. (According to U.N. estimates at the time, it would take at least fifty years.) A mere 10 percent thought it would take fifty years or more for the world population to double (the more accurate estimate). These numbers suggest that much of the American public is uninformed when it comes to population and related issues.

Chapters 1 and 2 provide a framework for the reader—the origins of the population debate and the underlying values and ethical dilemmas—without which it would be nearly impossible to understand the nature of the debate. The evolutionary divide between the neo-Malthusian and institutionalist mind-sets emerges, painting a literal and theoretical picture and enabling the reader to grasp the differing suppositions behind the population conundrum.

The first chapter provides the historical back and forth of the contextual divide. Ann Wolfgram and Maria Aguirre's essay, "Population, Resources, and Environment: A Survey of the Debate," introduces the complexity of the debate. The ordering of the various pieces is intentional and significant. Each essay is paired with another; both capture the differing perspectives of their respective eras. Thomas Malthus ("An Essay on the Principle of Population") is paired with Karl Marx, Paul R. Ehrlich with Julian Simon, and finally, Lester R. Brown, Gary Gardner, and Brian Halweil with Nicholas Eberstadt. All present classic arguments and familiarize the reader with some of the more recognized population scholars and their views.

In chapter 2, J. Philip Wogaman introduces the idea that the population issue is not merely "practical or technical." He explains that at nearly every level and from every angle, values are at stake. Joel E. Cohen, Garrett Hardin, and Julian Simon attempt to define some of these values and propose differing views on how best to rank them. The pieces in this chapter allow the reader to wrestle with his or her own population paradigm. What we value dictates our decision-making and ultimately our life's pursuits and priorities. Our perceptions and views regarding population are no exception to this truth.

Chapter One

FRAMING THE DEBATE

*Will humankind's propensity to multiply exhaust
the earth's ability to provide?*

Population, Resources, and Environment: A Survey of the Debate

Ann F. Wolfgram and Maria Sophia Aguirre

This selection was excerpted from "Population, Resources, and Environment: A Survey of the Debate" (available online at http://arts-sciences.cua.edu/econ/faculty/aguirre/ Harvard.doc).

FRAMING THE DEBATE

It is currently estimated that there is, or there will be shortly, 6 billion humans inhabiting the planet earth. The theme of population, and more specifically, overpopulation has been in the popular mind for the last thirty years or more. Schools, national governments, international legislative bodies, interest groups, and the media have all but ensured that the public sees the issue of population as a problem, and increasingly, in reference to natural resources and the environment. At the heart of the population-resources-environment debate lies the question: can the earth sustain 6 billion or more people? How one answers this question depends greatly on whether or not one sees population as a problem.

Is population a problem? Some would argue that yes, population is a problem in that the earth is limited, that it can only sustain a certain number of people (although no one knows what that particular number may be), that the more numerous we become, the poorer we will become. Others argue that, no, population is not a problem but that it is government policies, economic structures, and the organization of society that is the problem. Some contend that numbers in themselves do not equal poverty; rather, poorly structured societies and economies foster poverty.

How people perceive the issue of population is critical, for it is by these perceptions that international legislative policies are formed, economic development packages are crafted, federal social and economic programs are formulated, and local sex education classes are designed.

Thus, it is equally critical that people ensure that their perceptions are grounded not in rhetoric and emotion but in established scientific and empirical data. An accurate understanding of the data will enable people to think and act rationally with regard to population on a local, state, national, and international level.

PERSPECTIVES IN THE DEBATE TODAY

There are many groups taking part in the current population debate. All approach the question of population from very different points of view and with different motivations. A working knowledge of the parties and their underlying philosophies will allow one to sift through the diverse rhetoric and hold it up to the light of scientific data. Frank Furedi, in his book *Population and Development: A Critical Introduction* (New York: Palgrave Macmillan, 1997), has provided a brief outline of the variety of approaches to the issue of population.

The Developmentalist Perspective

Until the 1990s, this was one of the most influential perspectives. Its advocates argue that rapid population growth represents a major obstacle to development, because valuable resources are diverted from productive expenditure to the feeding of a growing population. Some also contend that development solves the problem of population. They believe that increasing prosperity and the modernization of lifestyles will create a demand for smaller families, leading to the stabilization of population growth. A classic account of this approach can be found in Coale and Hoover (1958). It is worth noting that at least until the early 1980s, this was the most prominent argument used by many leading demographers and most of the influential promoters of population control.

The Redistributionist Perspective

Those who uphold the redistributionist perspective are skeptical of the view that population growth directly causes poverty and underdevelopment. They often interpret high fertility as not so much the cause as the effect of poverty. Why? Because poverty, lack of economic security, the high mortality rates of children, the low status of women, and other factors force people to have large families. They also believe that population is a problem because it helps intensify the impoverishment of the masses. For some redistributionists, the solution to the problem lies in changing the status of poor people, particularly of women, through education and reform. Repetto (1979) and the World Bank (1984) provide a clear statement of this approach. This perspective is linked to the Women and Human Rights approach discussed below. Some proponents of redistribution contend that the population problem can only be solved through far-reaching social reform. (See Sen and Grown [1988] for a radical version of the redistributionist argument.)

The Limited Resources Perspective

This perspective represents the synthesis of traditional Malthusian concern about natural limits with the preoccupation of contemporary environmentalism. According to the limited resources perspective, population growth has a negative and potentially destructive impact on the environment. Its proponents argue that even if a growing population can be fed, the environment cannot sustain such large numbers; population growth will lead to the explosion of pollution, which will have a catastrophic effect on the environment. See Harrion (1993) for a clear statement of this position.

The Sociobiological Perspective

This approach politicizes the limited resources perspective. Its proponents present population growth as a threat not only to the environment but also to a way of life. They regard people as polluters and often define population growth as a pathological problem. In the West, the ruthless application of this variant of Malthusianism leads to demands for immigration control. Some writers call for the banning of foreign aid to the countries of the South, on the grounds that it stimulates an increase in the rate of fertility. Other writers believe that the number of people threatens the ecosystem, and even go so far as to question the desirability of lowering the rate of infant mortality. Abernethy (1993) and Hardin (1993) provide a systematic presentation of the sociobiological perspective.

The People-as-a-Source-of-Instability Perspective

In recent years, contributions on international relations have begun to discuss population growth in terms of its effect on global stability. Some writers have suggested that in the post–Cold War order, the growth of population has the potential to undermine global stability. Some see the rising expectations of large numbers of frustrated people as the likely source of violent protest and as a stimulus for future wars and conflicts. The key theme they emphasize is the differential rate of fertility between the North and South. From this perspective the high fertility regime of the South represents a potential threat to the fast-aging population of the North. See Kennedy (1993).

The Women and Human Rights Perspective

This perspective associates a regime of high birth rates with the denial of essential human rights. Those who advocate this approach insist that the subordination of women and their exclusion from decision-making has kept birthrates high. Some suggest that because of their exclusion from power and from access to safe reproductive technology, many women have more children then they otherwise would wish. The importance of gender equality for the stabilization of population is not only supported by feminist contributors but by significant sections of the population movement. At the Cairo Conference of 1994, this perspective was widely endorsed by the main participants. For a clear exposition of this approach see Correa (1994) and Sen, Germain, and Chen (1994).

The People-as-Problem-Solvers Perspective

In contrast to the approaches mentioned so far, this one does not believe that population growth constitutes a problem. On the contrary, its advocates believe that the growth of population has the potential to stimulate economic growth and innovation. From this perspective, more people means more problem solvers, since human creativity has the potential to overcome the limits of nature. Some believe that in the final analysis, the market mechanism can help establish a dynamic equilibrium between population growth and resources. Others emphasize the problem-solving abilities of the human mind. See Boserup (1993) and Simon (1981) for illustrations of this approach.

The Religious Pronatalist Perspective

Some of the most vocal opponents to population policy are driven by religious objections to any interference with the act of reproduction. They argue that population growth is not a problem and are deeply suspicious of any attempt to regulate fertility. Although some supporters of this perspective mobilize economic arguments to support their case, the relationship between population growth and development is incidental to their argument. For them, the argument that population growth is positive is in the first instance justified on religious grounds. See Kasun (1988) for a clear exposition of this perspective. Other pronatalist voices regard the growth of population in the South as a positive asset that will contribute to a more equitable relation of power with the North. They view population programs as an insidious attempt to maintain Western domination.

Not all people belong strictly to one perspective or another, as Furedi is also quick to point out. In fact, most people adopt different strands of argumentation pulled from the various perspectives. However, some approaches to the issue of population are more specific to particular aspects of the debate. For instance, the "People-as-a-source-of-instability" perspective only touches on resource and environment concerns and deals more specifically with issues of immigration and trade policy.

An Essay on the Principle of Population

Thomas Malthus

This selection was originally published as chapter I in *An Essay on the Principle of Population*, edited by Geoffrey Gilbert (Oxford: Oxford University Press, 1999).

It has been said that the great question is now at issue, whether man shall henceforth start forwards with accelerated velocity towards illimitable, and hitherto unconceived improvement, or be condemned to a perpetual oscillation between happiness and misery, and after every effort remain still at an immeasurable distance from the wished-for goal.

The most important argument that I shall adduce is certainly not new. The principles on which it depends have been explained in part by Hume, and more at large by Dr. Adam Smith. It has been advanced and applied to the present subject, though not with its proper weight, or in the most forcible point of view, by Mr. Wallace, and it may probably have been stated by many writers that I have never met with. I should certainly therefore not think of advancing it again, though I mean to place it in a point of view in some degree different from any that I have hitherto seen, if it had ever been fairly and satisfactorily answered.

The cause of this neglect on the part of the advocates for the perfectibility of mankind is not easily accounted for. I cannot doubt the talents of such men as Godwin and Condorcet. I am unwilling to doubt their candour. To my understanding, and probably to that of most others, the difficulty appears insurmountable. Yet these men of acknowledged ability and penetration scarcely deign to notice it, and hold on their course in such speculations with unabated ardour and undiminished confidence. I have certainly no right to say that they purposely shut their eyes to such arguments. I ought rather to doubt the validity of them, when neglected by such men, however forcibly their truth may strike my own mind. Yet in this respect it must be acknowledged that we are all of us too prone to err. If I saw a glass of wine repeatedly presented to a man, and he took no notice of it, I should be apt to think that he was blind or uncivil. A juster philosophy might teach me rather to think that my eyes deceived me and that the offer was not really what I conceived it to be.

In entering upon the argument I must premise that I put out of the question, at present, all mere conjectures, that is, all suppositions, the probable realization of which cannot be inferred upon any just philosophical grounds. A writer may tell me that he thinks man will ultimately become an ostrich. I cannot properly contradict him. But before he can expect to bring any reasonable person over to his opinion, he ought to shew that the necks of mankind have been gradually elongating, that the lips have grown harder and more prominent, that the legs and feet are daily altering their shape, and that the hair is beginning to change into stubs of feathers. And till the probability of so wonderful a conversion can be shewn, it is surely lost time and lost eloquence to expatiate on the happiness of man in such a state; to describe his powers, both of running and flying, to paint him in a condition where all narrow luxuries would be contemned, where he would be employed only in collecting the necessaries of life, and where, consequently, each man's share of labour would be light, and his portion of leisure ample.

I think I may fairly make two postulata.

First, That food is necessary to the existence of man.

Secondly, That the passion between the sexes is necessary and will remain nearly in its present state.

These two laws, ever since we have had any knowledge of mankind, appear to have been fixed laws of our nature, and, as we have not hitherto seen any alteration in them, we have no right to conclude that they will ever cease to be what they now are, without an immediate act of power in that Being who first arranged the system of the universe, and for the advantage of his creatures, still executes, according to fixed laws, all its various operations.

I do not know that any writer has supposed that on this earth man will ultimately be able to live without food. But Mr. Godwin has conjectured that the passion between the sexes may in time be extinguished. As, however, he calls this part of his work a deviation into the land of conjecture, I will not dwell longer upon it at present than to say that the best arguments for the perfectibility of man are drawn from a contemplation of the great progress that he has already made from the savage state and the difficulty of saying where he is to stop. But towards the extinction of the passion between the sexes, no progress whatever has hitherto been made. It appears to exist in as much force at present as it did two thousand or four thousand years ago. There are individual exceptions now as there always have been. But, as these exceptions do not appear to increase in number, it would surely be a very unphilosophical mode of arguing to infer, merely from the existence of an exception, that the exception would, in time, become the rule, and the rule the exception.

Assuming then my postulata as granted, I say, that the power of population is indefinitely greater than the power in the earth to produce subsistence for man.

Population, when unchecked, increases in a geometrical ratio. Subsistence increases only in an arithmetical ratio. A slight acquaintance with numbers will shew the immensity of the first power in comparison of the second.

By that law of our nature which makes food necessary to the life of man, the effects of these two unequal powers must be kept equal.

This implies a strong and constantly operating check on population from the difficulty of subsistence. This difficulty must fall somewhere and must necessarily be severely felt by a large portion of mankind.

Through the animal and vegetable kingdoms, nature has scattered the seeds of life abroad with the most profuse and liberal hand. She has been comparatively sparing in the room and the nourishment necessary to rear them. The germs of existence contained in this spot of earth, with ample food, and ample room to expand in, would fill millions of worlds in the course of a few thousand years. Necessity, that imperious all-pervading law of nature, restrains them within the prescribed bounds. The race of plants and the race of animals shrink under this great restrictive law. And the race of man cannot, by any efforts of reason, escape from it. Among plants and animals its effects are waste of seed, sickness, and premature death. Among mankind, misery and vice. The former, misery, is an absolutely necessary consequence of it. Vice is a highly probable consequence, and we therefore see it abundantly prevail, but it ought not, perhaps, to be called an absolutely necessary consequence. The ordeal of virtue is to resist all temptation to evil.

This natural inequality of the two powers of population and of production in the earth, and that great law of our nature which must constantly keep their effects equal, form the great difficulty that to me appears insurmountable in the way to the perfectibility of society. All other arguments are of slight and subordinate consideration in comparison of this. I see no way by which man can escape from the weight of this law which pervades all animated nature. No fancied equality, no agrarian regulations in their utmost extent, could remove the pressure of it even for a single century. And it appears, therefore, to be decisive against the possible existence of a society, all the members of which should live in ease, happiness, and comparative leisure; and feel no anxiety about providing the means of subsistence for themselves and families.

Consequently, if the premises are just, the argument is conclusive against the perfectibility of the mass of mankind.

I have thus sketched the general outline of the argument, but I will examine it more particularly, and I think it will be found that experience, the true source and foundation of all knowledge, invariably confirms its truth.

Marx and Engels on Malthus

Ronald L. Meek

This selection was excerpted from "Marx and Engels on Malthus," in *Marx and Engels on the Population Bomb*, edited by Ronald Meek (Berkeley, Calif.: Ramparts Press, 1971).

FOREWORD

Back in 1798—a year in which the French Revolution was still conjuring up hopes of the perfectibility of man and of society—the Reverend Thomas Robert Malthus issued his famous law of population: mankind's propensity to beget, he warned, would soon outstrip the earth's capacity to provide.

Half a century later another prophet branded the good parson "a shameless sycophant of the ruling classes" and "a bought advocate" of those who opposed a better life for Merrie England's poor. By arguing that poverty was a natural condition and misery a necessary check on growing numbers, the contemptible Malthus was, Karl Marx claimed, simply selling scientific and moral arguments to selfish opponents of reform. The real problem wasn't too many people or too little food, said Marx, but that private capitalists owned the means of meeting men's needs.

THE THEORY OF POPULATION

Marx, in a letter to Schweitzer of January 24, 1865, criticizing the work of Proudhon, made the following comment:

> In a strictly scientific history of political economy the book [Proudhon's *What is Property?*] would hardly be worth mentioning. But sensational works of this kind play their part in the sciences just as much as in the history of the novel. Take, for instance, Malthus's book *On Population*. In its first edition it was nothing but a "sensational pamphlet" and *plagiarism* from beginning to end into the bargain. And yet what a *stimulus* was produced by this *libel on the human race!*

The "stimulus" which the principle of population produced was indeed a strong and far-reaching one. There was probably no other idea which exercised so great an influence on economic theory and practice during the first half of the nineteenth century, and certainly no other which aroused such impassioned attacks and defenses. And it was destined to exercise considerable influence even outside the strictly economic sphere: for example, it was an important factor in the early development of Darwinism. The "stimulus" was strong from the beginning, and its strength is by no means exhausted today.

How did it come about that the Malthusian theory, which had few pretensions to scientific profundity and was shot through and through with fallacies, was able to exercise this enormous influence? One of the main reasons was that the *actual phenomenon* which Malthus described and which he tried to account for—the widespread poverty and pauperism among the working people—was a *real* phenomenon which could not be ignored and which was crying out for an explanation. Malthus was "right, in his way," said Engels, "in asserting that there are always more people on hand than can be maintained from the available means of subsistence"—although the pressure of population was really against the *means of employment* rather than against the means of subsistence. Malthus's critics might attempt to prove his principle of population to be wrong, but they could not "argue away the facts which led Malthus to his principle." Thus even apart from all questions of what Marx called "party interest," there was a presumption in favor of Malthus's explanation of the facts until a better one had been put forward.

"Party interest," however, played an important role in securing the wide acceptance of the theory in ruling-class circles. An explanation of human misery in terms of an "eternal law of nature," such as Malthus's principle of population, has an obvious appeal for political reactionaries, since it diverts attention from the part played in the creation of this misery by class exploitation in general and by particular systems of class exploitation such as capitalism. One cannot do away with an "eternal law of nature." If it is nature and not human society which is responsible for the misery, all one can do, at the very best, is to mitigate some of the effects of this "eternal law" and suffer the remainder with a good grace.

To Marx and Engels, interested as they were in discovering the basic laws of social change, and in particular the "law of motion" of bourgeois society, any explanation of social phenomena such as overpopulation under capitalism in terms of an "eternal law" was bound to appear superficial and inadequate. This was the basis of their main *general* criticism of Malthus's theory of population. As early as 1847, in his first economic work, Marx attacked the tendency of economists to "represent the bourgeois relations of production as eternal categories" and criticized Ricardo for applying the specifically bourgeois conception of rent to "the landed property of all ages and all countries." The Marxist position was stated by Engels in a letter to Lange of March 29, 1865:

> To us so-called "economic laws" are not eternal laws of nature but historic laws which arise and disappear; and the code of modern political economy, insofar as it has been drawn up with proper objectivity by the economists, is to us simply a summary of the laws and conditions under which alone modern bourgeois society can exist—in short the conditions of its production and exchange expressed in an abstract and summary way. To us also, therefore, none of these laws, insofar as it expresses *purely bourgeois conditions*, is older than modern bourgeois society; those which have hitherto been more or less valid throughout all history only express just those relations which are common to the conditions of all society based on class rule and class exploitation. To the former belongs the so-called law of Ricardo, which is valid neither for feudal serfdom nor ancient slavery; to the latter belongs what is tenable in the so-called Malthusian theory.

And even in the case of those laws and conditions which have had a limited validity throughout the whole history of class society, Marx and Engels maintained that the most interesting and important thing about them was the different ways in which they operated in different types of class society. Thus Marx and Engels denied that "the law of population is the same at all times and at all places." On the contrary, they maintained, "every stage of development has its own law of population."

It was not enough, of course, merely to assert this—it had to be *proved*. Marx and Engels do not seem to have made any direct attempt to formulate the laws of population appropriate to earlier forms of class society; had they done so, they would probably have framed these laws in terms of the particular form of pressure of the direct producers against the "means of employment" which was generated by each of these types of society. They considered that the most important job they had to do was to formulate the actual law of population peculiar to the present bourgeois stage of development, and to demonstrate that this new *specific* law fitted the contemporary facts better than the old *"eternal"* law that Malthus had put forward. Marx's main formulation of the law is reproduced below, and a brief summary—which necessarily does much less than justice to the original—is all that is required here.

To understand the reason for the emergence of "relative surplus population" under capitalism, says Marx, one must consider the influence of the *growth of capital* upon the lot of the laboring class. And here the most important factor is the composition of capital and the changes it undergoes in the course of the accumulation process. As accumulation proceeds, the value of the means of production (constant capital) tends to rise relatively to the sum total of wages (variable capital). "The accumulation of capital," says Marx, ". . . is effective . . . under a progressive qualitative change in its composition, under a constant increase of its constant, at the expense of its variable constituent." This relative diminution of the variable part of capital proceeds simultaneously with the progress of accumulation and the concentration of capital that accompanies it. Now "the demand for labor is determined not by the amount of capital as a whole, but by its variable constituent alone," so that the demand for labor "falls relatively to the magnitude of the total capital, and at an accelerated rate, as this magnitude increases." Although the demand for labor increases absolutely as the total capital increases, it does so "in a constantly diminishing proportion." Thus "it is capitalistic accumulation itself that constantly produces, and produces in the direct ratio of its own energy and extent, a relatively redundant population of laborers, i.e., a population of greater extent than suffices for the average needs of the self-expansion of capital, and therefore a surplus population." And after discussing briefly the various ways in which these changes may work themselves out, Marx sums the matter up as follows:

> The laboring population therefore produces, along with the accumulation of capital produced by it, the means by which itself is made relatively superflu-

ous, is turned into a relative surplus-population; and it does this to an always increasing extent. This is a law of population peculiar to the capitalist mode of production; and in fact every specific historic mode of production has its own special laws of population, historically valid within its limits alone. An abstract law of population exists for plants and animals only, and only insofar as man has not interfered with them.

It is on the basis of this central thesis that Marx goes on to discuss in greater detail, and with a wealth of historical illustration, the laws of the expansion and contraction of the "industrial reserve army" and the different forms that "relative surplus population" assumes in modern society. It was in this way that Marx and Engels completed their criticism of Malthus's law of population—by formulating a new law capable of replacing it.

Too Many People

Paul R. Ehrlich

This selection was excerpted from "Too Many People," in *The Population Bomb* (reprint, Cutchogue, N.Y.: Buccaneer Books, 1997).

Americans are beginning to realize that the underdeveloped countries of the world face an inevitable population-food crisis. Each year food production in these countries falls a bit further behind burgeoning population growth, and people go to bed a little bit hungrier. While there are temporary or local reversals of this trend, it now seems inevitable that it will continue to its logical conclusion: mass starvation. The rich may continue to get richer, but the more numerous poor are going to get poorer. Of these poor, a *minimum* of 10 million people, most of them children, will starve to death during each year of the 1970s. But this is a mere handful compared with the numbers that will be starving before the end of the century. And it is now too late to take action to save many of those people.

However, most Americans are not aware that the United States and other developed countries also have a problem with overpopulation. Rather than suffering from food shortages, these countries show symptoms in the form of environmental deterioration and increased difficulty in obtaining resources to support their affluence.

In a book about population, there is a temptation to stun the reader with an avalanche of statistics. I'll spare you most, but not all, of that. After all, no matter how you slice it, population is a numbers game. Perhaps the best way to impress you with numbers is to tell you about the "doubling time" — the time necessary for the population to double in size.

It has been estimated that the human population of 8000 B.C. was about 5 million people, taking perhaps 1 million years to get there from 2.5 million. The population did not reach 500 million until almost 10,000 years later — about A.D. 1650. This means it doubled roughly once every thousand years or so. It reached a billion people around 1850, doubling in some 200 years. It took only 80 years or so for the next doubling, as the population reached 2 billion around 1930. We have not completed the next doubling to 4 billion yet, but we now have well over 3.5 billion people. The doubling time at present seems to be about 35 years. Quite a reduction in doubling times: 1,000,000 years, 1,000 years, 200 years, 80 years, 35 years. Perhaps the meaning of a doubling time of around 35 years is best brought home by a theoretical exercise. Let's examine what might happen on the absurd assumption that the population continued to double every 35 years into the indefinite future.

If growth continued at that rate for about 900 years, there would be some 60,000,000,000,000,000 people on the face of the earth (60 million billion people). This is about 100 persons for each square yard of the earth's surface, land and sea. A British physicist, J. H. Fremlin, guessed that such a multitude might be housed in a continuous two-thousand-story building covering our entire planet. The upper thousand stories would contain only the apparatus for running this gigantic warren. Ducts, pipes, wires, elevator shafts, and so on, would occupy about half of the space in the bottom thousand stories. This would leave three or four yards of floor space for each person. I will leave to your imagination the physical details of existence in this ant heap, except to point out that all would not be black. Probably each person would be limited in his travel. Perhaps he could take elevators through all thousand residential stories but could travel only within a circle of a few hundred yards' radius on any floor. This would permit, however, each person to choose his friends from among some 10 million people! And, as Fremlin points out, entertainment on the worldwide TV should be excellent, for at any time "one could expect some 10 million Shakespeares and rather more Beatles to be alive."

Could growth of the human population of the earth continue beyond that point? Not according to Fremlin. We would have reached a "heat limit." People themselves, as well as their activities, convert other forms of energy into heat which must be dissipated. In order to permit this excess heat to radiate directly from the top of the "world building" directly into space, the atmosphere would have been pumped into flasks under the sea well before the limiting population size was reached. The precise limit would depend on the technology of the day. At a population size of 1 billion people, the temperature of the "world roof" would be kept around the melting point of iron to radiate away the human heat generated.

But, you say, surely Science (with a capital "S") will find a way for us to occupy the other planets of our solar system and eventually of other stars before we get all that crowded. Skip for a moment the virtual certainty that those planets are uninhabitable. Forget also the insurmountable logistic problems of moving billions of people off the earth. Fremlin has made some interesting calculations on how much time we could buy by occupying the planets of the solar system. For instance, at any given time it would take only about fifty years to populate Venus, Mercury, Mars, the moon, and the moons of Jupiter and Saturn to the same population density as earth.

What if the fantastic problems of reaching and colonizing the other planets of the solar system, such as Jupiter and Uranus, can be solved? It would take only about 200 years to fill them "earth-full." So we could perhaps gain 250 years of time for population growth in the solar system after we had reached an absolute limit on earth. What then? We can't ship our surplus to the stars. Professor Garrett Hardin of the University of California at Santa Barbara has dealt effectively with this fantasy. Using extremely optimistic assumptions, he has calculated that Americans, by cutting their standard of living down to 18 percent of its present level, could in *one year* set aside enough capital to finance the exportation to the stars of *one day's* increase in the population of the world.

Interstellar transport for surplus people presents an amusing prospect. Since the ships would take generations to reach most stars, the only people who could be transported would be those willing to exercise strict birth control. Population explosions on space ships would be disastrous. Thus we would have to export our responsible people, leaving the irresponsible at home on earth to breed.

Enough of fantasy. Hopefully, you are convinced that the population will have to stop growing sooner or later and that the extremely remote possibility of expanding into outer space offers no escape from the laws of population growth. If you still want to hope for the stars, just remember that, at the current growth rate, in a few thousand years everything in the visible universe would be converted into people, and the ball of people would be expanding with the speed of light! Unfortunately, even nine hundred years is much too far in the future for those of us concerned with the population explosion. As you will see, the next *nine* years will probably tell the story.

Of course, population growth is not occurring uniformly over the face of the Earth. Indeed, countries are divided rather neatly into two groups: those with rapid growth rates, and those with relatively slow growth rates. The first group, making up about two-thirds of the world population, coincides closely with what are known as the "underdeveloped countries" (UDCs). The UDCs are not industrialized, tend to have inefficient agriculture, very small gross national products, high illiteracy rates, and related problems. That's what UDCs are technically, but a short definition of underdeveloped is "hungry." Most Latin American, African, and Asian countries fall into this category. The second group consists of the "overdeveloped countries" (ODCs). ODCs are modern industrial nations, such as the United States, Canada, most European countries, Israel, the USSR, Japan, and Australia. They consume a disproportionate amount of the world's resources and are the major polluters. Most, but by no means all, people in these countries are adequately nourished.

Doubling times in the UDCs range around 20 to 35 years. Examples of these times (from the 1970 figures released by the Population Reference Bureau) are: Kenya, 23 years; Nigeria, 27; Turkey, 26; Indonesia, 24; Philippines, 21; Brazil, 25; Costa Rica, 19; and El Salvador, 21. Think of what it means for the population of a country to double in 25 years. In order just to keep living standards at the present inadequate level, the food available for the people must be doubled. Every structure and road must be duplicated. The amount of power must be doubled. The capacity of the transport system must be doubled. The number of trained doctors, nurses, teachers, and administrators must be doubled. This would be a fantastically difficult job in the United States — a rich country with a fine agricultural system, immense industries, and access to abundant resources. Think of what it means to a country with none of these.

Remember also that in virtually all UDCs, people have gotten the word about the better life it is possible to have. They have seen colored pictures in magazines of the miracles of Western technology. They have seen automobiles and airplanes. They have seen American and European movies. Many have seen refrigerators, tractors, and even TV sets. Almost all have heard transistor radios. They *know* that a better life is possible. They have what we like to call "rising expectations." If twice as many people are to be happy, the miracle of doubling what they now have will not be enough. It will only maintain today's standard of living. There will have to be a tripling or better. Needless to say, they are not going to be happy.

Doubling times for the populations of the ODCs tend to be in the 50-to-200-year range. Examples of 1970 doubling times are the United States, 70 years; Austria, 175; Denmark, 88; Norway, 78; United Kingdom, 140; Poland, 78; Russia, 70; Italy, 88; Spain, 70; and Japan, 63. These are industrialized countries that have undergone the so-called demographic transition—a transition from high to low growth rates. As industrialization progressed, children became less important to parents as extra hands to work on the farm and as support in old age. At the same time they became a financial drag—expensive to raise and educate. Presumably these were the reasons for the slowing of population growth after industrialization. They boil down to a simple fact—people just wanted to have fewer children.

It is important to emphasize, however, that the demographic transition does not result in zero population growth but in a growth rate that in many of the most important ODCs results in populations doubling every seventy years or so. This means, for instance, that even if most UDCs were to undergo a demographic transition (of which there is no sign), the world would still be faced by catastrophic population growth. *No growth rate can be sustained in the long run.*

Saying that the ODCs have undergone a demographic transition thus does not mean that they have no population problems. First of all, most of them are already overpopulated. They are overpopulated by the simple criterion that they are not able to produce enough food to feed their populations. It is true that they have the money to buy food, but when food is no longer available for sale, they will find the money rather indigestible. Similarly, ODCs are overpopulated because they do not themselves have the resources to support their affluent societies; they must co-opt much more than their fair share of the world's wealth of minerals and energy. And they are overpopulated because they have exceeded the capacity of their environments to dispose of their wastes. Remember, overpopulation does not normally mean too many people for the area of a country but too many people in relation to the necessities and amenities of life. *Overpopulation occurs when numbers threaten values.*

The ODCs also share with the UDCs serious problems of population distribution. Their urban centers are getting more and more crowded relative to the countryside. This problem is not as severe in the ODCs as it is in the UDCs (if current trends should continue, which they cannot, Calcutta would have 66 million inhabitants in the year 2000), but they are very serious and speedily worsening. In the United States, one of the more rapidly growing ODCs, we hear constantly of the headaches related to growing cities: not just garbage in our environment but overcrowded highways, burgeoning slums, deteriorating school systems, rising tax and crime rates, riots, and other social disorders. Indeed, social and environmental problems not only increase with growing population and urbanization, but they tend to increase at an even faster rate. Adding more people to an area increases the damage done by each individual. Doubling the population normally much more than doubles environmental deterioration.

Demographically, the whole problem is quite simple. A population will continue to grow as long as the birthrate exceeds the death rate—if immigration and emigration are not occurring. It is, of course, the balance between birthrate and death rate that is critical. The birthrate is the number of births per thousand people per year in the population. The death rate is the number of deaths per thousand people per year. Subtracting the death rate from the birthrate, ignoring migration, gives the rate of increase. If the birthrate is thirty per thousand per year, and the death rate is ten per thousand per year, then the rate of increase is twenty per thousand per year ($30 - 10 = 20$). Expressed as a percent (rate per hundred people), the rate of twenty per thousand becomes 2 percent. If the rate of increase is 2 percent, then the doubling time will be thirty-five years. Note that if you simply added twenty people per thousand per year to the population, it would take fifty years to add a second thousand people ($20 \times 50 = 1,000$). But the doubling time is actually much less because populations grow at compound interest rates. Just as interest dollars themselves earn interest, so do people added to population produce more people. It's growing at compound interest that makes populations double so much more rapidly than seems possible. Look at the relationship between the annual percent increase (interest rate) and the doubling time of the population (time for your money to double):

Annual Percent Increase	Doubling Time
1.0	70
2.0	35
3.0	24
4.0	17

Those are all the calculations—I promise. If you are interested in more details on how demographic figuring is done, you may enjoy reading Warren Thompson and David Lewis's excellent book, *Population Problems* (New York: McGraw-Hill, 1965), or my book, *Population, Resources, Environment* (San Francisco: W. H. Freeman and Co., 1970).

There are some professional optimists around who like to greet every sign of dropping birthrates with wild pronouncements about the end of the population explosion. They are a little like a person who, after a low temperature of five below zero on December 21, interprets a low of only three below zero on December 22 as a cheery sign of approaching spring. First of all, birthrates, along with all demographic statistics, show short-term fluctuations caused by many factors. For instance, the birthrate depends rather heavily on the number of women at reproductive age. In the United States the low birthrates of the late 1960s are being replaced by higher rates as more post–World War II "baby boom" children move into their reproductive years. In Japan, 1966, the Year of the Fire Horse, was a year of very low birthrates. There is widespread belief that girls born in the Year of the Fire Horse make poor wives, and Japanese couples try to avoid giving birth in that year because they are afraid of having daughters.

But, I repeat, it is the relationship between birthrate and death rate that is most critical. Indonesia, Laos, and Haiti all had birthrates around forty-six per thousand in 1966. Costa Rica's birthrate was forty-one per thousand. Good for Costa Rica? Unfortunately, not very. Costa Rica's death rate was less than nine per thousand, while the other countries all had death rates above twenty per thousand. The population of Costa Rica in 1966 was doubling every seventeen years, while the doubling times of Indonesia, Laos, and Haiti were all above thirty years. Ah, but, you say, it was good for Costa Rica—fewer people per thousand were dying each year. Fine for a few years perhaps, but what then? Some 50 percent of the people in Costa Rica are under fifteen years old. As they get older, they will need more and more food in a world with less and less. In 1983 they will have twice as many mouths to feed as they had in 1966, if the 1966 trend continues. Where will the food come from? Today the death rate in Costa Rica is low in part because they have a large number of physicians in proportion to their population. How do you suppose those physicians will keep the death rate down when there's not enough food to keep people alive?

One of the most ominous facts of the current situation is that over 40 percent of the population of the underveloped world is made up of people *under fifteen years old.* As that mass of young people moves into its reproductive years during the next decade, we're going to see the greatest baby boom of all time. Those youngsters are the reason for all the ominous predictions for the year 2000. They are the gunpowder for the population explosion.

How did we get into this bind? It all happened a long time ago, and the story involves the process of natural selection, the development of culture, and man's swollen head. The essence of success in evolution is reproduction. Indeed, natural selection is simply defined as the differential reproduction of genetic types. That is, if people with blue eyes have more children on the average than those with brown eyes, natural selection is occurring. More genes for blue eyes will be passed on to the next generation than will genes for brown eyes. Should this continue, the population will have progressively larger and larger proportions of blue-eyed people. This differential reproduction of genetic types is the driving force of evolution; it has been driving evolution for billions of years. Whatever types produced more offspring became the common types. Virtually all populations contain very many different genetic types (for reasons that need not concern us), and some are always outreproducing others. As I said, reproduction is the key to winning the evolutionary game. Any structure, physiological process, or pattern of behavior that leads to greater reproductive success will tend to be perpetuated. The entire process by which man developed involves thousands of millennia of our ancestors being more successful breeders than their relatives. Facet number one of our bind—the urge to reproduce has been fixed in us by billions of years of evolution.

Of course through all those years of evolution, our ancestors were fighting a continual battle to keep the birthrate ahead of the death rate. That they were successful is attested to by our very existence, because if the death rate had overtaken the birthrate for any substantial period of time, the evolutionary line leading to man would have gone extinct. Among our apelike ancestors, a few million years ago, it was very difficult for a mother to rear her children successfully. Most of the offspring died before they reached reproductive age. The death rate was near the birthrate. Then "the mother factor" entered the picture—cultural evolution was added to biological evolution.

Culture can be loosely defined as the body of nongenetic information which people pass from generation to generation. It is the accumulated knowledge that, in the old days, was passed on entirely by word of mouth, painting, and demonstration. Several thousand years ago the written word was added to the means of cultural transmission. Today culture is passed on in these ways, and also through television, computer tapes, motion pictures, records, blueprints, and other media. Culture is all the information man possesses except for that which is stored in the chemical language of his genes.

The large size of the human brain evolved in response to the development of cultural information. A big brain is an advantage when dealing with such information. Big-brained individuals were able to deal more successfully with the culture of their group. They were thus more successful reproductively than their smaller-brained relatives. They passed on their genes for big brains to their numerous offspring. They also added to the accumulating store of cultural information, increasing slightly the premium placed on brain size in the next generation. A self-reinforcing selective trend developed—a trend toward increased brain size.

But there was, quite literally, a rub. Babies had bigger and bigger heads. There were limits to how large a woman's pelvis could conveniently become. To make a long story short, the strategy of evolution was not to make a women bell-shaped and relatively immobile but to accept the problem of having babies who were helpless for a long period while their brains grew after birth. How could the mother defend and care for her infant during its unusually long period of helplessness? She couldn't, unless Papa hung around. The girls are still working on that problem, but an essential step was to get rid of the short, well-defined breeding season characteristic of most mammals. The year-round sexuality of the human female, the long period of infant dependence on the female, the evolution of the family group, all are at the root of our present problem. They are essential ingredients in the vast social phenomenon that we call sex. Sex is not simply an act leading to the production of offspring. It is a varied and complex cultural phenomenon penetrating into all aspects of our lives — one involving our self-esteem, our choice of friends, cars, and leaders. It is tightly interwoven with our mythology and history. Sex in human beings is necessary for the production of young, but it also evolved to ensure their successful rearing. Facet number two of our bind — our urge to reproduce is hopelessly entwined with most of our other urges.

Of course, in the early days the whole system did not prevent a high mortality among the young, as well as among the older members of the group. Hunting and food-gathering is a risky business. Cavemen had to throw very impressive cave bears out of their caves before people could move in. Witch doctors and shamans had a less than perfect record at treating wounds and curing disease. Life was short, if not sweet. Yet the total population size doubtless increased slowly but steadily as human populations expanded out of the African cradle of our species.

Then about ten thousand years ago a major change occurred — the agricultural revolution. People began to give up hunting food and settled down to grow it. Suddenly some of the risk was removed from life. The chances of dying of starvation diminished greatly in some human groups. Other threats associated with the nomadic life were also reduced, perhaps balanced by the new threats of disease and large-scale warfare associated with the development of cities. But the overall result was a more secure existence than before, and the human population grew more rapidly. Around 1800, when the standard of living in what are today the ODCs was dramatically increasing due to industrialization, population growth really began to accelerate. The development of medical science was the straw that broke the camel's back. While lowering death rates in the ODCs were due in part to other factors, there is no question that the "instant death control," exported by the ODCs, has been responsible for the drastic lowering of death rates in the UDCs. Medical science, with its efficient public health programs, has been able to depress the death rate with astonishing rapidity and at the same time drastically increase the birthrate; healthier people have more babies.

The power of exported death control can best be seen by examining the classic case of Ceylon's assault on malaria after World War II. Between 1933 and 1942 the death rate due directly to malaria was *reported* as almost two per thousand. This rate, however, represented only a portion of the malaria deaths, as many were reported as being due to "pyrexia." Indeed, in 1934–1935 a malaria epidemic may have been directly responsible for fully half of the deaths on the island. In addition, malaria, which infected a large portion of the population, made people susceptible to many other diseases. It thus contributed to the death rate indirectly as well as directly.

The introduction of DDT in 1946 brought rapid control over the mosquitoes that carry malaria. As a result, the death rate on the island was cut in half in less than a decade. The death rate in Ceylon in 1945 was twenty-two. It dropped 34 percent from 1946 to 1947 and moved down to ten in 1954. Since the sharp postwar drop, it has continued to decline and now stands at eight. Although part of the drop is due to the killing of other insects that carry disease and to other public health measures, most of it can be accounted for by the control of malaria.

Victory over malaria, yellow fever, smallpox, cholera, and other infectious diseases has been responsible for similar plunges in the death rate throughout most of the UDCs. In the decade 1940–1950 the death rate declined 46 percent in Puerto Rico, 43 percent in Formosa, and 23 percent in Jamaica. In a sample of eighteen undeveloped areas the average decline in death rate from 1945 to 1950 was 24 percent.

It is, of course, socially very acceptable to reduce the death rate. Billions of years of evolution have given us all a powerful will to live. Intervening in the birthrate goes against our evolutionary values. During all those centuries of our evolutionary past, the individuals who had the most children passed on their genetic endowment in greater quantities than those who reproduced less. Their genes dominate our heredity today. All our biological urges are for more reproduction, and they are all too often reinforced by our culture. In brief, death control goes with the grain, birth control against it.

In summary, the world's population will continue to grow as long as the birthrate exceeds the death rate; it's as simple as that. When it stops growing or starts to shrink, it will mean that either the birthrate has gone down or the death rate has gone up or a combination of the two. Basically, then, there are only two kinds of solutions to the population problem. One is a "birthrate solution," in which we find ways to lower the birthrate. The other is a "death rate solution," in which ways to raise the death rate—war, famine, pestilence—*find us.* The problem could have been avoided by *population control,* in which mankind consciously adjusted the birthrate so that a "death rate solution" did not have to occur.

Conclusion

Julian Simon

This selection was excerpted from "Conclusion," in *The Ultimate Resource II* (Princeton, N.J.: Princeton University Press, 1996).

- No food, one problem. Much food, many problems.

  Anonymous

- The humour of blaming the present, and admiring the past, is strongly rooted in human nature, and has an influence even on persons endued with the profoundest judgment and most extensive learning.

  David Hume, "Of the Populousness of Ancient Nations"

Raw materials and energy are getting less scarce. The world's food supply is improving. Pollution in the developed countries has been decreasing. Population growth has long-term benefits, though added people are a burden in the short run. Most important, fewer people are dying young.

These assertions, publicly stated in 1970 and then in the first edition of this book in 1981, have stood the test of time. The benign trends have continued until this edition. Our species is better off in just about every measurable material way. And there is stronger reason than ever to believe that these progressive trends will continue indefinitely.

Indeed, the trends toward greater cleanliness and less pollution of our air and water are even sharper than before, and cover a longer historical period and more countries (though the environmental disaster in eastern Europe has only recently become public knowledge). The increase in availability and the decrease in raw materials scarcity have continued unabated and have even speeded up. None of the catastrophes in food supply and famine that were forecast by the doomsayers have occurred; rather, the world's people are eating better than ever. The conventional beliefs of the doomsayers have been entirely falsified by events during past decades.

When we widen our scope beyond the physical matters of mortality, natural resources, and the environment . . . —to the standard of living, freedom, housing, and the like—we find that all the trends pertaining to economic welfare are also heartening. Perhaps most exciting, the amount of education that people obtain all over the world is sharply increasing, which means less tragic waste of human talent and ambition.

Many of the trends reported here are in fact commonplace among the scientists who study them. The consensus of agricultural economists has consistently been an optimistic point of view about food supply, and the consensus of natural resource economists has never been gloomy. But the scientific consensus about population growth largely changed in the 1980s. The consensus of population economists is now not far from what is written in this book; the profession and I agree that in the first few decades the effect of population growth is neutral. Such institutions as the World Bank and the National Academy of Sciences have recanted their former views that population growth is a crucial obstacle to economic development. (I am still in the minority when I emphasize the long-run benefits, on balance, of more people.)

The central issue is the effect of the number of people on the standard of living, with special attention to raw materials and the environment. On balance, the long-run effects are positive. The mechanism works as follows: Population growth and the increase of income expand demand, forcing up prices of natural resources. The increased prices trigger the search for new supplies. Eventually, new sources and substitutes are found. These new discoveries leave humanity better off than if the shortages had never occurred.

The vision that underlies and unifies the various topics is that of human beings who create more than they destroy. But even talented and energetic people require an incentive to create better techniques, better organizations, and better protection for the property that is the fruit of their labors. Therefore, the political-economic structure is the crucial determinant of the speed with which economic development occurs. In the presence of economic liberty and respect for property, population growth causes fewer problems in the short run and greater benefits in the short run than where the state controls economic activity.

In evaluating the effects of population growth, it is crucial to distinguish between the long run and the short run. Everyone agrees that in the short run additional people cause problems. When the pilgrims arrived in the United States, real problems arose for the Native Americans. ("There goes the neighborhood.") And when some Indians pointed out that there would be benefits in the long run, each of the others said, "Not in my hunting grounds." Babies use diapers and then schools before they become economically productive. Even immigrants need some services before they get to work.

In the short run, all resources are limited—natural resources, such as the pulpwood that went into making this book, created resources such as the number of pages Princeton University Press can allow me, and human resources such as the attention you will devote to what I say. In the short run, a greater use of any resource means pressure on supplies and a higher price in the market, or even rationing. Also in the short run, there will always be shortage crises because of weather, war, politics, and population movements. The results that an individual notices are sudden jumps in taxes, inconveniences and disruption, and increases in pollution.

But what about the effects in the longer run? What would life be like now if the Native Americans had managed to prevent immigration from Europe and there had been no population growth from then until now? Or if growth had stopped ten thousand years ago on earth when there were only a million people? Do you think that our standard of living would be as high as it is now if the population had never grown from about 4 million human beings perhaps ten thousand years ago? I don't think we'd now have electric light or gas heat or autos or penicillin or travel to the moon or our present life expectancy of over seventy years at birth in rich countries, in comparison with the life expectancy of twenty to twenty-five years at birth in earlier eras, if population had not grown to its present numbers.

The longer run is a very different story than the shorter run. The standard of living has risen along with the size of the world's population since the beginning of recorded time. And with increases in income and population have come less severe shortages, lower costs, and an increased availability of resources, including a cleaner environment and greater access to natural recreation areas. And there is no convincing economic reason why these trends toward a better life, and toward lower prices for raw materials (including food and energy), should not continue indefinitely.

Contrary to common rhetoric, there are no meaningful limits to the continuation of this process. There is no physical or economic reason why human resourcefulness and enterprise cannot forever continue to respond to impending shortages and existing problems with new expedients that, after an adjustment period, leave us better off than before the problem arose. Adding more people will cause us more such problems, but at the same time, there will be more people to solve these problems and leave us with the bonus of lower costs and less scarcity in the long run. The bonus applies to such desirable resources as better health, more wilderness, cheaper energy, and a cleaner environment.

This process runs directly against Malthusian reasoning and against the apparent common sense of the matter, which can be summed up as follows: the supply of any resource is fixed, and greater use means less to go around. The resolution of this paradox is not simple. Fuller understanding begins with the idea that the relevant measure of scarcity is the cost or price of a resource, not any physical measure of its calculated reserves. And the appropriate way for us to think about extracting resources is not in physical units, pounds of copper, or acres of farmland, but rather in the services we get from these resources—the electrical transmission capacity of copper, or the food values and gastronomic enjoyment the farmland provides. Following on this is the fact that economic history has not gone as Malthusian reasoning suggests. The prices of all goods and of the services they provide have fallen in the long run, by all reasonable measures. And this irrefutable fact must be taken into account as a fundamental datum that can reasonably be projected into the future, rather than as a fortuitous chain of circumstances that cannot continue.

Resources in their raw form are useful and valuable only when found, understood, gathered together, and harnessed for human needs. The basic ingredient in the process, along with the raw elements, is human knowledge. And we develop knowledge about how to use raw elements for our benefit only in response to our needs. This includes knowledge for finding new sources of raw materials such as copper, for growing new resources such as timber, for creating new quantities of capital such as farmland, and for finding new and better ways to satisfy old needs, such as successively using iron or aluminum or plastic in place of clay or copper. Such knowledge has a special property. It yields benefits to people other than the ones who develop it, apply it, and try to capture its benefits for themselves. Taken in the large, an increased need for resources usually leaves us with a permanently greater capacity to get them, because we gain knowledge in the process. And there is no meaningful physical limit—even the commonly mentioned weight of the earth—to our capacity to keep growing forever.

There is only one important resource that has shown a trend of increasing scarcity rather than increasing abundance. That resource is the most important of all—human beings. There are more people on earth now than ever before. But if we measure the scarcity of people the same way that we measure the scarcity of other economic goods—by how much we must pay to obtain their services—we see that wages and salaries have been going up all over the world, in poor countries as well as in rich countries. The amount that you must pay to obtain the services of a driver or a cook has risen in India, just as the price of a driver or cook—or economist—has risen in the United States over the decades. This increase in the price of services is a clear indication that people are becoming more scarce even though there are more of us.

The most dramatic evidence that the development of countries does not depend on their rates of population growth is shown by the economic histories from 1950 onward of the three pairs of countries that began with the same demographic rates as well as the same histories and cultures but were split into two very different political-economic systems: North and South Korea, East and West Germany, Taiwan and China. The countries with controlled economies and unfree societies have performed abysmally compared with their twins. The enormous influence of the political-economic system leaves nothing for population change to explain in these individual countries.

Many who oppose population growth assume that added people now would not have positive effects in the long run. Or, at least they put a low weight on those future positive effects. And they believe that more people now implies that the air will be dirtier than otherwise ten years in the future (say), and there will be less natural resources available. And they assume that the standard of living would be lower than otherwise.

An interesting aspect of this short-run view is that many who hold it are ecologically minded. Two of the great intellectual strengths of ecology are its long view of the consequences of present happenings and its propensity to search out the indirect and hard-to-see consequences, both of which tendencies it shares with economics. If we raise our eyes beyond the most immediate future, we see that the negative short-run effects are more than countered. This is seen in the trend evidence of long-run progress. And there is solid theory that fits these facts. That theory again is as follows: More people and increased income cause problems in the short run. The increased scarcity of resources causes prices to rise. The higher prices present opportunity and prompt inventors and entrepreneurs to search for solutions. Many fail, at a cost to themselves. But in a free society, solutions are eventually found. And in the long run the new developments leave us better off than if the problems had not arisen. That is, prices end up lower than before the increased scarcity occurred. We have seen many examples of this process, such as the energy transition from burning wood to coal to oil to nuclear power, and in the development of better ways to handle waste, not only reducing the scope of the problem but also converting "bad" waste to economic "goods."

At work is a general process that underlies all the specific findings in this book: humans on average build a bit more than they destroy and create a bit more than they use up. The process is, as physicists say, an "invariancy," applying to all metals, all fuels, all foods, and all other measures of human welfare, in almost all countries at almost all times; it can be thought of as a theory of economic history. The crucial evidence for the existence of this process is found in the fact that each generation leaves a bit more true wealth—the resources to create material and nonmaterial goods—than the generation began with. That is, the standard of living of each generation is on average higher than the generation before.

Indeed, it is necessarily so. If humankind did not have a propensity to create more than it uses, the species would have perished a long time ago. This propensity to build may be taken as a fundamental characteristic that is part of our evolution. This is the overarching theory that explains why events have turned out in exactly the opposite fashion from what Malthus and his followers foresaw.

Underlying the thinking of most writers who have a point of view different from mine is the concept of the fixity or finiteness of resources in the relevant system of discourse. This concept is central in Malthus, of course. But the idea probably has always been a staple of human thinking because so much of our situation must sensibly be regarded as fixed in the short run—the bottles of beer in the refrigerator, our paycheck, the amount of energy parents have to play basketball with their kids. But the *thema* underlying my thinking about resources (and the thinking of a minority of others) is that the relevant system of discourse has a long enough horizon that it makes sense to treat the system as not fixed, rather than finite in any operational sense. We see the resource system as being as unlimited as the number of thoughts a person may have or the number of variations that biological evolution may ultimately produce. That is, a key difference between the thinking of those who worry about impending doom and those who see the prospects of a better life for more people in the future is apparently whether one thinks in closed-system or open-system terms. For example, those who worry that the second law of thermodynamics dooms us to eventual decline necessarily see our world as a closed system with respect to energy and entropy; those who view the relevant universe as unbounded view the second law of thermodynamics as irrelevant to this discussion. I am among those who view the relevant part of the physical and social universe as open for most purposes. Which *thema* is better for thinking about resources and population is not subject to a scientific test. Yet it profoundly affects our thinking. I believe that here lies the root of the key difference in thinking about population and resources.

Why do so many people think of the planet and our presently known resources as a closed system, to which no resources will be added in the future? There are a variety of reasons. (1) Malthusian fixed-resources reasoning is simple and fits the isolated facts of our everyday lives, whereas the expansion of resources is complex and indirect and includes all creative human activity—it cannot be likened to our own larders or wallets. The same concepts, rhetoric, and even wording pop up in one resource and environmental scare after another—with respect to water as to oil, fluoridation of drinking water as with nuclear power, global warming as with acid rain as with the ozone layer. (2) There are always immediate negative effects from an increased pressure on resources, whereas the benefits only come later. It is natural to pay more attention to the present and the near future than to the more distant future. (3) There are often special-interest groups that alert us to impending shortages of particular resources such as timber or clean air. But no one has the same stake in trying to convince us that the long-run prospects for a resource are better than we think. (4) It is easier to get people's attention (and television time and printer's ink) with frightening forecasts than with soothing forecasts. (5) Organizations that form in response to temporary or nonexistent danger and develop the capacity to raise funds from public-spirited citizens and governments that are aroused to fight the danger do not always disband when the danger evaporates or the problem is solved. (6) Ambition and the urge for profit are powerful elements in our successful struggle to satisfy our needs. These motives, and the markets in which they work, often are not pretty, and many people would prefer not to have to depend on a social system that employed these forces to make us better off. (7) Associating oneself with environmental causes is one of the quickest and easiest ways to get a wide reputation for high-minded concern. It requires no deep thinking and steps on almost no one's toes.

The apparently obvious way to deal with resource problems—have the government control the amounts and prices of what consumers consume and suppliers supply—is inevitably counterproductive in the long run because the controls and price fixing prevent us from making the cost-efficient adjustments that we would make in response to increased short-run costs, adjustments that would eventually more than alleviate the problem. Sometimes governments must play a crucial role to avoid short-run disruptions and disaster and to ensure that no group consumes public goods without paying the real social cost. But the appropriate times for governments to play such roles are far fewer than the times they are called upon to do so by those inclined to turn to authority to tell us what to do, rather than allow each of us to respond with self-interest and imagination.

One of the main themes of this book, which this edition emphasizes even more than the first edition because there is now a greater weight of evidence behind it, is the proper role of government: to set market rules that are as impersonal and as general as possible, allowing individuals to decide for themselves how and what to produce and what to consume, in a manner that infringes as little as possible on the rights of others to do the same, and where each pays the full price to others of the costs to others of one's own activities. Support for this principle appears . . . as we view the history and the statistical data on such issues as food production, supply of natural resources, and the like.

It is not only the human mind and the human spirit that are crucial but also the framework of society. The political-economic organization of a country has the most influence upon its economics progress. In 1742 (first edition), the man whom I regard as the greatest philosopher who ever lived and one of the greatest economists of all time—David Hume—wrote this: "Multitudes of people, necessity, and liberty, have begotten commerce in Holland." In that one short sentence, Hume summarized everything important about economic progress: economic liberty, which comes from a country "ruled by laws rather than men" and allows people to make the most of their individual talents and opportunities; necessity—that is, in Holland's case, the lack of great stretches of fertile land on which to grow crops easily, and therefore the necessity of creating new fertile land by fighting the sea for that land; and multitudes of people—the human talent to invent new ways of doing things and of organizing an effective society. That is the heart of the story told in this book.

The greatest asset of the United States and of other economically advanced countries is the political, legal, and economic organization. Compare how easy it is to do business (for example, get inputs from suppliers) in the United States with the way it was in the Soviet Union, and as it will certainly continue to be in Russia for some years. . . .

But again, people look at the matter in the small rather than in the large, and don't see the long-run benefits of problems. Perhaps our willingness to believe that "clever" people can make sound decisions and render useful advice when in such positions as head of the World Bank or International Monetary Fund (IMF) is related to our belief that people can find a pattern even when there is no pattern. We are reluctant to think that we as human beings can do no better than chance in such matters.

I do not say that everything now is fine, of course. Children are still hungry and sick; some people live lives of physical and intellectual poverty and lack of opportunity; war or some new pollution may do us all in.

What I am saying is that for most of the relevant economic matters I have checked, the trends are positive rather than negative. And I doubt that it does the troubled people of the world any good to say that things are getting worse when they are really getting better. And false prophecies of doom can damage us in many ways.

Is a rosy future guaranteed? Of course not. There will always be temporary shortages and resource problems where there is strife, political blundering, and natural calamity—that is, where there are people. But the natural world allows, and the developed world promotes through the marketplace, responses to human needs and shortages in such a way that one backward step leads to 1.0001 steps forward, or thereabouts. That's enough to keep us headed in a life-sustaining direction.

Which should be our vision? The doomsayers of the population control movement offer a vision of limits, decreasing resources, a zero-sum game, conservation, deterioration, fear, and conflict, calling for more governmental intervention in markets and family affairs. Or should our vision be that of those who look optimistically on people as a resource rather than as a burden—a vision of receding limits, increasing resources and possibilities, a game in which everyone can win, creation, building excitement, and the belief that persons and firms, acting spontaneously in the search of their individual welfare, regulated only by rules of a fair game, will produce enough to maintain and increase economic progress and promote liberty?

And what should our mood be? The population restrictionists say we should be sad and worry. I and many others believe that the trends suggest joy and celebration at our newfound capacity to support human life—healthily, and with fast-increasing access to education and opportunity all over the world. I believe that the population restrictionists' hand-wringing view leads to despair and resignation. Our view leads to hope and progress, in the reasonable expectation that the energetic efforts of humankind will prevail in the future, as they have in the past, to increase worldwide our numbers, our health, our wealth, and our opportunities.

So to sum up the summary: In the short run, all resources are limited. An example of such a finite resource is the amount of time and attention you will devote to what I have written. The longer run, however, is a different story. The standard of living has risen along with the size of the world's population since the beginning of recorded time. There is no convincing economic reason why these trends toward a better life should not continue indefinitely.

The key theoretical idea is this: Increased population and a higher standard of living cause actual and expected shortages, and hence price rises. A higher price represents an opportunity that attracts profit-minded entrepreneurs and socially minded inventors to seek new ways to satisfy the shortages. Some fail, at a cost to themselves. A few succeed, and the final result is that we end up better off than if the original shortage problems had never arisen. That is, we need our problems, though this does not imply that we should purposely create added problems for ourselves.

Of course progress does not come about automatically. And my message certainly is not one of complacency, though anyone who predicts reduced scarcity of resources has always drawn that label. In this I agree with the doomsayers—that our world needs the best efforts of all humanity to improve our lot. I part company with them in that they expect us to come to a bad end despite the efforts we make, whereas I expect the successful efforts to continue. And I believe that their message is self-fulfilling, because if you expect your efforts to fail because of inexorable natural limits, then you are likely to feel resigned and therefore to literally resign. But if you recognize the possibility—in fact the probability—of success, you can tap large reservoirs of energy and enthusiasm.

Adding more people causes problems, but people are also the means to solve these problems. The main fuel to speed our progress is our stock of knowledge, and the brake is our lack of imagination. The ultimate resource is people—skilled, spirited, and hopeful people who will exert their wills and imaginations for their own benefit—and inevitably they will benefit not only themselves but the rest of us as well.

The Population Challenge

Lester R. Brown, Gary Gardner, and Brian Halweil

This selection was excerpted from "The Population Challenge," in *Beyond Malthus: Nineteen Dimensions of the Population Challenge* (New York: WW Norton & Company, 1999).

During the last half-century, world population has more than doubled, climbing from 2.5 billion in 1950 to 5.9 billion in 1998. Those of us born before 1950 are members of the first generation to witness a doubling of world population. Stated otherwise, there has been more growth in population since 1950 than during the 4 million preceding years since our early ancestors first stood upright.

This unprecedented surge in population, combined with rising individual consumption, is pushing our claims on the planet beyond its natural limits. Water tables are falling on every continent as demand exceeds the sustainable yield of aquifers. Our growing appetite for seafood has taken oceanic fisheries to their limits and beyond. Collapsing fisheries tell us we can go no further.

The earth's temperature is rising, promising changes in climate that we cannot even anticipate. And we have inadvertently launched the greatest extinction of plant and animal species since the dinosaurs disappeared.

Great as the population growth of the last half-century has been, it is far from over. U.N. demographers project an increase over the next half-century of another 2.8 billion people, somewhat fewer than the 3.6 billion added during the half-century now ending. In contrast to the last fifty years, however, all of the 2.8 billion will be added in the developing world, much of which is already densely populated.

Even as we anticipate huge further increases in population, encouraging demographic news seems to surface regularly. Fertility rates, the average number of children born to a woman, have fallen steadily in most countries in recent decades. Twice in the last ten years the United Nations has moderated its projections of global population growth, first in 1996 and then again in 1998. Unfortunately, part of the latter decline in population projections is due to rising mortality rather than declining fertility.

In contrast to the projected doublings and triplings for some developing countries, populations are stable or even declining in some thirty-two industrial nations. Compared with the situation at midcentury, when nearly all signs pointed to galloping population increases for the foreseeable future, today's demographic picture is decidedly more complex.

Anyone tempted to conclude that population growth is becoming a "nonissue" may find this book a reality check. Despite the many encouraging demographic trends, the need to stabilize global population is as urgent as ever. Although the rate of population growth is slowing, the world is still adding some 80 million people a year. And the number of young people coming of reproductive age—those between fifteen and twenty-four years old—will be far larger during the early part of the next century than ever before. Through their reproductive choices, this group will heavily influence whether population is stabilized sooner rather than later, and with less rather than more suffering.

In addition, population growth has already surpassed sustainable limits on a number of environmental fronts. From cropland and water availability to climate change and unemployment, population growth exacerbates existing problems, making them more difficult to manage. The intersection of the arrival of a series of environmental limits and a potentially huge expansion in the number of people subject to those limits makes the turn of the century a unique time in world demographic history.

As the global population locomotive hurtles forward—despite pressure applied to the demographic brakes—there are hazards on the tracks ahead. A number of limits to sustainability are being surpassed or are about to be.

By looking at the consequences of population growth for various environmental and social dimensions of the human experience, we are part of a long tradition dating back to 1798 when Thomas Malthus, a British clergyman and intellectual, warned in his "Essay on the Principle of Population" of the check on population growth provided by what he believed were coming constraints on food supplies. Noting that population grows exponentially while food supply grows only arithmetically, Malthus foresaw massive food shortages and famine as the inevitable consequence of population growth.

Critics of Malthus point out that his pessimistic scenario never unfolded. His supporters believe he was simply ahead of his time. On the bicentennial of Malthus's legendary essay, and in an era of environmental decline, we find his focus on the connection between resource supply and population growth to be particularly useful. We move beyond Malthus's focus on food, however, to look at several resources—such as water and forests—whose supply may be insufficient to support projected increases in population. We also examine social phenomena including disease and education and analyze the effect of population growth on these.

The results of our analysis offer further evidence that we are approaching—and increasingly broaching—any number of natural limits. We know that close to a tenth of world food production relies on the overpumping of groundwater, and that continuing this practice will mean a substantial decline in food production at some point in the future. We know that both atmospheric carbon dioxide concentrations and the earth's surface temperature are rising. We know that we are the first species in the planet's history to trigger a mass extinction, and we admit that we do not understand the consequences of such a heavy loss of plant and animal species. In short, we know enough to understand that the growth in our numbers and the scale of our activities is already redirecting the natural course of our planet, and that this new direction will in turn affect us.

The relationship between these natural limits and population growth becomes clear if we contrast key trends projected for the next half-century with those of the last one. For example, since 1950 we have seen a near fivefold growth in the oceanic fish catch and a doubling in the supply of fish per person, but people born today may well see the catch per person cut in half as population grows during their lifetimes. Marine biologists now believe we may have "hit the wall" in oceanic fisheries and that the oceans cannot sustain a catch any larger than today's.

Any meaningful assessment of the future pressures on resources must take into account both population growth and rises in affluence. Consumption per person of various resources among societies can vary from five to one for grain, as between the United States and India, for example, to easily twenty to one for energy. While population growth in some thirty-two countries has stabilized, and many more countries have stabilization as a goal, no country at any level of affluence has announced or even seriously contemplated limits on consumption per person.

The challenge to nations presented by continuing rapid population growth is not limited to natural resources. It also includes social and economic needs, including education, housing, and jobs. During the last half-century, the world has fallen further and further behind in creating jobs, leading to record levels of unemployment and underemployment. Unfortunately, over the next fifty years the number of entrants into the job market will be even greater, pushing the ranks of unemployment to levels that could be politically destabilizing. And as homelessness is already a serious problem in most large third world cities, the housing situation for added urban dwellers is increasingly dismal.

The earth is more crowded today than ever before. And although our numbers continue to grow, the size of the planet on which we live remains the same. Future population growth has the potential to further degrade and deplete resources, such as topsoil, groundwater, and forest cover, as well as to reduce the resources available to each person. Moreover, population growth strains the capacity of governments to provide basic social services, such as education and health care, for each citizen. This combination of environmental degradation and social shortfalls can ultimately result in any number of unpleasant scenarios that can undermine future progress.

Several questions stand out in trying to look beyond Malthus. Will countries with rapid population growth take control of their reproductive destinies and quickly shift to smaller families? Or will they fail to do so, and instead watch the resulting spread of disease, hunger, or social disintegration lead to rising death rates? In a world facing many problems as it prepares to enter the next century, stabilizing population may be the most difficult challenge of all.

Population, Resources, and the Quest to "Stabilize Human Population": Myths and Realities

Nicholas Eberstadt

This selection was excerpted from "Population, Resources, and the Quest to 'Stabilize Human Population': Myths and Realities," in *Global Warming and Other Eco-Myths*, edited by Ronald Bailey (New York: Random House, Inc., 2002).

THE IMPERATIVE OF "STABILIZING WORLD POPULATION": A WIDELY ACCEPTED NOTION

A demographic specter is haunting authoritative and influential circles in both the United States and the international community. This specter is the supposed imperative to "stabilize human population."

The quest to stabilize human population (or to stabilize world population, or sometimes just to stabilize population) is currently affirmed by the World Bank and many other multilateral and bilateral aid organizations in the international development community. That objective is likewise praised by the United Nations' current secretary general, Kofi Annan, and is now embraced by a panoply of subsidiary institutions in the United Nations family, including the United Nations Environmental Programme (UNEP), and the United Nations Children's Fund (UNICEF), and the United Nations Population Fund (UNFPA), which explicitly declares its mission to be the promotion of the "universally accepted aim of stabilizing world population."

Closer to home, the goal of stabilizing human population is championed by a broad network of population and environmental activist groups, including most prominently Planned Parenthood and the Sierra Club (the latter of which has established stabilizing world population as the fourth goal of its twenty-first century agenda). The objective, however, is not merely proclaimed by an activist fringe; to the contrary, it is broadly shared by many elements of what might be called the American estab-

lishment. Stabilizing world population, for example, is now a program-
matic effort for most of the prestigious multibillion-dollar American phil-
anthropic organizations that commit their resources to international
population activities, a list including, but not limited to, the Ford Foundation, the Hewlett Foundation, the MacArthur Foundation, the Packard
Foundation, and the Rockefeller Foundation. Further, stabilizing world
population is a prospect welcomed and financially supported by many of
America's most prominent and successful captains of industry, among
them, self-made multibillionaires Ted Turner, Warren Buffet, and Bill
Gates. The propriety—or necessity—of stabilizing global population has
been expounded by a wide array of respected writers, spokespersons, and
commentators in the U.S. and international media. Politically, the goal of
stabilizing world population has been approved by the U.S. State Department and USAID (America's foreign aid apparatus) for fully a generation.
The quest to stabilize world population, in fact, is championed in the
United States by political figures who are both influential and widely popular. One of America's most passionate and outspoken exponents of world
population stabilization, former Vice President Al Gore, very nearly won
the presidency in the closely contested 2000 election.

What, exactly, does "stabilizing human population" actually mean?
Though the objective is widely championed today, the banner itself is
somewhat misleading, for advocates of stabilizing population are in fact
not concerned with *stabilizing* human numbers. If they were, one would
expect champions of population stabilization to turn their attention to the
outlook for Europe and Japan, where populations are currently projected
to drop significantly over the next half-century. On a more immediate
front, human numbers have entered into an abrupt and as yet unchecked
decline in the Russian Federation over just the past decade. In 1999
alone, that country suffered almost 1 million more deaths than births. Yet
supporters of population stabilization have agitated for coordinated measures to lower Russia's death rate, raise its birthrate, and stanch its ongoing
demographic losses.

The reason for such seemingly curious insouciance about demographic decline by self-avowed population stabilizers is that their chosen
standard does not quite describe their true quest. For exponents of stabilizing human population do not simply look for population stabilization;

rather, as the former executive director of the UNFPA framed the goal, they strive "for stabilization of world population at the lowest possible level, within the shortest period of time."

On inspection, it is apparent that "stabilizing human population" is really code language, a new name for an old and familiar project. Today's call for stabilizing human population is actually a rallying cry for antinatalism. After all, its envisioned means of achieving stabilization is through limiting the prevalence, and reducing the level, of childbearing around the world, especially in the third world—implementing policies to reduce births, and thereby depressing fertility in various venues around the globe (and particularly where fertility levels are deemed to be unacceptably high).

The ongoing antinatal population crusade couches its arguments in the language of social science and invokes the findings of science to bolster its authority, but it cannot withstand the process of empirical review that lies at the heart of the rational scientific method. Whether they realize it or not, advocates of world population stabilization are devotees of an ideology, not followers of facts.

The Premises of "World Population Stabilization"

Reduced to its essence, the case for action to stabilize world population rests on four specific premises.

The first quite simply holds that we are manifestly in the midst of a world population crisis—a crisis defined by rapid population growth, which in turn is exacerbating overpopulation. Former Vice President Gore nicely illustrated this tenet of thinking in his best-selling book, *Earth in the Balance* (New York: Houghton Mifflin Co., 2000), and elsewhere when he stated that in today's global population trends "the absolute numbers are staggering" and that "we can't acquiesce in the continuation of a situation that adds another . . . China's worth of people every decade."

The second premise underpinning the population stabilization project is that current rates of world population growth are not only unsustainable over the long term but they also have direct and immediate adverse repercussions on living standards, resource availability, and even political stability today. In the estimate of the Planned Parenthood Federation of America, for example, "Slowing population growth helps poorer countries develop politically and economically." Gore is more vivid. He maintains that "population is pushing many countries over an economic cliff as their resources are stripped away and the cycle of poverty and environmental destruction accelerates" and that "societies cannot maintain stability with [that] kind of rapid, unsustainable [demographic] growth" that is being registered in many regions of the world; pointing to such strife-rent spots as Somalia, Rwanda, and the former Yugoslavia, Gore argues that "you can look at the contribution of rapid destabilizing population growth."

The third premise implicit in the agenda of stabilizing human population is that reduced birthrates constitute the solution to the population problems adduced by premises one and two. The fourth and final premise bolstering this agenda is the presumption that well-placed decision-makers can effectively and expeditiously engineer the desired changes in worldwide population patterns through deliberate policy interventions. Once again, Gore may have represented this presumption best. In his words, "we know how to stabilize world population" because "population specialists now know with a high degree of confidence what factors dramatically reduce birthrates."

However, all these premises are highly problematic. None of them are self-evidently true. And to the extent that any of these separate premises are testable, it would appear that they are demonstrably false.

"Overpopulation": A Problem Misdefined

Consider the first premise: that the world faces the crisis of being burdened by simply too many people. If that premise is offered as an aesthetic judgment, it is irrefutable. (By their very nature, subjective opinions are not falsifiable.) But how does it fare if treated as a testable proposition? Gore writes that an "overcrowded world is inevitably a polluted one"—a verdict that many of those worried about world population growth would accept without reservation. But overcrowding is not as easily established as some might suppose. Population density, for example, might seem to be a reasonable criterion for overcrowding. By that criterion, Haiti, India, and Rwanda (each with over six times the world's average population density) would surely qualify as overcrowded, and Bangladesh—with almost twenty times the inhabited globe's average density—would be manifestly "overcrowded." By that same criterion, however, Belgium (1998 population density per square kilometer: 335) would be distinctly more overcrowded than Rwanda (1998 population density per square kilometer: 272). Similarly, the Netherlands would be more overcrowded than Haiti, Bermuda would be more overcrowded than Bangladesh, and oil-rich Bahrain would be three times as overcrowded as India. But the most overcrowded country in the world would be Monaco: with a dire 32,894 persons per square kilometer in 1998, it suffers a population density almost forty times that of Bangladesh and more than seven hundred times the world average. Yet as we all know, population activists do not agitate themselves about the overcrowding problem in Monaco—or in Bermuda or in Bahrain.

Moreover, it is hardly self-evident that there is any association at the international level between population density and economic performance. The same holds true for the density of population with respect to arable land. It is impossible to distinguish any meaningful association— positive or negative—between a country's per capita output level and the number of people supported by each local hectare of farm- or pastureland. Surprising as it may sound to those convinced that the world is beset by overpopulation, the fact is that in our era, population density provides us with no information whatsoever for predicting a country's level of economic development or economic performance.

Do other demographic measures provide a better reading of the population problem that so many take to be so very obvious today? Perhaps we might look at rates of population growth. In the 1990s, sub-Saharan Africa was estimated to have the world's highest rate of population growth—the United Nations Population Division put its pace at over 2.5 percent a year for the period 1995 to 2000—and sub-Saharan Africa is clearly a most troubled area these days. However, if we look back in history, we will discover that the United States had an even higher rate of population growth at the end of the eighteenth century. In the decade 1790–1800, in fact, the U.S. pace of population growth was 3 percent a year. Some today may believe that sub-Saharan Africa has too many people—but would they say the same about early frontier America?

Fertility rates are hardly more illuminating. In *Earth in the Balance*, Gore expressly mentions Egypt, Kenya, and Nigeria as candidates for places with too many people (either today or in the decades immediately ahead). All three countries are thought to experience fertility levels above the current world average. According to the latest (May 2000) projections by the U.S. Census Bureau, in 1998 the total fertility rate (births per woman per lifetime under prevailing childbearing schedules) for the world as a whole was about 2.8, as against 3.4 in Egypt, 4.4 in Kenya, and 5.8 in Nigeria. But once again: fertility levels were far higher in the United States in the early years of the Republic than in any of these places today. Around 1800, according to estimates by the demographer Michael Haines ("The Population of the United States, 1790–1920," table 3), the total fertility rate for white Americans was just over *seven* births per woman per lifetime — yet Thomas Jefferson's America is not today widely regarded as a society in the throes of a population crisis. Clearly, fertility rates by themselves tell us very little.

We could continue combing for demographic measures that might help to clarify the nature, and pinpoint the epicenters, of the population crisis that Gore envisions. But as our exercise should already indicate, that would be a fruitless task. Additional demographic criteria will confront the same problem of obvious misidentification of presumptive regions suffering from too many people because demographic criteria cannot by themselves unambiguously describe overpopulation. This is a basic fact, recognized by every trained demographer. And that basic fact raises correspondingly basic questions about the concept of overpopulation.

The alleged population crisis that advocates of world population stabilization wish to resolve is impossible to define in demographic terms because it is a problem that has been misdefined. In most minds, the notions of overpopulation, overcrowding, or too many people are associated with images of hungry children, unchecked disease, squalid living conditions, and awful slums. Those problems, sad to say, are all too real in the contemporary world. But the proper name for those conditions is *human poverty*. And the correspondence between human poverty and demographic trends, as we shall see in a moment, is by no means as causal and clear-cut as some would suppose.

If we are to make inroads against the problems of humanity, it is important that we begin by calling those problems by their proper names.

The problem of global poverty, in and of itself, cannot in an empirical sense be defined as a world population crisis—unless one means it is a crisis that so many people today should be suffering from poverty. But it is a fundamental lapse in logic to assume that poverty is a population problem simply because it is manifest today in large numbers of human beings. The proper name for that logical error is the *fallacy of composition.*

Population Growth, Development, and Political Stability

Let us now consider the second premise of world population stabilization: that rapid population growth and high fertility levels cause or exacerbate poverty, resource scarcity, and political instability. If we wish to treat this premise as an empirically testable proposition (rather than an unchallengeable tenet of faith), we will recognize immediately the complexity of the processes we propose to observe. The relationships between population change and economic or political change encompass an extraordinarily broad and complicated set of interactions with an array of multidirectional influences and consequential second-, third- and even higher-order impacts.

Describing these interactions comprehensively and accurately is a tremendous and subtle challenge. And researchers who have approached this challenge with care and objectivity typically have described the economic impact of demographic changes in nuanced and qualified terms. Typical of such work are the findings of econometrician Dennis Ahlburg, who concludes that "it is not clear whether population growth causes poverty in the long run or not, [although] high fertility leading to rapidly growing population will increase the number of people in poverty in the short run" ("Population Growth and Poverty," in *Population and Development: Old Debates, New Conclusions* [New Brunswick, N.J.: Transaction Publishers, 1994]). Development economist Robert Cassen accurately describes the state of current research when he notes "the issue of whether per capita economic growth is reduced by population growth remains unsettled. Attempts to demonstrate such an effect empirically have produced no significant and reliable results" ("Population Policy: A New Consensus" [Washington, D.C.: Overseas Development Council, 1994]).

Even so, we need not rely on the judgment of experts, or attempt to replicate their efforts at model building, to appreciate the flaws inherent in this premise.

We can begin by recalling the reason for the twentieth century's population explosion. From 1900 to 2000, human numbers almost quadrupled, leaping from about 1.6 billion to more than 6 billion; in pace or magnitude, nothing like that surge had ever previously taken place. But why exactly did we experience a world population explosion in the twentieth century? It was not because people suddenly started breeding like rabbits—rather, it was because they finally stopped dying like flies.

Between 1900 and the end of the twentieth century, the human life span likely doubled: from a planetary life expectancy at birth of perhaps thirty years to one of more than sixty years. By this measure, the overwhelming preponderance of the health progress in all of human history took place during the last hundred years.

Over the last half-century, worldwide progress in reducing death rates has been especially dramatic. Between the early 1950s and the late 1990s, according to estimates in "UN World Population Prospects" (2000 revision) by the United Nations Population Division (UNPD—not to be confused with UNFPA), the planetary expectation of life at birth jumped by almost nineteen years, or two-fifths, from under forty-seven years to sixty-five years. For the low-income regions, the leap was even more dramatic. Taken together, average life expectancy in these areas surged up by well over two decades, a rise of more than 50 percent. Even troubled sub-Saharan Africa—despite its protracted postindependence-era political and economic turmoil and the advent of a catastrophic HIV/AIDS epidemic—is thought to have enjoyed an increase in local life expectancy of nearly a third. (Practically the only countries to register no appreciable improvements in life expectancy over this period were the handful of European territories in what was once the Soviet Union; in the Russian Federation in particular, gains over these four and a half decades were almost negligible.)

Among the most important proximate reasons for the global surge in life expectancy was the worldwide drop in infant mortality rates. In the early 1950s, according again to UNPD estimates, 167 out of every thousand children born around the world did not survive their first year of life; by the late 1990s, that toll was down to 60 per thousand. In developed countries, infant mortality is thought to have fallen by five-sixths during those decades, and by almost two-thirds in the collectivity of developing countries. Even in troubled regions, great advances in infant survival were achieved; in sub-Saharan Africa, for example, the infant mortality rate is thought to have declined by nearly half, and Russia's infant mortality rate probably fell by more than 80 percent.

This radical drop in mortality is entirely responsible for the increase in human numbers over the course of the twentieth century; the population explosion, in other words, was really a health explosion.

Now, with respect to economic development, the implications of a health explosion—of *any* health explosion—are, on their face, hardly negative. Quite the contrary: A healthier population is clearly going to be a population with greater productive potential. Healthier people are able to learn better, work harder, and engage in gainful employment longer and contribute more to economic activity than their unhealthy, short-lived counterparts. Whether that potential actually translates into tangible economic results will naturally depend on other factors, such as social and legal institutions or the business and policy climate. Nevertheless, the health explosion that propelled the twentieth century's population explosion was an economically auspicious phenomenon rather than a troubling trend.

All other things being equal, one would have expected the health explosion to contribute to the acceleration of economic growth, the increase of income, and the spread of wealth. And as it happens, the twentieth century witnessed not only a population explosion and a health explosion but also a prosperity explosion. Estimates by the economic historian Angus Maddison, who has produced perhaps the most authoritative reconstruction of long-term global economic trends presently available, demonstrate this ("Monitoring the World Economy: 1820–1992" [Paris: Organization for Economic Cooperation and Development, 1995] and "The World Economy: A Millennial Perspective" [Paris: Organization for Economic Cooperation and Development, 2001]).

Though specialists may quibble over particular figures in Maddison's detailed long-term series, the overall economic picture that his calculations paint and the general trends they outline are not matters of dispute among serious students of economic history today.

Between 1900 and 1998, by Maddison's reckoning, global gross domestic product (GDP) per capita (in internationally adjusted 1990 dollars) more than quadrupled. Gains in productivity were globally uneven. In both relative and absolute terms, today's Organization for Economic Cooperation and Development (OECD) states enjoyed disproportionate improvement. Nonetheless, every region of the planet became richer. Africa's economic performance, according to Maddison, was the most dismal of any major global region over the course of the twentieth century. Yet even there, per capita GDP was approximated to be more than two and a half times higher in 1998 than it had been in 1900.

Suffice it then to say that the twentieth century's population explosion did not forestall the most dramatic and widespread improvement in output, incomes, and living standards that humanity has ever experienced. Though severe poverty still endures in much of the world, there can be no doubt that its incidence has been markedly curtailed over the past hundred years, despite a near quadrupling of human numbers.

Maddison's estimates of global economic growth highlight another empirical problem with the second premise of the population stabilization project. With a near quadrupling of the human population over the course of the twentieth century, and a more than fourfold increase in human GDP per capita over those same years, global economic output has taken an absolutely amazing leap. Maddison's own figures suggest world GDP might have been more than eighteen times higher in 1998 than it was in 1900. But GDP is a measure of economic output—and for the world as a whole, economic output and economic demand must be identical. If the demand for goods and services has multiplied nearly twentyfold during the twentieth century, humanity's demand for, and consumption of, natural resources has also rocketed upward. But despite humanity's tremendous new pressures on planetary resources, the relative prices of virtually all primary commodities have *fallen* over the course of the twentieth century, and many of them, quite substantially.

Despite the tremendous expansion of the international grain trade over the past century, for example, the inflation-adjusted, dollar-denominated international price of each of the major cereals—corn, wheat, and rice—fell by over 70 percent between 1900 and 1998. By the same token, The *Economist* magazine's industrials price index—a weighted composite for fourteen internationally traded metals and non-food agricultural commodities—registered a decline in inflation-adjusted dollars of almost 80 percent between 1900 and 1999. Perhaps the most comprehensive index of long-term real primary commodity prices was the one constructed by Enzo Grilli and Maw Cheng Yang ("Primary Commodity Prices, Manufactured Goods Prices, and the Terms of Trade of Developing Countries: What the Long Run Shows," *World Bank Economic Review*, 1988). Their series encompassed twenty-four internationally traded nonfuel primary commodities, plus coal and oil. Their calculations extend from 1900 only up to 1986, but their results are nevertheless arresting. For that eighty-six-year period, Grilli and Yang found that real prices of nonfuel primary commodities—renewable resources like cereals and nonrenewable resources such as metals—fell substantially, trending downward by an average of 0.6 percent a year. When fuels were included in the series, the picture changed only slightly. With energy included in their primary commodity index, real overall prices still trended downward at a pace of 0.5 percent a year. On that trajectory, real primary commodity prices would be expected to decline by nearly 40 percent over the course of a century.

The paradox of exploding demand for resources and simultaneous pronounced declines in real resource price will appear curious and compelling to any observer, but it should be especially arresting to a viewer with the essentially Malthusian sensibility of ideological environmentalism. In the most fundamental sense, after all, price data are meant to convey information about scarcity—and by the sorts of information that they convey, they seem to indicate that the resources humanity makes economic use of grew *less scarce* over the course of the twentieth century. There are, to be sure, explanations for this paradox—but the stabilization project's second premise, which holds that population growth must result in resource scarcity, is hardly able to provide it.

The dilemma can be stated even more starkly: if the presumptions incorporated in that premise regarding the interplay between population growth, living standards, and resource scarcity were valid, the twentieth century should not have occurred.

What about the supposed relationship between rapid population growth and political strife? The hypothesis that population growth could affect political stability is certainly worth entertaining. It is plausible, after all, to conjecture that instability is more of a risk for governments that do not cope well with change—and population growth, whatever else it may be, is also inescapably a form of social change.

The vision of the link between rapid population growth and political destabilization, however, is sometimes undercut by the very evidence adduced to support it. Take Gore's aforementioned attribution of the carnage in the former Yugoslavia in the early 1990s to rapid population growth. The problem with this argument is that the former Yugoslavia was characterized neither by especially rapid rates of population growth nor by particularly high levels of fertility.

Consider Bosnia and Herzegovina, which suffered war, horrific ethnic cleansing, and other atrocities in the early 1990s. Over the three decades before pandemonium erupted (i.e., 1961 to 1991), Bosnia and Herzegovina recorded a population growth rate of about 1 percent a year—slower than the United States's 1.1 percent per annum rate over the same period, and barely half the average worldwide pace of 1.9 percent during those years. Moreover, in 1991—on the eve of its descent into chaos—Bosnia's estimated total fertility rate was 1.7 births per woman per lifetime—well below the replacement level. Estimates by the UNPD suggest that Bosnia and Herzegovina's fertility levels had been below replacement throughout the 1980s as well. The situation is little different in the other fragments of the former Yugoslavia. Fertility levels and population growth rates were even lower than Bosnia's in Croatia and Slovenia and only marginally higher in Macedonia; Serbia's fertility level was slightly higher, but its rate of population growth was slightly lower. (Today, incidentally, all the countries carved out of the former Yugoslavia report fertility levels far below the replacement.)

One can only wonder, if the former Yugoslavia is an example of a region rent by demographically driven political turmoil, exactly how low are population growth rates supposed to fall, and birthrates to sink, before a region is safe from this purported menace? It is perfectly true that political conflict cannot take place without human populations—but it does not follow that the surest and soundest way of preventing political conflict is simply to prevent the existence of people in the first place.

"World Population Stabilization" through Scientific Population Policies?
The third premise of world population stabilization—that birthrates must be lowered to alleviate the world population crisis and to mitigate the adverse economic, political, and resource-related consequences of rapid population growth—requires absolutely no substantiation if one is a true believer in the antinatalist dogma of ideological environmentalism. To the antinatalist way of thinking, the purposeful reduction of birthrates (and especially birthrates in poorer regions) is an incontestably worthy policy objective—for to this way of thinking it is axiomatic that fewer births translate directly into benefits for present and future generations. For those who must be convinced that a problem exists before consenting to the public action proposed to redress it, that conclusion rests on the first two premises—and for the empirically inclined, as we have seen, those are shaky foundations indeed.

But even if we were convinced of the pressing need to take public action to lower worldwide birthrates, it would not necessarily follow that the desired result could be achieved, or achieved at an acceptable cost, or achieved voluntarily. Here lies the pivotal importance of the fourth premise of world population stabilization, for this tenet maintains that it is an established fact that population specialists know how international birthrates can be lowered and that these specialists can consequently provide policymakers with reliable advice about the precise interventions that will bring about fertility declines.

But once again, the final premise underpinning the quest for stabilizing world population is badly flawed. The plain fact is that students of contemporary and historical child-bearing patterns have *not* uncovered the magic formula that explains why fertility changes have occurred in the past, much less identified the special levers that can determine how these trends will unfold in the future.

The trouble with the mission to identify universal and reliable determinants of fertility decline goes back literally to the origins of the phenomenon. Secular fertility decline—the sustained, long-term shift from big families to small ones—began for the first time in Europe, about two hundred years ago. But it did not begin in England and Wales, then perhaps the most open, literate, and industrialized part of the Continent, if not the world. Instead, it began in France, a country then impoverished, overwhelmingly rural, predominantly illiterate—and, not to put too fine a point on it, Catholic. Clearly, the modernization model does not plausibly explain the advent of fertility decline in the modern world. And unfortunately, alternative models do not really fare much better. Reviewing the theories of fertility decline in western Europe and the evidence adduced to support them, the historian Charles Tilly wrote that "[t]he problem is that we have too many explanations which are plausible in general terms, which contradict each other to some degree and which fail to fit some significant part of the facts" (*Historical Studies of Changing Fertility* [Princeton, N.J.: Princeton University Press, 1978]). But what was true for western Europe at the onset of this process holds equally for the rest of the world today.

Al Gore's best-seller, *Earth in the Balance*, exemplifies the thinking of many current proponents of world population stabilization in describing the factors that he holds to be instrumental in achieving sustained fertility reductions:

> High literacy rates and education levels *are important, especially for women; once they are empowered intellectually and socially they make decisions about the number of children they wish to have. Low infant mortality rates give parents a sense of confidence that even with a small family, some of their children will grow to maturity . . . and provide physical security when they are old. Nearly ubiquitous access to a variety of affordable birth control techniques gives parents the power to choose when and whether to have children.* [emphasis in the original]

Each of these three desiderata may qualify as a social objective in its own right, entirely irrespective of its influence on demographic trends. As purported determinants of fertility change, however, the explanatory and predictive properties of these three factors largely fail.

Data from the 2000–2001 edition of the World Bank's *World Development Report* underscore the problem. According to the World Bank's figures, the adult illiteracy rate for both males and females was higher in

1998 in Mongolia than in Tanzania—but Tanzania's fertility level in 1998 was reportedly over twice as high as Mongolia's (5.4 versus 2.5 births per woman). Tunisia and Rwanda were said to have almost identical rates of adult female illiteracy (42 percent versus 43 percent), yet Tunisia's fertility level is put at just over replacement (2.2) while Rwanda's is almost three times higher (6.2). And although Bangladesh's female illiteracy rate is still placed at more than 70 percent, the country's fertility level is said to have fallen by almost half from 1980 to 1998. Iran's total fertility rate is said to have plummeted by a remarkable 60 percent, from 6.7 to 2.7, over those same eighteen years. But presumably the Iranian revolution was not quite what Gore and other ideological environmentalists had in mind in arguing that the intellectual and social empowerment of women would lead to smaller families.

Infant mortality provides scarcely more information about fertility levels or fertility change. By the UNPD's projections, for example, Jordan's infant mortality rate was about the same as Thailand's in the early 1990s. But where the Thailand fertility level at that time was below replacement, Jordan's was above five births per woman per lifetime. By the same token, although infant mortality rates were said to be almost identical in Bangladesh and Yemen in the late 1990s, Yemen's total fertility rate at that time was twice as high as Bangladesh's (7.6 versus 3.8)—and while fertility levels had dropped substantially in Bangladesh over the previous generation, movement in Yemen's fertility rate had yet to be detected. Historically, the onset of sustained fertility decline in France took place during a period (1780–1820) when the country suffered an estimated average of almost two hundred infant deaths for every thousand births. No country in the contemporary world suffers from such a brutally high infant mortality rate, but a number of present-day countries with considerably lower infant mortality rates than prevailed in Napoleonic France apparently have yet to enter into fertility decline. Conversely, literally dozens of contemporary low-income countries with much more favorable infant and child survival schedules than prevailed in that bygone France have yet to report fertility levels as low as the four births per woman per lifetime estimated for French society around 1800.

As for the relationship between fertility and the availability of modern contraceptives (or national programs to subsidize or encourage their use), inconvenient facts must once again be faced. To start with, the utilization rates for modern contraceptive methods are not an especially reliable indicator of a society's fertility level. In the early 1990s, among married women ages fifteen to forty-nine, Zimbabwe's rate of modern contraceptive use was three times as high as Romania's (42 percent versus 14 percent), yet Romania's total fertility rate was about 1.4 whereas Zimbabwe's was about 4.1. Syria's 1993 rate of modern contraceptive use was likewise higher than Lithuania's rate for 1994 to 1995 (29 percent versus 22 percent), yet the total fertility rate was also three times the Lithuanian level (4.6 versus 1.5). Further such examples abound.

For another thing, the independent influence of national population programs on national birthrates appears to be very much more limited than enthusiasts are willing to recognize. A comparison of Mexico and Brazil, Latin America's two most populous countries, illustrates the point. Since 1974, Mexico has sponsored a national family planning program expressly committed to reducing the country's rate of population growth. Brazil, by contrast, has never implemented a national family planning program. In the quarter century after the introduction of Mexico's national population program, Mexican fertility levels fell by an estimated 56 percent. In Brazil, during the same period, fertility is estimated to have declined by 54 percent—an almost identical proportion. And despite the absence of a national family planning program, Brazil's fertility levels today remain lower than Mexico's.

In the final analysis, the single best international predictor of fertility levels turns out to be *desired* fertility levels: the number of children that women say they would like to have. Perhaps this should not be surprising. Parents tend to have strong opinions about important matters pertaining to their families; parents tend to act on the basis of those opinions; and even in poor developing countries, parents do not believe that babies are found under cabbages. The primacy of desired fertility explains why birthrates can be higher in regions where contraceptive use rates are also higher, because it is parents, not pills, that make the final choice about family size.

For advocates of stabilizing world population, the predominance of parental preferences in determining national and international birthrates poses an awkward dilemma. If parental preferences really rule, and a government sets official population targets for a truly voluntary family planning program, those targets are not likely to be met. Indeed, if parents are genuinely permitted to pursue the family size they personally desire, national population programs can only meet preestablished official demographic targets by complete and utter chance.

On the other hand, if a government sets population targets and wishes to stand a reasonable chance of achieving them, the mischievous independence of parental preferences means that wholly voluntary population programs cannot be relied on. If states, rather than parents, are to determine a society's preferred childbearing patterns, governments must be able to force parents to adhere to the officially approved parameters.

Thus, whether they recognize it or not, every advocate of antinatal population programs must make a fateful choice. They must either opt for voluntarism, in which case their population targets will be meaningless. Or else they must opt for attempting to meet their population targets, in which case they must embrace coercive measures. There is no third way.

Chapter Two

ETHICAL DIVIDE

To what degree should ethics influence optimum population decisions?

The Contribution of Ethics

J. Philip Wogaman

This selection was excerpted from "The Contribution of Ethics," in *The Population Crisis and Moral Responsibility* (New York: Public Affairs Press, 1973).

The unprecedented size and growth of world population has clearly emerged as one of the most basic problems facing mankind in the closing decades of the twentieth century. The basic facts concerning this problem are well enough known, and most of them need not be reviewed here. It is sufficient to remember that world population has doubled in the last half century and that, at present growth rates, it will continue to double every thirty-five years until either nature or human action intervene. This rapid growth rate affects nearly every aspect of man's social, economic, political, and cultural life. It creates some new problems and greatly exacerbates old ones. It can be argued that population size is already a factor in the suffering of hundreds of millions of people in developing countries and in the environmental problems of more highly developed areas.

In the past, human increase has largely been kept within bounds by the natural forces of disease and famine, supplemented occasionally by war and primitive forms of birth control. But disease, famine, and war are immensely destructive of human values. Medical and agricultural revolutions have to some extent limited disease and famine for twentieth century man. Therefore, despite some diminishing of crude birthrates in many countries, the world population has been moving ahead dramatically. While the carrying capacity of the planet for humans has yet to be determined, that capacity may have already been stretched to the breaking point from the standpoint of quality of life.

This basic situation has evoked widespread discussion among population experts, ecologists, governmental officials, and others. Many thoughtful people believe that a *laissez faire* approach is a luxury we can no longer afford. They are beginning to ask how humankind will be able to halt population growth by using means that are not dehumanizing, and whether we will be able to do so in time to prevent further suffering and hardship. Some twenty-one governments of developing countries have responded to what they regard as the population crisis by adopting official policies. Governments of more highly developed countries, such as the United States, have been slower to respond, but even here official concern has increased notably in the past few years. The report of the U.S. Commission on Population Growth and the American Future in 1972 signaled greater interest in official as well as unofficial circles. Many different kinds of governmental policies have been proposed in the United States and in other parts of the world. Even without such evidence of interest, the objective consequences of the population growth rate are likely to create pressures to which governments must react in some way.

Population problems and policies are not purely practical or technical. At most points they also require consideration on the humanistic level where our values become involved. Our very definition of problems suggests the points at which we believe our values to be threatened, and our approach to policy questions is usually dominated by our efforts to achieve or protect these values. For this reason, I do not believe we can bypass serious consideration of ethical issues in dealing with population problems and policies.

Ethics can be understood as the attempt to clarify the source and meaning of basic values and to apply them to the world of practical experience. All people have values and seek, in one way or another, to apply them. But the clarification of values and the analysis of practical problems in applying them demands considerable acquaintance with the great religious and humanistic traditions and with past and present approaches to ethical analysis. People who take ethics seriously must be concerned simultaneously with a deeper understanding of value traditions and with accurate factual understanding of problems. They must work constantly at the task of relating the one to the other. Where this is not done, we may be led to believe that we cannot deal with our problems successfully without abandoning our values, or that faithfulness to our values requires us to ignore the practical problems. Either way, the result is likely to produce personal and cultural crisis and disintegration rather than increased integrity and maturity.

The population crisis poses unusual new problems for ethical analysis. Issues of population policy that we now face have been too largely neglected in the past by ethics. It is important that we not neglect them any longer. Increasingly, society will have to develop realistic policies. The question is whether these policies will be consonant with important moral values. I believe that where social policies are widely regarded as both necessary and immoral, some cultural disintegration is a likely consequence.

It cannot be assumed in advance that any particular policy approach is either ethical or unethical without examining it carefully in the light of basic values. Our formulation of these values can itself change in an interaction with policy. But where carefully done, ethical inquiry can clarify the value implications of alternative solutions to problems for the guidance of policymakers and laymen alike.

The concept of "optimum population" tests most directly whether ethics has a contribution to make to population policy questions. The term "optimum" itself is meaningless apart from value judgment. It suggests that some number of people is "best" or "better" in relation to a physical or social environment. Moreover, any given viewpoint of optimum population provides an important clue to its author's basic ethical and even religious assumptions — whether he or she is conscious of this or not. The point can be illustrated by referring to several discernible models of optimum population in recent debates.

One quite widely accepted model could be called *the laissez faire position*: the view that optimum population size is that which results from the uncoerced decisions and activities of all potential parents. Occasionally in recent debates the point has been expressed that it is both disruptive and unnecessary for government to attempt any planning in this field. People can be counted on to do what is desirable for them, and the sum total of the results of this will be what is desirable for society as a whole. The "Family Planning" movement emphasizes that its sole aim is to make it possible for each individual family planning unit to have the number of children (no more and no less) that it wishes to have. It is assumed that the results of this will be beneficial to society as a whole. That assumption may or may not be well-founded factually in a particular instance. In any case it is a non sequitur to suppose that *because* individual families find a particular family size desirable, it is therefore desirable for society that they have that family size. This approach is in fact similar to the classical economic faith in the "invisible hand." It tends to absolutize the value of freedom, to neglect the possibility that freedom can be used for selfish as well as benevolent ends. It may be based on the view that whatever is done by people is good (in the literature of ethics this is called the "naturalistic fallacy") or on the view that whatever is done by people does not matter. Or it may simply hold that what happens to society as a whole is unimportant. Such views touch ethics and religion at the root.

Another model is based on the *maximization of national power*. It is an old assumption that group size is an index to social power. A column by economist Henry C. Wallich (*Newsweek*, June 29, 1970) illustrates the continuing popularity of this viewpoint. While contesting the attitude of the Zero Population Growth movement, Wallich develops a picture of an America increasingly overwhelmed by the growth of other countries and predicts "we would be less well-prepared to defend our position as we became increasingly outnumbered." "A nation's power does not depend exclusively on population size," he writes, "but numbers obviously have something to do with it." To some extent this thinking is parallel to that of ethnic spokesmen who regard all talk of population limitation as being genocidal. There are, of course, factual difficulties in equating mere numbers of people with social power. (Were this not the case, China and India would be the leading superpowers simply because of their numbers.) Even were this not so, the chauvinistic ethical roots of this position are more than evident. The power supremacy of a particular nation or group is not self-evidently a good at all—much less the supreme good. When treated as the basic value, it is a form of what H. Richard Niebuhr has called henotheism: a form of idolatry that takes some aspect of humanity as the organizing center of value and that correspondingly neglects the *whole* of reality. I am not suggesting that this is not a popular ethical viewpoint but that it is not self-evidently the right one.

Another model is based on the *maximization of economic productivity*. It treats as best that population size which contributes most to production. There are overtones of this view in Joseph J. Spengler's argument that "the optimum population is that which enables a people 'to obtain, in return for whatever expenditure of effort [they] may regard as normal and proper, the largest, permanently practicable *per capita* product'" ("Population

Optima," in *The 99th Hour,* ed. Daniel O. Price [Chapel Hill, N.C.: University of North Carolina Press, 1967]). Others have noted the relationship between population growth and expanding labor pools and markets, urging continuing population growth as a way of maintaining the upward movement of the Gross National Product. This, of course, implies that products are of greater importance than people. A reasonable theory of optimum population must surely regard economic productivity as an important variable, but this is not the same as treating it as the central point in a theory of value.

Another model is based on *happiness and pleasure*: that number of people is optimum that contributes most to the maximization of pleasure and avoidance of pain. Wayne H. Davis recently referred to America as being overpopulated because "we have far more people now than we can continue to support at anything near today's level of affluence" (*Readings in Human Population Ecology* [Englewood Cliffs, N.J.: Prentice-Hall, 1971])—thus implicitly regarding a high level of affluence as the governing moral norm. In a more elaborate fashion, S. Fred Singer has devised a formula for determining the optimum based on the same kind of assumption. He writes that "one definition often proposed defines optimum as the 'highest quality of life for the largest percentage of population.' This puts the burden on defining 'quality of life,' and on devising a yardstick for measuring it. In our society, where material comforts are important and contribute to what people perceive of as happiness, a loose definition might be 'having as much money as possible left over after taking care of the basic necessities, and having the necessary time and opportunities for spending it in a pleasant way.' It means also having the maximum range of choices for a way of life. This definition . . . tells you how to measure quality of life in terms of dollars by calculating the potential consumption and assigning a monetary value to free time" (*Is There an Optimal Level of Population?* [New York: McGraw-Hill, 1971]).

The nineteenth and early twentieth century discussions of optimum population are replete with comparable appeals to the happiness principle. While happiness as such is difficult to oppose, it also raises difficulties when taken by itself as the basis for other values. If the objective of individuals in approaching questions of population policy should be their own *private* happiness, the goal would be understandable, though selfish and of doubtful ethical standing in the long run. If, on the other hand, the goal should be the happiness of the greatest number of people, an ethical principle broader than happiness would be required to account for the obligation to make *other* people happy. That broader ethical principle has been assumed, in a rather confused way, by thinkers who try to use the utilitarian formula ("greatest good for the largest number") while basing it on pleasure as the ultimate norm.

Still another model is based on *minimum disruption of the environment.* The attempt to correlate population optima with ecological considerations may be the most novel contribution of recent discussion. It has emerged with force in the writings of Paul Ehrlich, Garrett Hardin, and others. It is illustrated by Walter Orr Roberts's statement that "the optimum is that level of population at which the growth of population has ended and society has firmly established its determination to live in harmonious balance with the environment" ("There Is an Optimum Population Level," in *Is There an Optimal Level of Population?* ed. S. Fred Singer [New York: McGraw-Hill, 1971]). The well-being of the environment surely must also be a consideration in any defensible approach; but if the well-being of nature per se should become the governing consideration (as it is not quite in the Roberts statement, but as it sometimes seems to be in the more visceral contributions of the ecology movement), then it is clearly the case that the fewer people there are, the better off nature will be. On this basis we might fittingly declare that the optimum population is really no population at all. Short of this, the term "harmonious balance with the environment" is both helpful and inconclusive. It is helpful because it acknowledges that whatever dangers there are from overpopulation do in fact accrue from disruption and overuse of the natural world and that man's life on this planet does in fact depend on his living in harmony with nature. But it is inconclusive because it cannot tell us what a "harmonious balance with the environment" might be without introducing other value questions. The word "harmonious" begs the question of what *kind* of harmony.

There is a very wide range of possible balances between man and nature, between the point where man is completely excluded and the point where man's overwhelming numbers threaten the very existence of nature. Moreover, the concept of harmony with nature presupposes a theory of the moral significance of nature. Of what intrinsic value is a tree or a bird or water and air? Are these to be regarded simply as human life-support systems, and does "harmonious" refer to that relationship between man and environment which best provides for human support? Or does it refer to some degree of human respect for different aspects of nature, regarded as valuable in their own right? A defensible theory of optimum population must begin, not end, with such questions.

These various models illustrate and pose the problem: how are we best to apply ethical insight to the determination of optimum?

A striking note in recent population discussions is the emergence of some explicitly ethical writing. Daniel Callahan's writings are particularly worthy of mention. His small monograph *Ethics and Population Limitation* (New York: The Population Council, 1971) reviews several basic problems and proposes formal criteria for ethical decision-making in this field. He suggests that three formal values (freedom, justice, and security/survival) should be treated as norms and that "in cases of conflict, one is obliged to act in such a way that any limitation of one or more of the three fundamental values . . . continues to respect the values and can be justified because it promises to increase the balance of good over evil." It is unclear in context whether good and evil are defined by the presence or absence of the three values or whether good and evil have a meaning related to but also transcending those values.

This approach is interesting for our purposes because while explicitly ethical it is also apparently successful in avoiding religious or theological questions. It raises the question whether religion or theology have anything in particular to add. General values, such as freedom and justice, belong to the mainstream of Western ethical tradition and can be given meanings concerning which persons of differing faiths can agree. One does not need to be a Christian or a Jew or, for that matter, the adherent of any other religious tradition, to acknowledge the importance of freedom and justice. Nevertheless, a problem develops when we wish to say why we regard such general values as normative. We can, along with Callahan, validate them through reference to still other values: "Freedom," he writes, "is a prized value because it is a condition for self determination and the achievement of knowledge. Justice, particularly distributive justice, is prized because it entails equality of treatment and opportunity and an equitable access to those resources and opportunities necessary for human development. Security/survival is prized because it constitutes a fundamental ground for all human activities."

But why, then, are self-determination, knowledge, equality of treatment, and so forth, important, and why, in particular, should we be concerned about whether *other* people have such values?

This kind of question suggests to me that until we have come to terms with our *center* of value—the ultimate object of all our valuing—we cannot really validate any lesser or abstract value-claim. Freedom, justice, security/survival, or any other such general values must be viewed in their ultimate context. The question is, what view of ultimate reality do particular ways of understanding and applying these values presuppose?

Such a question is properly called theological. It is an inquiry into the center of value in which we place our faith. Does it require intellectual arrogance? Quite the opposite. Theological views cannot in the final analysis be validated with certainty. Since they pertain to the nature of the whole of reality and since the whole of reality cannot be known by anyone, such views are based on those experiences and symbols that people consider to be decisive clues to the nature of the whole. It is by faith that we acknowledge that the character of the whole is most fully disclosed in this or that part. The way we understand or use abstract values, like freedom and justice, necessarily owes much to our overall view of things. Therefore, the attempt to treat such values as universal apart from theological dependency merely conceals what is in fact operative. I do not mean to say that there is no place in ethics for an appeal to particular values that are not in themselves theological. I mean only that such values are incomplete until they can be related explicitly to central theological foundations.

If this is true, we cannot offer a satisfactory theory of optimum population until we have in some way begun to relate population size to ultimate concerns. This is not to say that optimum population must be Christian or Jewish or based on any particular theological tradition in order to be satisfactory. No particular tradition can prove its final superiority. It is to say that *some* theological commitment must be made in an adequate theory of optimum population. The ecumenical and interfaith movements of our time have partially validated the hope that the dialogue among people who are clear about their differing theological commitments greatly contributes to the foundations for practical cooperation on common concerns while at the same time clarifying the genuine, as distinct from merely apparent, points of difference. Perhaps this can also be true in discussions of ethics and population policies.

Human Choices

Joel E. Cohen

This selection was excerpted from "Human Choices," in *How Many People Can the Earth Support?* (New York: WW Norton & Company, 1995).

WHAT HAPPENS WHEN MORAL VALUES CONFLICT?

Tastes and moral values that affect the earth's human carrying capacity commonly conflict. Here is a striking example from the Harvard demographer Nathan Keyfitz: "Every couple has a right to as few or as many children as it wishes. That sounds fair enough, until one meets up with the parallel assertion that every child has the right to adequate nutrition. Suppose the world is made in such a way that these two rights cannot both exist once density goes above a certain point? Such incompatibilities of moral principles are not usually acknowledged in official documents" ("Population and Development within the Ecosphere: One View of the Literature," *Population Index* 57, no. 1: 5–22).

I will cite some additional examples, mention some proposed responses (not necessarily responses I accept), and suggest one way of organizing conflicts of values.

Kristin Shrader-Frechette, a philosopher at the University of Florida, Gainesville, analyzed three ethical issues: first, should the wealth and environmental well-being of the world be distributed primarily according to egalitarian, utilitarian, or libertarian values? Egalitarian principles would aspire to give future generations and today's poor equal opportunities to compete with today's rich and powerful for a share of the world's pie. The underlying axiom of egalitarianism is "that all human beings, within and among different generations and countries, share a social contract according to which all are to be treated as morally equal" ("Environmental Ethics and Global Imperatives," in *The Global Possible: Resources, Development, and the New Century*, ed. Robert Ropetto [New Haven, Conn.: Yale University Press, 1985]). Of course, the notion and practice of equality are far subtler than these simple words suggest. Utilitarian principles would aspire to maximize the well-being of all people, even if equal opportunity and equal treatment have to be sacrificed in the short term because they would delay eventual social improvement. Libertarian principles would aspire to fairness (no enslavement, theft, fraud, or force) in the procedures by which the world pie is divided, whatever the equity or social utility of the resulting distribution of goods.

The second ethical problem Shrader-Frechette analyzed was, do the rights of individuals have priority over the rights of governments and groups, or vice versa? For example, does a government have the right to sanction industrial emissions of dangerous pollutants on the grounds that further reductions are not cost-effective, or do individuals have the right not to be exposed to the risks of cancer caused by those pollutants? Does a state, or do potential parents, have the ultimate right to control the number and spacing of children? Present-day Hutterites and Amish consider the control of marital fertility by conscious choice to be immoral. What if they are surrounded by a majority who, like John Stuart Mill, regard "the producing of large families . . . with the same feelings as drunkenness or any other physical excess"? (Quoted in *Population, Environment, and People*, ed. Noel Hinrichs [New York: McGraw-Hill, 1971].)

More generally, what if the childbearing decisions by independent couples or women lead to a level of fertility that the society decides it does not want (however the society arrives at and expresses its wants)? In Nepal, because of high fertility, people in the hill areas were gathering more fuelwood than forest growth was replacing, and were clearing the forests to grow food. People were then migrating to lowland resettlement areas called *terai*. Children, as added helping hands, became economically more valuable in the hill areas when traditional environmental monitoring and communal support broke down. Children, again as laborers, also became economically more valuable in the *terai* because the mixed communities of immigrants lacked traditional communal support and environmental monitoring. Density itself brought about social changes that made families find large size more attractive; large family size aggravated the problems of density. Similarly, families in Bangladesh confronted with recurrent famines and floods sustained high fertility to counterbalance the economic and mortal risks. By trying to reduce their own vulnerability to disaster, families collectively worsened the risk and magnitude of disaster.

Again, if farmers try to produce more food to feed more people by short-ening fallow periods, soil fertility may decline and food production may fall. Does the farmer have the right to do as he or she sees fit, or does a gov-ernment have the right to compel agricultural practices that it sees as more beneficial?

In 1992, then-senator Al Gore proposed a solution to the conflict be-tween individuals and groups that some might accept: "The emphasis on the rights of the individual must be accompanied by a deeper under-standing of the responsibilities to the community that every individual must accept if the community is to have an organizing principle at all" (*Earth in the Balance: Ecology and Human Spirit* [New York: Houghton Mifflin, 1997]). Will this hortatory principle solve some of the practical conflicts just described?

The third ethical conflict Shrader-Frechette raised was, should poli-cies regarding population and the environment center on the values of people, all sentient beings (including animals, who are evidently capable of suffering), all living beings (including trees and viruses and fungi), everything on the earth (do rocks have rights?), or whole ecosystems? Shrader-Frechette argued that anthropocentric values are theoretically preferable and practically more workable than ecocentric values. By con-trast, a high government official, N. H. Biegman, writing in 1992 as Di-rector General for International Cooperation of the Netherlands Ministry of Foreign Affairs, preferred ecocentric values:

I, personally, find it hard to accept the tendency passed down to us by the Jewish, Christian and Islamic religions to see man as the centre and the measure of all things on earth. I think that even without man the earth would be a very worth-while place and that as a latecomer on the scene man should show the necessary modesty. If one takes this view, the protection of nature and the environment requires no further argument. Nature can manage very nicely without man, but man cannot manage without nature ("Population, Environment, and Development: Govern-ment's View," in *Population, Environment, and Development*, ed. Everett van Imhoff, Ellen Themmen, and Frans Willekins [Berwyn, Penn.: Sweets and Zeitlinger, 1992]).

Edwin Dobb, a magazine editor writing on humankind's place in na-ture, argued that seeing an opposition between humans and nature is itself the problem, and the dichotomy is a false one: ". . . any definition of nature that excludes people and their works has always been indefensible, as has any definition of humanity that excludes nature. Wherever we stand, in the Gila Wilderness or in Times Square, we stand at the intersection of nature and culture" ("Cultivating Nature," *The Sciences* [New York: Academy of Sciences, January/February 1992]).

The World Health Organization (WHO) Commission on Health and Environment (1992) gave an important example of a conflict between values held by itself:

Priority given to human health raises an ethical dilemma if "health for all" conflicts with protecting the environment. Two extreme positions may be envisaged. The first stresses individual rights, societal good being seen as the aggregate of everyone's personal preferences and any controls over the individual's use of resources as an infringement of the individual's freedom. The other extreme—a response to increasing environmental degradation—gives priority to the environment and to the maintenance of the ecosystem. All species are seen as having rights as people do, environmental welfare thus coming before human welfare. A middle ground between these extremes can be found by distinguishing between first-order and second-order ethical principles. Priority to ensuring human survival is taken as a first-order principle. Respect for nature and control of environmental degradation is a second-order principle, which must be observed unless it conflicts with the first-order principle of meeting survival needs.

And who decides which principles are first order, which are second order? The WHO Commission on Health and Environment also identified short-term local conflicts between improving health by the cheapest means and maintaining a clean environment. Power stations that burn coal or oil can reduce local air pollution by venting combustion products through tall chimneys; doing so increases acid deposition elsewhere. A country rich enough to import minerals and timber transfers the environmental costs of mining and logging to the exporting country.

Humans seem to resolve conflicts of values by personal and social processes that are poorly understood and virtually unpredictable at present. How such conflicts are resolved can materially affect human carrying capacity, and so there is a large element of choice and uncertainty in human carrying capacity.

I emphasized that the earth's human carrying capacity depends on human choices, including human values. Not all of those choices are free choices. Natural constraints restrict the possible options.

Living on a Lifeboat

Garrett Hardin

This selection first appeared in *Journal of Bio Sciences* (Bangalore, India: Indian Academy of Sciences, 1974).

No generation has viewed the problem of the survival of the human species as seriously as we have. Inevitably, we have entered this world of concern through the door of metaphor. Environmentalists have emphasized the image of the earth as a spaceship—Spaceship Earth. Kenneth Boulding is the principal architect of this metaphor. It is time, he says, that we replace the wasteful "cowboy economy" of the past with the frugal "spaceship economy" required for continued survival in the limited world we now see ours to be ("The Economics of the Coming Spaceship Earth," in *Environmental Quality in a Growing Economy*, ed. H. Jarrett [Baltimore: Johns Hopkins Press, 1966]). The metaphor is notably useful in justifying pollution control measures.

Unfortunately, the image of a spaceship is also used to promote measures that are suicidal. One of these is a generous immigration policy, which is only a particular instance of a class of policies that are in error because they lead to the tragedy of the commons (Garrett Hardin, "The Tragedy of the Commons," *Science* 162 [1968]: 1243–1248). These suicidal policies are attractive because they mesh with what we unthinkingly take to be the ideals of "the best people." What is missing in the idealistic view is an insistence that rights and responsibilities must go together. The "generous" attitude of all too many people results in asserting inalienable rights while ignoring or denying matching responsibilities.

For the metaphor of a spaceship to be correct, the aggregate of people on board would have to be under unitary sovereign control (William Ophuls, "The Scarcity Society," *Harper's* 243 [1974]: 47–52). A true ship always has a captain. It is conceivable that a ship could be run by a committee. But it could not possibly survive if its course were determined by bickering tribes that claimed rights without responsibilities.

What about Spaceship Earth? It certainly has no captain and no ex-ecutive committee. The United Nations is a toothless tiger, because the signatories of its charter wanted it that way. The spaceship metaphor is used only to justify spaceship demands on common resources without ac-knowledging corresponding spaceship responsibilities.

An understandable fear of decisive action leads people to embrace "incrementalism"—moving toward reform by tiny stages. As we shall see, this strategy is counterproductive in the area discussed here if it means ac-cepting rights before responsibilities. Where human survival is at stake, the acceptance of responsibilities is a precondition to the acceptance of rights, if the two cannot be introduced simultaneously.

LIFEBOAT ETHICS

Before taking up certain substantive issues let us look at an alternative metaphor, that of a lifeboat. In developing some relevant examples the fol-lowing numerical values are assumed. Approximately two-thirds of the world is desperately poor, and only one-third is comparatively rich. The people in poor countries have an average per capita gross national product (GNP) of about $200 per year; the rich, of about $3,000. (For the United States it is nearly $5,000 per year.) Metaphorically, each rich nation amounts to a lifeboat full of comparatively rich people. The poor of the world are in other, much more crowded, lifeboats. Continuously, so to speak, the poor fall out of their lifeboats and swim for a while in the water outside, hoping to be admitted to a rich lifeboat or in some other way to benefit from the "goodies" on board. What should the passengers on a rich lifeboat do? This is the central problem of "the ethics of a lifeboat."

First we must acknowledge that each lifeboat is effectively limited in capacity. The land of every nation has a limited carrying capacity. The exact limit is a matter for argument, but the energy crunch is convincing more people every day that we have already exceeded the carrying capac-ity of the land. We have been living on "capital"—stored petroleum and coal— and soon we must live on income alone.

Let us look at only one lifeboat, ours. The ethical problem is the same for all, and is as follows. Here we sit, say 50 people in a lifeboat. To be gen-erous, let us assume our boat has a capacity of 10 more, making 60. (This, however, is to violate the engineering principle of the "safety factor." A new plant disease or a bad change in the weather may decimate our population if we don't preserve some excess capacity as a safety factor.)

The 50 of us in the lifeboat see 100 others swimming in the water outside, asking for admission to the boat or for handouts. How shall we respond to their calls?

There are several possibilities.

One. We may be tempted to try to live by the Christian ideal of being "our brother's keeper" or by the Marxist ideal "from each according to his abilities, to each according to his needs" (Karl Marx, "Critique of the Gotha Program," in *The Marx-Engels Reader*, ed. R. C. Tueker [New York: Norton, 1972]). Since the needs of all are the same, we take all the needy into our boat, making a total of 150 in a boat with a capacity of 60. The boat is swamped and everyone drowns. Complete justice, complete catastrophe.

Two. Since the boat has an unused excess capacity of 10, we admit just 10 more to it. This has the disadvantage of getting rid of the safety factor, for which action we will sooner or later pay dearly. Moreover, which 10 do we let in? "First come, first served?" The best 10? The neediest 10? How do we *discriminate*? And what do we say to the 90 who are excluded?

Three. Admit no more to the boat and preserve the small safety factor. Survival of the people in the lifeboat is then possible (though we shall have to be on our guard against boarding parties).

The last solution is abhorrent to many people. It is unjust, they say. Let us grant that it is.

"I feel guilty about my good luck," say some. The reply to this is simple: *Get out and yield your place to others.* Such a selfless action might satisfy the conscience of those who are addicted to guilt, but it would not change the ethics of the lifeboat. The needy person to whom a guilt-addict yields his place will not himself feel guilty about his sudden good luck. (If he did, he would not climb aboard.) The net result of conscience-stricken people relinquishing their unjustly held positions is the elimination of their kind of conscience from the lifeboat. The lifeboat, as it were, purifies itself of guilt. The ethics of the lifeboat persist, unchanged by such momentary aberrations.

This then is the basic metaphor within which we must work out our solutions. Let us enrich the image step by step with substantive additions from the real world.

REPRODUCTION

The harsh characteristics of lifeboat ethics are heightened by reproduction, particularly by reproductive differences. The people inside the lifeboats of the wealthy nations are doubling in numbers every eighty-seven years; those outside are doubling every thirty-five years, on the average. And the relative difference in prosperity is becoming greater.

Let us, for a while, think primarily of the U.S. lifeboat. As of 1973, the United States had a population of 210 million people who were increasing by 0.8 percent per year, that is, doubling in number every eighty-seven years.

Although the citizens of rich nations are outnumbered two to one by the poor, let us imagine an equal number of poor people outside our lifeboat—a mere 210 million poor people reproducing at a quite different rate. If we imagine these to be the combined populations of Colombia, Venezuela, Ecuador, Morocco, Thailand, Pakistan, and the Philippines, the average rate of increase of the people "outside" is 3.3 percent a year. The doubling time of this population is twenty-one years.

Suppose that all these countries, and the United States, agreed to live by the Marxist ideal, "to each according to his needs," the ideal of most Christians as well. Needs, of course, are determined by population size, which is affected by reproduction. Every nation regards its rate of reproduction as a sovereign right. If our lifeboat were big enough in the beginning, it might be possible to live *for a while* by Christian-Marxist ideals. *Might.*

Initially, in the model given, the ratio of non-Americans to Americans would be one to one. But consider what the ratio would be eighty-seven years later. By this time Americans would have doubled to a population of 420 million. The other group (doubling every twenty-one years) would now have swollen to 3,540 million. Each American would have more than eight people to share with. How could the lifeboat possibly keep afloat?

All this involves extrapolation of current trends into the future and is consequently suspect. Trends may change. Granted, but the change will not necessarily be favorable. If—as seems likely—the rate of population increase falls faster in the ethnic group presently inside the lifeboat than it does among those now outside, the future will turn out to be even worse than mathematics predicts, and sharing will be even more suicidal.

RUIN IN THE COMMONS

The fundamental error of the sharing ethic is that it leads to the tragedy of the commons. Under a system of private property, the man (or group of men) who own property recognize their responsibility to care for it, for if they don't they will eventually suffer. A farmer, for instance, if he is intelligent, will allow no more cattle in a pasture than its carrying capacity justifies. If he overloads the pasture, weeds take over, erosion sets in, and the owner loses in the long run.

But if a pasture is run as a commons open to all, the right of each to use it is not matched by an operational responsibility to take care of it. It is no use asking independent herdsmen in a commons to act responsibly, for they dare not. The considerate herdsman who refrains from overloading the commons suffers more than a selfish one who says his needs are greater. (As Leo Durocher says, "Nice guys finish last.") Christian-Marxist idealism is counterproductive. That it *sounds* nice is no excuse. With distribution systems, as with individual morality, good intentions are no substitute for good performance.

A social system is stable only if it is insensitive to errors. To the Christian-Marxist idealist a selfish person is a sort of "error." Prosperity in the system of the commons cannot survive errors. If *everyone* would only restrain himself, all would be well; but it takes *only one less than everyone* to ruin a system of voluntary restraint. In a crowded world of less than perfect human beings—and we will never know any other—mutual ruin is inevitable in the commons. This is the core of the tragedy of the commons.

One of the major tasks of education today is to create such an awareness of the dangers of the commons that people will be able to recognize its many varieties, however disguised. There is pollution of the air and water because these media are treated as commons. Further growth of population and growth in the per capita conversion of natural resources into pollutants require that the system of the commons be modified or abandoned in the disposal of "externalities."

The fish populations of the oceans are exploited as commons, and ruin lies ahead. No technological invention can prevent this fate: in fact, all improvements in the art of fishing merely hasten the day of complete ruin. Only the replacement of the system of the commons with a responsible system can save oceanic fisheries.

The management of western rangelands, though nominally rational, is in fact (under the steady pressure of cattle ranchers) often merely a government-sanctioned system of the commons, drifting toward ultimate ruin for both the rangelands and the residual enterprisers.

No workable answers can be found if we ignore population problems. And—if the argument of this essay is correct—so long as there is no true world government to control reproduction everywhere, it is impossible to survive in dignity if we are to be guided by Spaceship ethics. Without a world government that is sovereign in reproductive matters, mankind lives, in fact, on a number of sovereign lifeboats.

For the foreseeable future survival demands that we govern our actions by the ethics of a lifeboat. Posterity will be ill served if we do not.

Ultimately, What Are Your Values?

Julian Simon

This selection was excerpted from *The Ultimate Resource II* (Princeton, N.J.: Princeton University Press, 1996).

A small number of academics—many of them biologists and almost none of them economists—have convinced a great many politicians and laymen that rational population policies on fertility, mortality, and immigration can be deduced directly from actual or supposed facts about population and economic growth. The persuaded politicians believe it is "scientific truth" that countries should reduce their population growth. And the persuading academics want the politicians and the public to believe that such judgmental propositions really are "scientific." For example, the front page of the canon book of the population control movement in the United States, *The Population Bomb*, says: "Paul Ehrlich, a qualified scientist, clearly describes the dimensions of the crisis . . . overpopulation is now the dominant problem . . . population control or race to oblivion?"

But it is scientifically wrong—outrageously wrong—to say that "science shows" there is overpopulation (or underpopulation) in any given place at any given time. Science can only reveal the likely effects of various population levels and policies. Whether population is now too large or too small or is growing too fast or too slowly cannot be decided on scientific grounds alone. Such judgments depend on our values, a matter on which science does not bear.

Whether you think that it is better for a country to have a population of, say, 50 million human beings at a $4,000 per capita yearly income or 100 million at $3,000 is strictly a matter of what you consider important. And further, please keep in mind that if the empirical studies and my theoretical analysis are correct, the world can have both a larger population and higher per capita income. This is as true for less-developed as for more-developed countries. But the judgments about whether this is good news or bad news, whether population is growing too fast or too slowly, or whether population is now too large or too small depends on values. This is reason enough to say that science does not show that there is overpopulation or underpopulation anywhere.

Because of the belief that population policies can be deduced from scientific studies alone, particular values enter implicitly into policy decisions, without explicit discussion of whether the values really are those that the decision-makers and the community desire to have implemented. For a leading example, because almost all economic analyses of "optimum" rates of economic growth take per capita income as the criterion, this criterion implicitly becomes the community goal and the guideline for policymakers. In some cases values are smuggled in consciously, though without discussion; in other cases the values enter without any conscious recognition.

SOME VALUES RELEVANT TO POPULATION POLICY

The Rate of Discounting for Futurity

The relative importance given to the nearer term versus the further future affects investment decisions. It enters into every weighing of the costs and benefits of resource use and population growth.

The proposition that we should focus on the short run and not pay attention to the benefits of more people that accrue in the long run because "in the long run we're all dead"—Keynes's famous foolish phrase—has a curious similarity to the thinking of young children. For children there really is a free lunch—consuming without having to work to pay for the goods—for twenty years. And children are not predisposed to invest and save for the future; every parent knows how hard it is to induce children to study now in order to have the benefits of education in adulthood, and to know the virtues of saving money. But the activity that children find least natural—hard work—becomes emotionally necessary to most of us later on in the life cycle. The need to work, and to create, may be seen most purely in gardening, where the work is almost its only reward. It is as if we need to cultivate and produce in order to give back what we have earlier taken in during our lives. The psychological explanation here is mere speculation, of course, but the need to work even when the product of that work makes no material difference to the worker is as much a plain undeniable fact as is the need of children to play. The attitude that we should consume without attending to what we leave behind, or without considering how many and which persons we will leave behind, is analogous to the childhood stage of the life cycle.

There is a curious contradiction in the thinking of the population control–environmentalist movement with respect to the future. On the one hand, they say they want to "save the planet" for our children and grandchildren. On the other hand, they want to reduce as much as possible the number of children and grandchildren for whom the planet is to be "saved."

The Inherent Value of Human Life

Can some people's lives be so poor and their standard of living so low that they would have been better off had they never been born? "Humane Society and health officials say that feral cats lead miserable, disease-ridden lives and that killing them is more humane than leaving them on the streets." Many have values about poor people exactly similar to these values about cats, but since Nazi times the view is applied publicly only to the unborn rather than to people already born.

A contrasting value is that no life is so poor in goods that it does not have value. Still others believe that only the individual should be allowed to decide whether his or her own life is worth living. Surprisingly to me, the issue of these conflicting values, which is crucial (though usually only implicit) in deliberations about population policy, is rarely the subject of explicit discussion. At least one economist developed a model in which he made explicit the assumption that some people's lives have "negative utility"—a truly amazing piece of economic analysis, to my mind. But this technically elegant essay raised no furor of backlash in the literature.

The Acceptability of Various Methods of Preventing Life

To some people, abortion or contraception or infanticide are acceptable; for others, any of these may be unacceptable.

A *Value for Numbers of People*

Both the Bible, which urges people to be fruitful and multiply, and the utilitarian philosophy of "the greatest good for the greatest number" lead to a value for more people. This value may be held by those who do not believe in a personal God as well as by those who do. Many people of all theological beliefs do not share this value. (It would be unsound for the reader to infer from anything written in this book that I hold any particular theological belief, though several have ventured to do so in print.)

Animals and Plants versus People

According to the Bible, "And God said, Let us make man in our image, after our likeness, and let them have dominion over the fish of the sea, and over the fowl of the air, and over the cattle, and over all the earth. . . . Be fertile and increase, fill the earth and master it and rule the fish of the sea, the birds of the sky, and all the living things that creep on earth" (Genesis 1:26–28). (This does not imply that humans should treat the world about them with lack of care: "Replenish the earth," says Genesis 1:28.)

In sharp contrast is the view of some environmentalists. Consider, for example, the "Greenpeace philosophy" of the whale-protecting group: "Ecology teaches us that humankind is not the center of life on the planet. Ecology has taught us that the whole earth is part of our 'body' and that we must learn to respect it as we respect life — the whales, the seals, the forests, the seas. The tremendous beauty of ecological thought is that it shows us a pathway back to an understanding and appreciation of life itself — an understanding and appreciation that is imperative to that very way of life."

Many of the environmentalist views are held and expressed with quasi-religious fervor, and as others have noted, a sharp shift in values has occurred over the decades: Thus the nineteenth-century child was taught that nature is animated with man's purposes. God designed nature for man's physical needs and spiritual training. Scientific understanding of nature will reveal the greater glory of God, and the practical application of such knowledge should be encouraged as part of the use God meant man to make of nature. Besides serving the material needs of man, nature is the source of man's health, strength, and virtue. He departs at his peril from a life close to nature. At a time when America was becoming increasingly industrial and urban, agrarian values which had been a natural growth in earlier America became articles of fervent faith in American nationalism. The American character was formed in virtue because it developed in a rural environment, and it must remain the same despite vast environmental change. The existence of a bounteous and fruitful frontier in America, with its promise not only of future prosperity but of continued virtue, offers proof that God has singled out the United States above other nations for His fostering care. The superiority of nature to man-made things confers superiority on the American over older civilizations. That Uncle Sam sooner or later will have to become a city dweller is not envisaged by these textbook writers, although their almost fanatical advocacy of rural values seems to suggest an unconscious fear that this might be so.

This shift in values can be seen neatly in the wonderful book *Birds of America*, published in 1917 (T. Gilbert Pearson, ed. [New York: Garden City Books]). The descriptions of many birds include evaluations of their effects on humanity in general and on farmers in particular; a bird that helped agriculture was more highly valued than a bird that harmed it. Today naturalists often evaluate humankind for our effect on birds rather than vice versa.

The shift in values can also be seen in the 1990s call for the return of wolves to Yellowstone National Park about seventy years after Congress passed a law to eradicate them because of their danger to cattle and humans.

Individual Freedom versus Community Coercion

Another important value in debates about population is the willingness to coerce others to attain one's ends with respect to conservation, the environment, and population growth.

Eugenics

The belief that the human race can, and should, be improved by selective breeding was rife in the 1920s and 1930s. Along with this belief has gone the belief in the benefit of race-selective immigration policies. These beliefs bulked large in the thinking of Margaret Sanger when she began the organizational activities that led to Planned Parenthood. Earlier on, eugenics and the Eugenics Society of London had been one of the main channels of thought that led to the founding of the Population Investigation Committee in Great Britain, as important a population research center as any in the world. J. M. Keynes began as a strong supporter of eugenics, which went hand-in-hand with his then-Malthusian economic outlook. When he later invented Keynesian economics, which saw a benefit in a larger market, he flip-flopped and favored larger populations for a while. He later flip-flopped again, and came to worry about population growth. But all this time he remained a strong supporter of eugenics, serving as a director of the society from 1937 to 1944, and as vice president in 1937. So the connection between Malthusianism and population control is close historically.

Some of the main population institutions in the United States, too, arose from an interest in eugenics—for example, the Population Reference Bureau and Planned Parenthood. Since Hitler's demise this idea has dropped out of public statements, and I do not assert that the present officials of these groups are eugenicists (though I would like to hear them deny it publicly). But their original aim of population control in poor countries and among poor people continues unchanged. And the association between the ideas of eugenics and population control are joined together in the writings of such persons as Garrett Hardin.

The Value of Progress

Of all the values that I have long held without examination, the value for progress—and the value of human life, no matter whose it is—are perhaps the most important. Perhaps my unthinking acceptance of these values is at least partly a result of my being an American; these values have been associated with both political parties, in early as well as in present times.

Thomas Jefferson wrote:

We are bound with peculiar gratitude . . . that [we are] permitted quietly to cultivate the earth and to practice and improve those arts which tend to increase our comforts . . . to direct the energies of our nation to the multiplication of the human race, and not to its destruction. ("First Annual Message to Congress" [1801] [New York: Bureau of National Literature, Inc., 1897])

A very different sort of political thinker wrote something quite similar:

The settlement of this great and generous land and the development of its resources created a diverse and expansive American republic of hope, opportunity, experimentation, mobility, and personal freedom.

It has come as a surprise to me that many others do not, as a matter of course, consider it desirable that people should have greater access to educational and economic opportunity, better health, and the material goods that constitute the standard of living. Perhaps it is not surprising that the Duke of Wellington commented on the first railroad in Great Britain that it would "enable the lower orders to go uselessly wandering about the country." And the present Duke of Wellington inveighs against the birth of additional people who might share the pleasures of life in England and on the planet with him. But there are also many who are not members of the "nobility" who associate negative spiritual and metaphysical values with various aspects of progress. For example, when "progress" in painkilling drugs is mentioned, they mention drug abuse in return. And their views are in no manner inherently illogical or foolish, though they may be unpalatable to others.

Values Masquerading as Rights or Other Entitlements

The concept of rights—apart from any specific body of secular law—has become used widely in the discussion of subjects related to people and other species. Such rights are often asserted without explicit justification, as if they are undeniable. A typical example is a letter to the editor following a (facetious) article about a man's battle with moles in his lawn: "What makes him think that he owns the world and has more right to inhabit it than moles? Were your readers supposed to chuckle over his escapades of trying to poison, gas and shish kebab a helpless animal? Who really cares what Mr. Sautter's lawn looks like?"

Or this from the Indian ambassador to the United States:

The view that the human race is endowed with the divine right to ruthlessly exploit planetary resources for its own short term benefit is no longer valid and must be decisively rejected . . . we must shed the quaint belief that ours is a race in some special way entitled to exploit this planet infinitum for its own selfish purpose.

The likening of the human species to cancer and other virulent diseases has long been a common piece of rhetoric. Now AIDS has become a favorite analogy to people. "We, the human species, have become a viral epidemic to the earth . . . the AIDS of the earth." And "If radical environmentalists were to invent a disease to bring human populations back to sanity, it would probably be something like AIDS." Author William Vollmann is quoted in *Publishers Weekly*: "[T]he biggest hope that we have right now is the AIDS epidemic. Maybe the best thing that could happen would be if it were to wipe out half or two-thirds of the people in the world." *The Economist* wrote in an editorial: "The extinction of the human species may not only be inevitable, but a good thing." And in another article the eminent biologist E. O. Wilson writes: "The sin our descendants are least likely to forgive us is the loss of biological diversity." There is an interesting contradiction here, as Robert Nelson pointed out. On the one hand, *Homo sapiens* is said to be no different from other species; on the other hand, it is the only species whom the environmentalists ask to protect other species. They attribute to us a special duty but not a special privilege.

CONCLUSION

My aim here is not to discuss the above values, but simply to point out that they operate importantly in discussions of these matters. Their universal validity is usually taken for granted by those who assert them, though to others they may seem to be simply odd preferences that may be atypical, unhallowed by tradition, quite arguable, and perhaps no more than one person's tastes.

POPULATION AND NATURAL RESOURCES

PART II: QUICK FACTS

"America is sauntering through her resources, and through the mazes of her politics with an easy nonchalance; but presently there will come a time when she will be surprised to find herself grown old—a country, crowded, strained, perplexed—when she will be obliged to pull herself together, husband her resources, concentrate her strength, steady her methods, sober her views, restrict her vagaries."

Woodrow Wilson, "Bryces American Commonwealth Review" (1889)

"There are no such things as limits to growth, because there are no limits on the human capacity for intelligence, imagination and wonder."

Ronald Reagan, "Address to the University of South Carolina" (1983)

■ Although water is the most widely occurring substance on earth (70 percent of the earth's surface is water), only 2.53 percent is fresh water and the remainder is salt water.

United Nations, *World Water Development Report* (2003)
(See figure 2.1 for a detailed look at global freshwater resources.)

■ Air pollution declined 25 percent over the past thirty years in the United States while the U.S. population grew 39 percent and gross domestic product rose 161 percent.

U.S. Environmental Protection Agency, *Report Card* (2003)

■ While global population has increased by more than 70 percent over the past three decades, per capita food consumption is nearly 20 percent higher.

Food and Agricultural Organization of the United Nations,
Agriculture: Towards 2015/2030 (2002)
(See figure 2.3 for the proportion of undernourished in the total population.)

■ Approximately 12 percent of the land surface is generally suitable for food and fiber production, 24 percent is used for grazing, 31 percent is forested, and the remaining 33 percent has too many constraints for most uses.

U.S. Department of Agriculture, *Global Land Resources and Population Supporting Capacity* (1999)
(See figure 2.4 for historical and projected changes in land use and population.)

■ The use of fossil fuels (e.g., coal, oil, and natural gas) accounts for 77 percent of world energy consumption, followed by hydro and traditional biomass at 15 percent, nuclear at 6 percent, and new renewables at 2 percent.

Worldwatch Institute, *State of the World 2003* (2003)

(See figures 2.5 and 2.6 for more detailed information on world energy consumption and production.)

INTRODUCTION

Population and Natural Resources

Human activity affects every aspect of the natural world, posing great possibilities and perhaps dangers for the quality and sustainability of our planet. Have the actions of the past century set us on a collision course with the environment, or has human ingenuity brought us this far and therefore will continue to ensure the well-being of future generations? The purpose of part 2 is to explore these questions in relationship to water, pollution, food, land, and energy.

In chapter 3 Sandra Postel claims that "Water scarcity is the 'sleeping tiger' of our environmental problems, but the tiger is waking up, and we had better wake up too." In contrast, Terry L. Anderson and Pamela S. Snyder explain in "Priming the Invisible Pump" that these fears are not legitimate when factoring in the earth's total demand and supply of water. They contend that water markets are the solution to keeping the supply of water flowing. Will the increasing demand for fresh water make desalinization an attractive market? "Cities Look to Sea for Fresh Water" provides one perspective.

Evidence suggests that humankind has altered the atmosphere on a small scale throughout time. In recent decades, however, concern has grown that people are changing the atmosphere on a global scale—changes that may be detrimental and irreversible. An air pollution study by the American Association for the Advancement of Science (AAAS) reports that today's industrial processes degrade ecosystems and threaten to transform the climate. Bjørn Lomborg counters, demonstrating that careful analysis of the data illustrates that air pollution is getting better not worse over time. The emission of greenhouse gases (see figure 2.2 for detailed description) serves as a case study in chapter 4. Is climate change occurring and if so what kind of an impact will it have on the population?

Technological advances tripled the productivity of world cropland during the twentieth century but can this rate be maintained in the new millennium? Lester Brown argues in chapter 5 that the limits to continued growth in food productivity are significant enough that there is a good chance that the supply of food will fall behind population growth unless the population is stabilized. D. Gale Johnson maintains that world food productivity will continue to improve and exceed demand. Thus, the growing world population will not suffer from food shortages.

Management of land has been central to human society since its earliest civilizations and continues to be a priority today. Many advances have been made over the past fifty years in land management but where that leaves us in relation to the population conundrum is the focus of chapter 6. Anthony Young, in "Concern for Land," argues that growing populations place ever-increasing pressures on scarce land, implying that improved land management practices, such as minimizing degradation, should be a top priority. Julian

Simon, however, claims in "Are We Losing Ground?" that there is no need to panic because less land is needed as the decades pass, and, in fact, taken as a whole, the amount of arable land is increasing. This chapter concludes by diving deeper into the debate by examining the changing demands on the world's forests.

The United States and the rest of the world have many decisions to make regarding appropriate energy sources for the future. In chapter 7, the authors of *State of the World 2003* make a case for renewable energy. A shift toward greater reliance on renewables will help alleviate increasing concerns over the rising demand for energy, fuel supplies, global security, and the threat of climate change. Conversely, in an article by Dave Gorak, Robert L. Bradley Jr. asserts that the real threat to energy sustainability in the twenty-first century "is the environmental activists who seek to replace affordable and reliable energy sources with inferior and costlier substitutes."

The interplay between humankind and the environment is unavoidable. The point of part 2, however, is to explore what level of interaction is most advantageous.

Chapter Three

WATER

Will future demand for water exhaust existing supplies?

Governments Failing to Protect Societies from Spreading Water Scarcity

Worldwatch Institute

This selection was excerpted from the Worldwatch press release for *Last Oasis: Facing Water Scarcity* (Washington, D.C.: Worldwatch Institute, 1997).

Spreading water scarcity will make meeting the drinking water, food, and material needs of an expected world population of 8 billion one of our most difficult challenges over the next thirty years, reports the Worldwatch Institute.

"Water scarcity is the 'sleeping tiger' of our environmental problems, but the tiger is waking up, and we had better wake up, too," says Sandra Postel, director of the Global Water Policy Project in Amherst, Massachusetts, and author of *Last Oasis: Facing Water Scarcity* (New York: WW Norton and Company, 2nd edition, 1997).

"Additional water supplies equal to 20 Nile rivers could be needed over the next 30 years just to satisfy new food requirements for a still-growing global population," Postel said, "and it's not clear where that water will come from on a sustainable basis. Boosting water productivity by roughly half is essential to avoid costly water shortages, food shortfalls, and a severely degraded environment."

Major food-producing regions are now plagued by chronic groundwater overpumping, dried-up rivers, and salt buildup in soils. In addition, an imbalance between growing populations and finite water supplies may shut off the option of food self-sufficiency for a growing number of countries. Of the twenty-eight countries in Africa and the Middle East that have crossed the "water stress" threshold, nineteen already import at least 20 percent of their grain. In less than thirty years, Africa and the Middle East will have more than 1.3 billion people living in water-stressed countries, more than triple the number today.

"Given these facts, it's not easy to be optimistic about future food security," Postel said. "An all-out effort is needed to raise the water productivity of the global crop base, both irrigated and rainfed." She recommends pricing and other policies to improve irrigation efficiency, to better match crops to local climates and varying qualities of water, to promote the re-use of urban wastewater for crop irrigation, and to breed new crop varieties that are more salt tolerant, drought resistant, and water efficient.

The report also calls for greater investments to repair and protect rivers, streams, wetlands, and deltas, which have been degraded by decades of large-scale water engineering, escalating water demands, and mounting pollution. These systems sustain fisheries, process society's waste, maintain soil fertility, and create habitat for a rich diversity of aquatic life. The total global value of these freshwater "ecosystem services" almost certainly amounts to several trillion dollars annually, according to the report.

Several large restoration attempts are planned or under way, including projects in the Everglades, the San Francisco bay and delta, and a portion of central Asia's shrinking Aral Sea. But greater efforts are needed to slow the degradation of the planet's freshwater assets.

"Each time we build a dam, drain a wetland, siphon off too much river flow, or pave a critical watershed, we lose valuable ecological functions that we end up paying for later," Postel said. "Governments have the responsibility to protect public resources when the market fails to do so, and this is a clear case where government action is warranted."

The report sees hopeful signs in growing efforts to leave more water "instream" and to make habitat protection a more explicit goal of water management. The U.S. government—in a shift that could be repeated elsewhere—has reallocated eight hundred thousand acre-feet of water annually from a large federal irrigation project in California to maintain fish and wildlife habitat and other ecosystem functions.

In several international river basins, there are promising steps to defuse tensions that have threatened regional "water wars." In December 1996, India and Bangladesh signed a treaty on sharing the dry-season flow of the Ganges River, which has begun to dissipate a generation-old dispute. Israel, Jordan, and the Palestinians have begun to move toward water sharing, but the challenging task remains of equitably allocating Jordan basin waters. And Nile basin countries have met annually since 1993 to foster cooperation and have agreed to work toward "equitable allocation of the Nile waters."

In contrast, little concrete progress is evident in the Tigris-Euphrates basin, where Turkey is moving ahead with dam plans that will reduce the Euphrates' flow into Syria and Iraq.

"With supplies unlikely to get much bigger, and with demand continuing to rise, our challenge is to use the water we have more efficiently, and to divide it in ways that satisfy basic human needs, protect vital ecosystems, and avert conflict," Postel said.

Reaching these goals, Postel cautions, could be made more difficult by the growing trend toward governments turning over the construction, operation, and sometimes even the ownership of water systems to the private sector. Ensuring that the poor get water at affordable prices and that rivers, lakes, and watersheds are adequately protected takes strong regulation—but it is often lacking in such privatization schemes. Yet in the last decade, such shifts valued at more than $400 billion have been proposed, started, or completed in the urban water sector alone. Buenos Aires, Casablanca, Dakar, and Mexico City are among the large cities in the developing world that have privatized all or part of their water systems.

Incentives to use water more efficiently, share it more equitably, and protect its ecological functions are urgently needed, yet this report finds that no national government has a comprehensive strategy firmly founded on these pillars of sustainability. Inappropriate pricing still makes it cheaper to waste than to conserve it; inadequate regulations permit valuable ecosystem services to be lost, and gross inequalities persist between rich and poor. Postel concludes: "Every day we delay, we consign ourselves to more difficult and expensive solutions, greater human insecurity, and a more degraded world. It is now time—indeed past time—for government leaders and citizens worldwide to face these problems head-on."

Priming the Invisible Pump

Terry L. Anderson and Pamela S. Snyder

This selection originally appeared in *Priming the Invisible Pump*, PERC Policy Series, no. PS-9 (Bozeman, Mont.: Property and Environment Research Center, 1997).

> "Throughout the West, water markets are evolving—not always fast enough for the thirsty cities and too quickly for some rural irrigators. But the discussions . . . are much more strongly pro-market today than they were five years ago."
>
> *Water Strategist*
> Winter 1996

"We are running out of water!" This theme echoes through environmental publications and the popular press. For example:

- The Worldwatch Institute predicts that by the year 2025 "as many as 3 billion people could be living in countries experiencing water stress or chronic water scarcity" ("Forging a Sustainable Water Strategy," in *State of the World 1996* [New York: WW Norton and Company, 1996]).
- "From the slums of Mexico to the overburdened farms of China, human populations are outstripping the limited stock of fresh water," says *Time* magazine. "Mankind is poisoning and exhausting the precious fluid that sustains all life" ("The Last Drops," August 20, 1990).

ARE THESE FEARS LEGITIMATE?

Not if we are talking about the earth's total demand for and supply of water. While less than 1 percent of the world's total water supply is fresh water available for human consumption, humans are only using between 38 percent and 64 percent of the readily available water. This is true even though global water use has tripled since 1950, and shot up 500–800 percent in the United States since the turn of the century.

The problem is that clean water is not always in the right place at the right time. Many developing nations are water-scarce. In these poor countries, especially in Africa and the Middle East, available water is often contaminated. Diarrheal diseases, which kill more than 3 million people a year, mostly children, are often caused by unsanitary water.

We contend that water markets are the solution to this problem. Here are a few examples of what water markets can do.

- In 1991, at the height of a drought in California, the state established an Emergency Drought Water Bank to purchase water from farmers at $125 per acre-foot and sell it to municipal and other agricultural users for $175 per acre-foot. "By the end of June, 1991, the Drought Water Bank had purchased about 750,000 acre-feet of water. . . . It was a surprise to many people that such large quantities of water became available so quickly," according to Peter Rogers, the author of *America's Water: Federal Roles and Responsibilities* (Cambridge, Mass.: MIT Press, 1993).

- Buck Hollow Creek near Dalles, Oregon, had become a trickle of water in the summer due to irrigation, and the once-plentiful steelhead run had dwindled to thirty pairs or fewer. But in 1994, the newly formed Oregon Water Trust leased a local farmer's water rights and left the water flowing for fish. The price was $6,600, the cost of the seventy-eight tons of hay the farmer would have grown had he irrigated his land.

- Chile's new constitution, passed in 1980 and modified in 1988, established secure, transferable water rights. According to Renato Schleyer: "The freedom to buy and sell or 'rent' water has given farmers greater flexibility to shift crops according to market demand. Efficiency in urban water and sewage services has been greatly increased with no impact on prices . . ." ("Chile's Market-Oriented Water Policy: Institutional Aspects and Achievements," in *Water Policy and Water Markets* [Washington, D.C.: World Bank, 1994]).

Unfortunately, these examples are exceptions in a world where public policy hinders the use of water markets. The good news is that we are on the brink of a revolution in water marketing. As our forthcoming book, *In Pursuit of Water Markets: Priming the Invisible Pump* (Washington, D.C.: Cato Institute, 1997), will show, water rights are coming full circle—once again returning to a system that allows trade. In spite of many impediments, water is being more freely traded than in the past. Markets are providing agricultural and urban users with more reliable supplies and with an incentive to conserve, and are enabling environmentalists to purchase instream flows to protect fish and recreational opportunities.

CONCLUSION

Gloom-and-doom predictions of future water crises will probably always plague us. Fortunately, predictions of natural resource shortages are often wrong because they ignore the impact of market forces on supply and demand. Despite predictions that we will run out of everything from copper to tungsten and that we will have shortages of everything from energy to food, markets—imperfect as they may be—have worked well to avert crises. Higher prices induce suppliers to find new sources of supply and users to conserve and search for substitutes.

Water allocation is no exception. If governments send the wrong signals to suppliers and users by subsidizing water storage and delivery, exponential growth in consumption will inevitably run into environmental and fiscal constraints. But if progress toward greater reliance on markets continues, water supplies and efficiency will increase as users trade with one another, and consumption will be tamed by higher prices.

Today in the western United States, water rights have come full circle. From private property rights freely transferable like any other property on the western frontier, they became public rights governed by legislatures and courts. Now they are becoming tradable property rights once again. States and the federal government, recognizing the practicality of markets for reallocating water, are taking steps to liberate water rights from burdensome rules and regulations. Although the "water is public" and "water is unique" paradigms remain strong, irrigators, environmentalists, urban dwellers, and other water users are overcoming obstacles to markets with innovative arrangements involving voluntary transactions.

SNAPSHOT: Desalination

Cities Look to Sea for Fresh Water

John Ritter

This selection originally appeared in *USA Today* (*USA Today*, November 11, 2002).

SAN RAFAEL, California—Water is a precious commodity even here in one of the nation's most affluent counties. Low-flush toilets, low-volume showerheads, and drip sprinklers are the norm in a region wholly dependent on winter rains and imported river water.

But spiraling demand for water and the threat of drought have officials in Marin County considering an idea long thought to be too expensive and impractical: a plant that turns ocean saltwater into high-quality drinking water.

Bordering the Pacific north of San Francisco, Marin is one of many jurisdictions across the United States giving desalination a serious look. "There are huge red flags about the reliability of our supply in drought years," says Jared Huffman, chairman of the Marin County Water District. "Desalination looks very attractive considering the alternatives."

In Tampa, the nation's first major plant will open in January, producing 25 million gallons of drinking water a day, 10 percent of a three-county area's needs. Five Southern California cities, including Los Angeles and San Diego, are seeking subsidies from their wholesale water provider to build desalination plants. Texas Governor Rick Perry is pushing a plan offering state financial backing for plants, most on the Gulf Coast. Ten proposals are in the works, including two from El Paso and San Antonio, inland cities that want to treat brackish, or slightly salty, groundwater.

Desalination is common in other parts of the world, particularly the Middle East, where Israel and Saudi Arabia have built plants to provide much of their drinking water. Worldwide, more than 13,500 plants are operating.

But desalination never took hold in the United States because plentiful fresh water supplies and high costs kept it from being competitive.

Today, however, population growth in coastal areas is straining traditional water sources in California, Texas, Florida, and other regions.

Technological advances have nudged the cost of desalinated water closer to that of lakes, rivers, and aquifers, natural underground water storage that serves millions of people. In some regions, desalination can squeeze more out of depleted supplies by treating groundwater that's naturally brackish.

"Nobody wants to do desalination. Everyone would rather have an abundant mountain stream they can get great-quality water from, "says consultant John Tonner, a board member of the International Desalination Association, a non-profit group that promotes converting saltwater for drinking supplies. "But the economics can work in places with dwindling water or where the water is getting worse."

STRAIN ON SUPPLIES

The fear is that future demand will exhaust existing supplies. "The state of Texas will almost double by 2050 to 40 million people, but water is not going to double," says Carla Daws, staff member of the Texas Water Development Board. "Combine that with our history of drought, and we have to figure out ways to use our water more carefully."

Pressure will intensify most heavily in coastal areas, where 53 percent of U.S. residents live on 17 percent of the land. A study by the National Oceanic and Atmospheric Administration estimates that 27 million more people will live on the coasts by 2015.

Nowhere is the pressure more acute than in California, whose 35 million population is expected to exceed 50 million by 2020. "California's water infrastructure is basically unchanged since the state was 15 million," says David Sunding, natural resource economics professor at the University of California, Berkeley. "Something's got to give. Either water becomes a limiting factor for growth, which nobody wants, or you need to look to new mechanisms to enhance supply. Desalination is definitely a promising part of the mix."

Price competitiveness makes it so. Water from Tampa's $208 million plant will sell for $1.88 per thousand gallons, officials say, compared with

$1.50 to $1.75 from traditional sources. Tampa Bay Water, Florida's largest wholesale agency, is under a state mandate to cut groundwater pumping next year in order to help restore damaged aquifers and wetlands. Further cutbacks loom in 2007. Desalinated water will make up part of the loss.

Tampa Bay Water says its desalinated water will be the world's cheapest. Prices have risen elsewhere because of higher energy costs and other factors. Large amounts of electricity are needed to force water through membranes that filter out salt in a process called reverse osmosis. West Coast costs run higher because the Pacific is colder and saltier than the Gulf of Mexico or the Atlantic Ocean.

Proponents say desalination is far more benign to the environment than building dams and aqueducts. The main environmental issue is returning the brine left from osmosis to the sea. Experts say that's a problem only when brine is flushed into a confined body of water with marginal flows.

COSTS SHOULD DECLINE

Some experts think desalination costs will fall further as technology improves and engineers gain experience. Tampa Bay's plant, for example, will save money because it is next to a power plant, allowing it to share water intake and discharge pipes.

Even at costs as much as 80 percent above Tampa Bay's, California officials say desalination will take pressure off expensive imported supplies, such as water from the Colorado River.

The cities of Long Beach and Los Angeles, Orange and San Diego counties, and a water district in southern Los Angeles County have proposals before the region's wholesaler to build desalination plants.

Some or all of them will be approved next year. The cost of water from these plants is estimated to vary from $2.63 to $3.37 per thousand gallons.

"We'll add the equivalent of two Chicagos to Southern California in the next 20 years," says Steven Erie, political science professor at the University of California, San Diego. "Desalination is the long-term solution." Erie says conservation, recycling, and transfers of water from farms to cities are only "short-term, finite fixes."

FIGURE 2.1.   Global Freshwater Resources: Distribution by Region

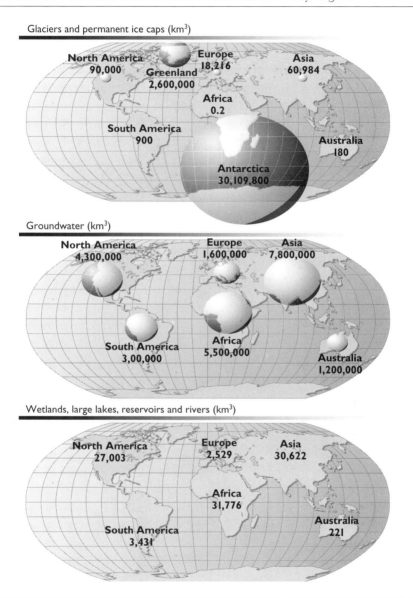

Glaciers and permanent ice caps (km³)

North America 90,000
Europe 18,216
Greenland 2,600,000
Asia 60,984
Africa 0.2
South America 900
Australia 180
Antarctica 30,109,800

Groundwater (km³)

North America 4,300,000
Europe 1,600,000
Asia 7,800,000
South America 3,00,000
Africa 5,500,000
Australia 1,200,000

Wetlands, large lakes, reservoirs and rivers (km³)

North America 27,003
Europe 2,529
Asia 30,622
Africa 31,776
South America 3,431
Australia 221

Source: Igor A. Shiklomanov, State Hydrological Institute and United Nations Educational, Scientific and Cultural Organisation (UNESCO), 1999; World Meteorological Organisation (WMO); International Council of Scientific Unions (ICSU); World Glacier Monitoring Service (WGMS); United States Geological Survey (USGS).

But Sunding at Berkeley says that with three-quarters of the state's water used by farms, transfers are a potentially large new urban source, especially because the water could come from low-value crops such as cotton, alfalfa, and rice.

Marin County's costs will be higher than Southern California's—$5 per thousand gallons or more—because the county has no power plants that a $60 million desalination facility could be built next to.

Still, desalination would "significantly improve our drought preparedness," says Huffman of the water district.

A quarter of Marin's supply is piped in from the Russian River to the north. But a contract obligates the county to buy that water even in wet years when Marin's reservoirs meet demand. And there's no guarantee that Russian River water will always be available.

"Desalination is very cost-competitive with our other options because we can turn it off when we don't need it," Huffman says.

Taste is no issue. When residents tried desalinated water in a blind test, 95 percent of them preferred it to reservoir water.

Chapter Four

POLLUTION

What has happened to air pollution over time?

Population and Atmosphere

Paul Harrison and Fred Pearce

This selection originally appeared in *The AAAS Atlas of Population and Environment* (Berkeley, Calif.: University of California Press, 2001).

People have been altering the atmosphere on a small scale ever since they learned to make fire. But today's fires and industrial processes create so much smoke, gas, and particulate matter that they can degrade ecosystems hundreds of kilometers away and threaten to transform climate worldwide.

Wherever humans have lived in dense settlements, pollution from smoke and gases has been a problem. The first attempt to ban coal burning to reduce smoke in London was in 1273. But during the industrial age the amount of fossil-fuel burning—in the form of coal, oil, and gas—has risen steeply. All these fuels generate smoke and gaseous compounds when burned, producing a series of chemical reactions with oxygen in the air to create sulfur dioxide (SO_2), oxides of nitrogen (NO_x), and carbon dioxide (CO_2). Between 1800 and the mid-1990s, the world population increased sixfold, while global CO_2 emissions rose 800-fold over the same period, notably from burning fossil fuels. Growing wealth and new fuel-burning technologies, particularly for generating electricity and powering the internal combustion engine, drove this.

Industrialization has also added to the range of pollutants in the air. A variety of synthetic compounds, invented mostly in the twentieth century, are now widely dispersed in the atmosphere. These include certain pesticides and compounds containing chlorine and bromine used as inert gases in refrigerators and sprays and as solvents. The volume of all these emissions to the air, and the persistence of some of them, has caused their buildup and transformation in the atmosphere to levels that cause ecological damage on a wide, and sometimes global, scale.

SO_2 and NO_x both acidify water droplets in the air. The resulting acid deposition (through rain, fog, or snow) may fall locally or travel long distances in clouds. Below a pH of four, it can acidify soils and leach metals from them, poisoning trees. And it can make lakes and streams too acidic for some fish, such as the brown trout. In the nineteenth century, European acidification of ecosystems was confined to regions close to industrial centers, such as the German Hartz mountains and the English Pennines, where tree growth became patchy. But in the mid-twentieth century increased fossil-fuel burning caused the first internationally recognized case of transboundary air pollution—with German, British, and Polish pollution causing acid deposition and fish deaths, particularly in Scandinavia.

In other atmospheric chemical transformations, NO_x reacts with hydrocarbons in sunlight to create a new range of photochemical pollutants, notably low-level ozone, the component of smog most dangerous to human health and crops. Atmospheric emissions of nitrogen compounds also add to those from intensive agriculture, sewage discharges, and the cultivation of leguminous crops to disrupt the global nitrogen cycle, causing overfertilization of both marine and terrestrial ecosystems.

In the latter half of the twentieth century, it became clear that other pollutants were accumulating globally. Pesticides such as DDT and toxaphene, and industrial synthetic compounds such as polychlorinated biphenyls (PCBs), collectively known as persistent organic pollutants (POPs), have been recognized as dangerous since the early 1960s—they are toxic, soluble in fat, and accumulate in body tissue. But in the 1990s two further concerns emerged, first, that they are "endocrine disrupters," disrupting hormone systems and threatening the health of both wildlife and humans, and second, that many are now accumulating in ecosystems globally—sometimes at higher concentrations than are present where they are first released. In a process known as "global distillation," many of these substances evaporate into the air where they are released and then preferentially settle out in the colder air of the polar regions. Though global emissions of most POPs are falling, their presence in Arctic ecosystems continues to rise, and concentrations in the diets of some Arctic inhabitants exceed tolerable daily intakes. POPs are currently the subject of negotiations intended to bring them under a global agreement, with some being phased out and others tightly controlled.

Chlorofluorocarbons (CFCs), halons, and other chlorine and bromine compounds were identified as a potential threat to stratospheric ozone in the 1970s. By the late 1980s, they had thinned the ozone layer at all latitudes by around 5 percent, and in the freezing air over the Arctic and Antarctic, created ozone "holes" in which 50 to 80 percent of the ozone was destroyed for several weeks each spring.

The current use of ozone-depleting chemicals is strongly regulated by international political agreement—notably, the Montreal Protocol of 1987—which called for production phaseout in the developed world by 1996, with a more gradual phaseout in developing countries. Though production phaseout in developed nations has been partly counterbalanced by growing production in developing nations, particularly China, production in these countries has been frozen at 1999 levels and must be phased out for most uses by 2009. The ozone layer itself will take another half century to recover.

The most fundamental effect of atmospheric pollution has been on the global carbon cycle. Carbon is a key element for life. It makes up half the mass of plants and animals and, as CO_2, is a major "greenhouse gas" responsible for maintaining the atmospheric temperature at levels fit for those organisms.

In the past 150 years, human activity has released more than 350 billion tons of carbon into the air in the form of CO_2. Though up to a half is currently absorbed by oceans or terrestrial ecosystems, this has been sufficient to raise CO_2 concentrations in the air by 30 percent since preindustrial times. Carbon is also present in the second most important anthropogenic greenhouse gas, methane, produced in agricultural activities such as rice paddies, the domestication of ruminants, and the clearance of natural vegetation. The industrial age has seen a 145 percent rise in methane concentrations in the atmosphere.

The cumulative effect of different air pollution is reducing the atmosphere's ability to cleanse itself. Most pollutants are removed from the atmosphere through oxidation by the hydroxyl radical. Some research suggests that hydroxyl levels in the atmosphere, particularly temperate northern latitudes, are falling. As a result, some compounds are lasting longer in the air than before, causing ever more pollution.

Take a Deep Breath . . . Air Quality Is Getting Better

Bjørn Lomborg

This selection originally appeared in *Guardian Unlimited* (London: Guardian Newspapers Unlimited, August 15, 2001).

Of all the different types of pollution affecting human health, by far the most important is air pollution. Of all the major U.S. Environmental Protection Agency statute areas (air, water, pesticides, conservation, drinking water, toxic control, liability), and even by the agency's own reckoning, 86 to 96 percent of all social benefits stem from the regulation of air pollution.

We often assume that air pollution is a modern phenomenon and that it has got worse in recent times. However, air pollution has been a major nuisance for most of civilization, and the air of the Western world has not been as clean as it is now for a long time. In ancient Rome, the statesman Seneca complained about "the stink, soot, and heavy air" in the city. In 1257, when Henry III's wife visited Nottingham, she found the stench of smoke from coal burning so intolerable that she left for fear of her life, and in 1285 London's air was so polluted that Edward I established the world's first air pollution commission. Shelley wrote: "Hell must be much like London, a smoky and populous city."

For London, the consequences were dire. In the eighteenth century it had twenty foggy days a year, but this had increased to almost sixty by the end of the nineteenth century: this meant that London got 40 percent less sunshine than the surrounding towns, and the number of thunderstorms doubled in London from the early eighteenth to the late nineteenth century.

We have data for air pollution in London since 1585, estimated from coal imports till 1935, and adjusted to measured pollution from the 1920s till today. These data show how levels of smoke and sulphur pollution increased dramatically over the three hundred years from 1585, reaching a maximum in the late nineteenth century, only to have dropped even faster ever since, such that the levels of the 1980s and 1990s were below the levels of the late sixteenth century. And despite increasing traffic, particulate emissions in the United Kingdom are expected to decrease over the next ten years by 30 percent. Smoke and particles are probably by far the most dangerous pollutant, and London's air has not been so free of them since the middle ages.

Generally, the data indicate that this picture holds true for all developed countries. Although air pollution is increasing in many developing countries, analyses show that they are merely replicating the development of industrialized countries. When they grow sufficiently rich they, too, will start to reduce their air pollution.

But even with this drastic reduction in particulate pollution, it still costs many lives: in the United Kingdom, the number of excess deaths from particle pollution today can be estimated at about sixty-four thousand a year—much higher than the number of deaths from road accidents (3,581 lives in 1998). Thus, cutting particle pollution even further would make good sense, especially for diesel cars, which make up only 6 percent of the total number of cars but contribute 92 percent of all vehicle particle emissions.

Careful analysis of the data on air pollution shows us where our preconceptions are wrong (not a new phenomenon getting worse but an old phenomenon getting ever better) and allows us to focus on the most important area where we still need to make progress: particle pollution from diesel cars.

SNAPSHOT: Global Warming

Greenhouse Gas Emissions and Climate Change

United Nations Population Fund

This selection is an excerpt from Footprints and Milestones: Population and Environmental Change *(United Nations Population Fund, 2001).*

Carbon dioxide and other greenhouse gases trap heat in the atmosphere and raise average global surface temperatures (see figure 2.2, p. 130). Emissions of carbon dioxide grew twelvefold between 1900 and 2000, from 543 million metric tons per year in 1900 to 6.59 billion metric tons in 1997.

In the same period, human population nearly quadrupled, from 1.6 billion to 6.1 billion, progressively consuming greater quantities of fossil fuels—oil, gas, and coal. Expanded agriculture, destruction of forests, and increased production of certain chemicals also increase greenhouse gases in the atmosphere.

It is unlikely that the human population could ever have reached its present size without the energy provided by fossil fuels. Conversely, the needs of the growing population have provided an ever-expanding market for exploration and production.

Climate change will have a serious impact. The Intergovernmental Panel on Climate Change (IPCC) estimates that the earth's atmosphere will warm by as much as 5.8 degrees Celsius over the coming century, a rate unmatched over the past ten thousand years. The IPCC's "bests estimate" scenario projects a sea level rise of about half a meter by 2100 (with a range of fifteen to ninety-five centimeters), substantially greater than the increase over the last century ("Third Assessment Report [TAR]," 2001).

The human and ecological impacts of rising oceans include increased flooding, coastal erosion, salinization of aquifers, and loss of coastal cropland, wetlands, and living space. The intensity and frequency of hurricanes and other hazardous weather may also increase, endangering the growing human population in coastal areas.

Rising global surface temperatures and changes in precipitation magnitude, intensity, and geographical distribution may well redraw the world renewable resources map. Whether or not these climate changes affect net global agricultural production, they are almost certain to shift productivity among regions and countries, and within nations.

For example, recent projections suggest that while total U.S. agriculture production may not diminish, certain regions of the country are likely to suffer substantially relative to others, as a result of changes in precipitation and temperature. Climate change policy will have to address changing regional and national fortunes, as well as the global economic and biological impact.

A warming climate also poses a significant public health threat. The redistribution of precipitation would markedly increase the number of people living in regions under extreme water stress—a problem compounded by increasing population. The geographical range of temperature-sensitive tropical diseases, such as malaria and dengue fever, would also expand. Higher average temperatures mean longer and more-intense heat waves, with a corresponding rise in heat-related health problems.

The combined effects of population growth and climate change could produce regional resource shortages, which in turn could result in the exploitation of environmentally sensitive areas such as hillsides, flood plains, coastal areas, and wetlands. These conditions may also increase environmental refugees, international economic migration, and associated sociopolitical challenges. Climate and environmental policy should address the geographical distribution and movement of people in the twenty-first century, as well as their absolute numbers.

Box 2.1 Equity and Environmental Intervention

As the earth's atmosphere warms, the impacts will be felt in all the world's regions, although not with equal force. While there may be some benefits, for example, warmer temperatures and an extended growing season in some northern regions, many more negative consequences can be expected. These include

- An average global sea level rise of as much as 0.88 meters from warming oceans and melting glaciers; this may engulf low-lying coastal cities and smaller settlements.

- Decreasing agricultural and fisheries productivity in warm, subtropical, and tropical areas.

- Less predictable, more common, and more severe storms, floods, droughts, heat waves, avalanches, and windstorms, with accompanying threats to human health.

- Larger zones for insect-borne infectious diseases such as malaria and dengue fever.

- Increased soil erosion, drying out and shrinking of tropical forests, and invasions of exotic species, including fast-growing weeds.

- Accelerated extinction rates as plants and animals fail to adapt or migrate; many species are at risk, particularly those whose habitats are isolated or fragmented by human activity; up to a third of existing plant and animal habitats could be lost by 2100.

- Southern countries in ecologically vulnerable tropical regions, small islands, or large deserts are likely to be hardest hit by climate change and also least able to adapt.

The Scientific Case against the Global Climate Treaty

S. Fred Singer

This selection is excerpted from "The Scientific Case against the Global Climate Treaty," in *Hot Talk, Cold Science: Global Warming's Unfinished Debate* (Oakland: The Independent Institute, 1999).

A driving force behind the push for a global climate treaty has been the United Nations' Intergovernmental Panel on Climate Change (IPCC). Through a series of well-publicized reports—co-authored by teams of scientists and policy specialists—the IPCC has come to be viewed by many governmental agencies, environmental policy organizations, and the media as the leading source of scientific information on climate change. It is for this reason that I focus much of my attention on reports issued by this esteemed organization.

The major conclusion of the United Nations' Intergovernmental Panel on Climate Change (IPCC WG-I 1996)—that "the balance of evidence suggests a discernible human influence on global climate"—cannot and should not be used to validate current Global Circulation Models (GCMs). The growing discrepancy between weather satellite observations, backed by balloon radiosonde data, and the results of computer models, throws doubt on the models' adequacy to predict a future warming. An earlier IPCC (1990) conclusion that observed and calculated temperature changes are "broadly consistent" is no longer accepted; the current IPCC explanation of the acknowledged discrepancy in terms of cooling effects from anthropogenic (man-made) sulfate aerosols is being increasingly disputed. There exist different, competing views about the cause(s) of the discrepancy—including exogenous factors like solar variability and endogenous factors like clouds or water vapor distribution—all inadequately treated by current computer models. The models do not include a variety of human influences, ranging from possible climate effects of air traffic to the diversion of fresh water from the Mediterranean.

Even if a moderate warming were to materialize, its consequences would be largely benign—for other climate parameters, for sea level changes, and for agricultural production. The goal of the Global Climate Treaty—avoiding a "dangerous" level of greenhouse gases—cannot as yet be scientifically defined; higher greenhouse gas levels may well produce a more stable climate. Therefore, the prudent course is to practice a "no regrets" policy of conservation and efficiency improvements and rely on adaptation to meet any damaging effects of climate change. At the same time, building on successful initial experiments, the capability of ocean fertilization to draw down atmospheric CO_2 should be demonstrated.

The chief points of this overview are as follows:

1. The major conclusion of the 1996 report of the U.N.-sponsored science advisory group, the Intergovernmental Panel on Climate Change, is that "the balance of evidence suggests a discernible human influence on global climate" (IPCC WG-I 1996, chap. 8). This innocuous but ambiguous phrase has been (mis)interpreted to mean that computer models predicting a future warming have now been validated. But such a connection is specifically denied in the body of the IPCC report (IPCC WG-I 1996, p. 34)—although not in the politically approved IPCC Summary for Policymakers (SPM).

On the contrary, the global temperature record of this century, which shows both warming and cooling, can best be explained by natural climate fluctuations caused by the complex interaction between atmosphere and oceans, and perhaps stimulated by the variations of solar radiation that drive the earth's climate system. The satellite record of global temperature, spanning nearly twenty years, does not show a global warming—much less one of the magnitude predicted by General Circulation Models (GCMs). The gap between the satellite observations and existing theory is so large that it throws serious doubt on all computer-modeled predictions of future warming. Yet this discrepancy is never mentioned in the IPCC report's summary—nor does the SPM even admit the existence of satellites.

If one were to extrapolate the maximum allowed temperature trend from satellites to the year 2100, allowing for a further increase in atmospheric carbon dioxide and other greenhouse gases, one might estimate the increase in global average temperature at about 0.5° C (U.S. General Accounting Office 1995)—about one-fourth of the "best" IPCC value—hardly detectable and completely inconsequential.

Any future warming would be reduced further by the cooling effects of volcanoes—a factor not specifically considered by the IPCC. Even though we cannot predict the exact dates of future volcanic eruptions, we have sufficient statistical information about past eruptions to estimate an average cooling effect.

2. Even if global warming were to occur, it would most likely lead to positive benefits overall, rather than to disbenefits. Human activities, especially agriculture, have always thrived during warm periods and faltered during cold periods. Greenhouse warming should lead to a reduction in severe storms. Furthermore, it seems likely that global warming would lower, rather than raise, sea levels, because more evaporation from the ocean would increase precipitation and thereby thicken the ice caps of Greenland and Antarctica.

3. Finally, no credible attempt has been made to define what constitutes a "dangerous" level of atmospheric CO_2; thus the goal of the U.N. Climate Treaty (the Framework Convention on Climate Change [FCCC]) is arbitrary. If one chooses as the target the present concentration, about 30 percent higher than the preindustrial CO_2 level of 280 parts per million by volume (ppmv), emission rates must be cut by over 60 percent on a worldwide basis, according to IPCC modeling (IPCC WG-I 1990, p. xi).

The policy of adaptation to a possible climate change should be considered, rather than energy rationing. If it becomes advisable to limit the growth of atmospheric CO_2, it may be more cost-effective to speed up CO_2 absorption into the ocean, rather than by reducing emissions. In fact, by fertilizing the ocean with micronutrients, it may be possible to increase phytoplankton and fish populations and thereby derive commercial benefits from the excess atmospheric CO_2.

Box 2.2 Some Benefits of Increased CO_2 Levels

It should be noted that little, if any, of the more than $2 billion a year environmental research budget has been used to identify, document, or quantify the possible benefits of adding CO_2 to the atmosphere or any of the other consequences of man's activities. This bias in itself has contributed greatly to the public perception that these activities pose serious threats. That there are benefits from adding CO_2 to the atmosphere is undeniable:

1. *Fertilization of the biosphere:* CO_2 is essential to plant life. At the last glacial maximum (eighteen thousand years before the present), the CO_2 level dropped to ~190 parts per million by volume, which is close to the level where plants would begin to experience propagation failure.

2. *Longer frost-free growing season:* Any greenhouse warming will be due to reduced radiative cooling of the surface and thus will be greatest in winter, at higher latitudes, and at night. That is, minimum temperatures will be affected much more than maximum temperatures, leading to longer frost-free growing seasons and little, if any, additional summer afternoon heat stress.

3. *Greater water efficiency for plants:* Except in already arid subtropics, precipitation is predicted to increase. Increased CO_2 allows plants to ingest the CO_2 they need with less opening of their stomata, thus making it possible to survive with less water since less is lost by evapotranspiration.

4. *Health:* The increase of minimum temperatures with little effect on maximum temperatures will be beneficial both in reducing cold stress on health and in reducing the requirements for space heating. S. B. Idso (*Carbon Dioxide and Global Change: Earth in Transition* [Tempe, Ariz.: IBR Press, 1989]) has suggested that "the significant downturn in circulatory heart disease experienced worldwide over the past two decades" is a possible consequence of the 25 percent increase in CO_2 in the atmosphere. Respiration is controlled by the concentration of CO_2 (rather than of oxygen) in the blood. Thus CO_2-stimulated deeper breathing may have reduced the strain on the circulatory system.

Box 2.3 Rio to Johannesburg: Ten Years of Climate Change Negotiations

The U.N. Framework Convention on Climate Change (FCCC), which was signed at the 1992 Earth Summit and entered into force in March 1994, established the objective of stabilizing atmospheric concentrations of greenhouse gases at levels that will avoid "dangerous anthropogenic interference with global climate" and allow economic development to proceed. The treaty recognizes several basic principles:

- that scientific uncertainty must not be used to avoid precautionary action;
- that nations have "common but differentiated responsibilities"; and
- that industrial nations, with the greatest historical contribution to climate change, must take the lead in addressing the problem.

The agreement commits all signatory nations to addressing climate change, adapting to its effects, and reporting on the actions they are taking to implement the convention. It also requires industrial countries and economies in transition to formulate and submit regular reports on their climate policies and their greenhouse gas inventories. It commits these nations to aim for a voluntary goal of returning emissions to 1990 levels by the year 2000 and to provide technical and financial assistance to other nations. Today 181 nations and the European Union (EU) are party to the U.N. FCCC.

In 1995, signatories to the U.N. FCCC concluded that its commitments were inadequate, and launched talks on a legally binding protocol to the convention. These negotiations culminated in the 1997 Kyoto Protocol, which collectively committed industrial and former Eastern bloc nations—termed Annex B nations—to reducing their greenhouse gas emissions by 5.2 percent below 1990 levels during 2008–2012. The agreement includes several measures designed to lessen the difficulty of meeting the target, such as "flexibility mechanisms" that allow the trading of emissions permits, the use of forests and other carbon "sinks," and the earning of credits through a Clean Development Mechanism or joint implementation projects (carbon-saving initiatives that take place in developing or Annex B nations, respectively). The protocol also commits developing countries to further their existing commitments to monitor and address their emissions.

In 1998, governments agreed to a plan of action and timeline for finalizing the rules on the protocol's implementation. At negotiations in The Hague, Netherlands, in late 2000, disagreement between the United States and the EU over several key provisions led to a breakdown in the talks. Following a U.S. withdrawal

Box 2.3 *(Continued)*

from the negotiating process in March 2001, 178 nations reached agreement in July in Bonn, Germany, on several key elements of the protocol's rules. Many details of the Bonn agreement concerned compromises on emissions trading, sinks, and compliance that allow additional flexibility in meeting the Kyoto targets. Governments also established a special fund to help developing nations adapt to the impacts of climate change. Outstanding issues were deferred to negotiations in Marrakesh, Morocco, from October 29 to November 9, 2001.

FIGURE 2.2.   The Greenhouse Effect

Our Changing Atmosphere

Energy from the sun drives the earth's weather and climate, and heats the earth's surface; in turn, the earth radiates energy back into space. Atmospheric greenhouse gases (water vapor, carbon dioxide, and other gases) trap some of the outgoing energy, retaining heat somewhat like the glass panels of a greenhouse. Without this natural "greenhouse effect," temperatures would be much lower than they are now, and life as known today would not be possible. Instead, thanks to greenhouse gases, the earth's average temperature is a more hospitable 60°F. However, problems may arise when the atmospheric concentration of greenhouse gases increases.

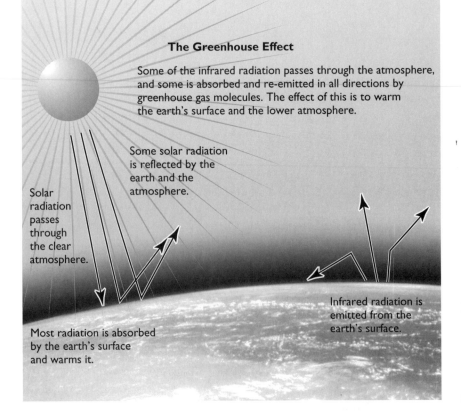

The Greenhouse Effect

Some of the infrared radiation passes through the atmosphere, and some is absorbed and re-emitted in all directions by greenhouse gas molecules. The effect of this is to warm the earth's surface and the lower atmosphere.

Some solar radiation is reflected by the earth and the atmosphere.

Solar radiation passes through the clear atmosphere.

Infrared radiation is emitted from the earth's surface.

Most radiation is absorbed by the earth's surface and warms it.

Source: The United States Environmental Protection Agency (2002). Available via the Internet: http://www.epa.gov/globalwarming/climate/index.html.

Chapter Five

FOOD

Can food productivity enhanced by technological advances continue to adequately feed the projected population?

Feeding Nine Billion

Lester R. Brown

This selection was excerpted from "Feeding Nine Billion," in *State of the World 1999* (Washington, D.C.: Worldwatch Institute, 1999).

When this century began, each American farmer produced enough food to feed seven other people in the United States and abroad. Today, a U.S. farmer feeds ninety-six people. Staggering gains in agricultural productivity in the United States and elsewhere have underpinned the emergence of the modern world as we know it. Just as the discovery of agriculture itself set the stage for the emergence of early civilization, these gains in agricultural productivity have facilitated the emergence of our modern global civilization.

This has been a revolutionary century for world agriculture. Draft animals have largely been replaced by tractors; traditional varieties of corn, wheat, and rice have given way to high-yielding varieties; and world irrigated area has multiplied sixfold since 1900. The use of chemical fertilizers—virtually unheard of in 1900—now accounts for an estimated 40 percent of world grain production.

Technological advances have tripled the productivity of world cropland during this century. They have helped expand the world grain harvest from less than 400 million tons in 1900 to nearly 1.9 billion tons in 1998. Indeed, farmers have expanded grain production five times as much since 1900 as during the preceding ten thousand years since agriculture began.

This impressive century of growth unfortunately has not translated into adequate food supplies for all the earth's inhabitants. An estimated 841 million people remain hungry and undernourished, a number that approaches the population of the entire world when Thomas Malthus warned about the race between food and people some two hundred years ago. Unless the world can move quickly to stabilize population, the ranks of the hungry and undernourished could increase as the new millennium unfolds.

Historically, we have depended on three basic systems for our food supply: oceanic fisheries, rangelands, and croplands. With oceanic fisheries and rangelands, two essentially natural systems, the world appears to have "hit the wall." After increasing nearly fivefold since midcentury, the oceanic fish catch appears to be at or near its sustainable yield limit. Overfishing is now the rule, not the exception. The same can be said about the world's rangelands: after tripling from 1950 to 1990, the production of beef and mutton has increased little in recent years as overgrazing has lowered rangeland productivity in large areas of the world.

Continued population growth is the dominant source of the mounting pressure on these natural systems. Some countries, such as Ethiopia, Nigeria, and Pakistan, are projected to nearly triple their populations by 2050. Nigeria is expected to have 339 million people in 2050—more than there were in all of Africa in 1950. Ethiopia, controlling a large share of the headwaters of the Nile, which is in effect the food lifeline for the Sudan and Egypt, is projected to increase its population from 62 million at present to 213 million in the year 2050. India, a country with nearly a billion people and water tables falling almost everywhere, is due to add another 600 million by 2050. And China, even with its efforts to slow population growth, is still slated to add some 300 million people, more than currently live in the United States, before its population stabilizes in 2040.

CHANGING COURSE

As we prepare for the new millennium, there is a rising tide of concern about the long-term food prospect. This can be seen in the frustration of plant breeders who are running into physiological constraints as they attempt to develop the new higher-yielding varieties needed to restore rapid growth in the world food supply. And it can be seen in the apprehensiveness of political leaders in countries where the food supply depends heavily on irrigation, but the aquifers are being depleted.

This mounting concern is also evident in the intelligence community in Washington, where the National Intelligence Council (NIC), the umbrella over all U.S. intelligence agencies, has commissioned a major interdisciplinary assessment of China's food prospect by a prominent group of scientists. This research effort was triggered by the realization that if China were to turn to the world market for massive quantities of grain, it could drive world grain prices up to a level that would create unprecedented political instability in third world cities. The NIC study ("China Agriculture: Cultivated Land Area, Grain Projections, and Implications" [Washington, D.C.: NIC, 1997])—the most comprehensive interdisciplinary assessment ever undertaken of China's food prospect—concluded in its "most likely" scenario that by 2025 China would need to import 175 million tons of grain. This quantity, which approaches current world grain exports of 200 million tons, could overwhelm the capacity of exporting countries.

Two major food issues face the world as it enters the twenty-first century. One is how to feed adequately those who suffer from chronic hunger and malnutrition, people who do not get enough protein and energy to develop their full physical and mental potential. The second is how to maintain the price stability needed in world grain markets if economic progress is not to be disrupted.

The worst mistake political leaders can make entering the new millennium is to underestimate the dimensions of the food challenge. To begin with, oceanic fisheries and rangelands—the two leading sources of growth in the animal protein supply over the last half-century—have both apparently reached their limits. This means that all future growth in the world food supply must come from croplands, but irrigation water supplies may not expand much further and the response to additional fertilizer is diminishing in many countries. The backlog of unused technology to raise land productivity is shrinking. This does not mean that food production cannot be increased. It can be and it will. But it is becoming much more difficult to sustain the rapid growth needed to keep up with increased demand.

Given these challenging new dimensions of the food prospect, governments facing continuing population growth need to calculate their future population carrying capacity by projecting the land available for crops, the amount of water that will be available for irrigation over the long term, and the likely yield of crops, based on what the most agriculturally advanced countries with similar growing conditions have achieved. This will provide the basis for a public dialogue on population policy.

Once projections of future food supplies are completed, societies can consider what combination of population size and consumption levels they want, recognizing that there are tradeoffs between the two.

Supply-side initiatives are still important in achieving an acceptable balance between food and people. But victory in the battle to eradicate hunger and malnutrition may now depend heavily on demand-side initiatives. The world still needs to invest more in agricultural research, in agricultural infrastructure, and in providing credit to small farmers, especially women in agriculture. But in addition, there is now a need for substantial demand-side initiatives in slowing population growth and using grain and water more efficiently.

The most recent U.N. population projections show the world adding 3.3 billion people during the first half of the next century. All these people will be added in the developing world, with a disproportionate share being added in countries that are already densely populated. A review of the U.N. projections shows some of the biggest increases slated for the Indian subcontinent and sub-Saharan Africa—the two regions where most of the world's hungry people are concentrated. As noted earlier, India is projected to add nearly 600 million people to its current population during the next half-century. Pakistan, meanwhile, will go from 148 million to 357 million by 2050. In Africa, Nigeria will go from 122 million at present to 339 million, while Ethiopia will more than triple its population, going from 62 million to 213 million.

Given the limits to the carrying capacity of each country's land and water resources, every national government needs a carefully articulated and adequately supported population policy, one that takes into account the country's carrying capacity at whatever consumption level citizens decide on. As Harvard biologist Edward O. Wilson observes in his landmark book *The Diversity of Life* (New York: WW Norton and Company, 1993), "Every nation has an economic policy and a foreign policy. The time has come to speak more openly of a population policy. . . . What, in the judgment of its informed citizenry, is the optimal population?"

Adequately feeding the projected increases in population poses one of the most difficult challenges that modern civilization faces. With little prospect of achieving an acceptable balance between food and people by supply-side initiatives alone, the time has come to focus on the demand side of the food equation as well. This means finding ways to accelerate the shift to smaller families, particularly in those countries where many are already hungry and malnourished, and it means moving down the food chain for those who are consuming unhealthily large amounts of livestock products.

Food Security and World Trade Prospects

D. Gale Johnson

This selection originally appeared in the *American Journal of Agricultural Economics*, vol. 80, no. 5 (United Kingdom: Blackwell Publishing Ltd., 1998).

Food security depends on available world supplies of food, the income of the designated population, and the population's access to the available supplies. Consequently, though seldom recognized in national food security policies, there is a direct relationship between food security, world trade in food, and the domestic policies that govern access to international markets for food. On all three scores, I believe we can be optimistic about improvement in world food security over the next quarter century.

Over the next quarter century, the world's supply of food will grow somewhat more rapidly than will the demand for it, leading to lower real prices of food. Thus, the trend of food prices, as measured by grain prices, is likely to continue the trend of the current century, though at a slower rate of decline. The remarkable reduction in the international price of grain that has occurred in the twentieth century is given all too little emphasis in discussions of the world food situation, certainly so in the discussions of the food pessimists.

I am confident that the real per capita income of the majority of the population in the developing countries will continue to increase, contributing to an improvement in food security. Finally, I believe that, with the changes in agricultural policies in major industrial countries, world trade in farm products, especially grains, will be further liberalized in the future. In addition, more and more developing countries are reducing barriers to trade, thus increasing access to world food supplies. Thus, all the broad trends point to an improvement in world food security and a reduction in the number of persons adversely affected by both long- and short-term inadequate access to food.

This does not mean that in every country food security will improve. Some governments may continue to follow national and trade policies related to food that restrict domestic food production, limit the growth of per capita incomes, and restrict access to the available world food supplies. When this happens, food security and adequacy will not be improved or not improved as much as they potentially could be. At this time, there can be little doubt that the poor performance of agriculture and the insecurity of food supplies in sub-Saharan Africa over the past quarter century have been due primarily to inappropriate policies—to policies that discriminated against agriculture and resulted in large-scale governmental intervention in international trade. Misgovernment plus civil and ethnic wars have exacted and continue to exact a heavy toll on the people of Africa.

There are those who argue that Africa's agricultural problems stem from the low and declining real prices of their major exportable products. But even a casual analysis indicates that the prices of agricultural exports from the region declined no more, in real terms, than did the prices of wheat, corn, and rice. Until policies are changed—and they are changing in a number of countries—and peace prevails, there will be little improvement in food security in this region. When policies are inappropriate, farmers find themselves at an enormous disadvantage in making effective use of their natural and human resources.

A BRIEF LOOK AT THE PAST

Before looking to the future, let us briefly look at the developments in world food supplies during the last half of the twentieth century. During these years, there has been more improvement in the available supplies of food for the world and in the developing countries than in all of previous human history. Much of the improvement occurred after 1960. From 1960 to 1990, the per capita caloric supplies in developing countries increased by 27 percent, reaching an average of 2,473 in 1988–1990 (Food and Agriculture Organization [FAO]). The improvement in per capita caloric supplies occurred while population growth was at the highest rate ever recorded and while the real prices of grains in international markets declined by approximately 40 percent from their levels in the late 1950s. Was it not quite remarkable that per capita food supplies in developing countries reached their historic peak while grain prices fell to their lowest level in the twentieth century, and while population was growing rapidly? This certainly does not support the view that supply lagged behind demand.

What brought about this remarkable development? Basically, it was the application of modern biological and chemical sciences to agriculture, first in the developed countries and, with a lag, in the developing countries. I doubt if there are many who know that, during the last half of the 1930s, the grain yields per hectare were the same in developing and developed countries at 1.15 tons per hectare—world yields are now nearly 2.5 times that amount (FAO). A yield differential soon emerged between the developed and developing countries, reaching 59 percent in 1961–1965 but declining to 29 percent in 1990–1992. I believe that it is reasonable to assume that the differential will narrow even further in the future.

SUCCESS GOES UNRECOGNIZED

It is perhaps useful to pause at this time to ask why it was that, during a period with such positive developments, there were repeated claims that the growth of demand for food was outpacing the growth of supply. True, since 1960 there have been three price spikes—in 1972–1974, 1979–1981, and 1995–1996. The spikes lasted no more than two or three years and did not interrupt the long-term decline in real grain prices. Yet throughout this period, doom and gloom made the headlines—Lester Brown's repeated and erroneous predictions, Paul Ehrlich's claim that there would be mass starvation in the world in the 1970s, and the Club of Rome's prophecies of doom—to name a few of the doomsayers.

It is quite remarkable that, in 1994, researchers at three international agencies—the Food and Agriculture Organization (*FAO Production Yearbook* [Rome: FAO]), the International Food Policy Research Institute (*Population and Food in the Early Twenty-First Century: Meeting Future Food Demand of an Increasing Population*, ed. N. Islam [Washington, D.C.: International Food Policy Research Institute, 1994]), and the World Bank (E. Bos et al., *World Population Projections: Estimates and Projections with Related Demographic Statistics* [Baltimore, Md.: Johns Hopkins Press, 1994])—independently published studies of prospective trends in food demand and supply and came to the same conclusion. This conclusion was that the world food situation would continue to improve over the next two or so decades and that world grain prices would continue to decline (Islam). Yet these three competent studies received hardly any notice in the world's press while claims by Lester Brown that the world faced food shortages were widely reported, and even greater attention was given to his fanciful paper "Will China Starve the World?" (Worldwatch, 1994). What does it prove? A promising view of the future is not news, but a pessimistic view or prediction of a calamity is news. Bad news sells; good news doesn't.

PROSPECTIVE GROWTH OF FOOD SUPPLY AND DEMAND

It is difficult to believe that, given the record of the last four or five decades, there should be significant doubt about the world's ability to expand the supply of food more rapidly than the growth of demand over the next quarter century. Some argue that the rate of growth of food supply in the future will be slower than in the recent past—and they will be right. The rate of demand growth over the next three decades will be substantially less than between 1960 and 1990. True, real per capita incomes are anticipated to increase, and this will increase the per capita demand for food, especially through the shift toward livestock products. However, the big shifter of total demand for food is population growth. While you wouldn't believe it from what you read in the press, the rate of growth of population has slowed down, not by a little but by a lot. No country in Europe except Albania is now reproducing its population, and a considerable number of developing countries now have fertility rates below the replacement level as well—South Korea, Taiwan, Singapore, Hong Kong—and Turkey, Sri Lanka, and China have reached or are approaching that level.

The consensus estimate of the three major studies referred to above is that the annual growth in grain use (as a proxy for total food use) for 1990 to 2010 is projected at 1.5 to 1.7 percent. This compares with a growth of 2.46 percent for 1960–1990 and represents a 30 to 40 percent decrease in the rate of growth of world grain use. This is a very large decline.

The projections for 1990 to 2010 of an annual increase in grain production and use can be moved ahead for a further decade. The 1.5 to 1.7

percent projected annual increase in grain production and consumption was based on a projected population growth rate of 1.5 percent annually. The population projections that Islam used have already been reduced from an annual rate of 1.5 to 1.385 percent. For 2010 to 2020, the projected annual rate of population growth is now about 1.1 percent. If the population projections hold true, the growth of per capita consumption in developing countries will be greater than projected in these studies or, more likely, the growth in world demand will be lower than projected.

Nonetheless, let us return to the original studies, accepting their data as then known. Their projections imply no increase in world per capita production and consumption of grain. How can this be? Does this bear out the predictions of the food pessimists? How can world per capita use or production of grain remain constant if the developing countries have income growth and increase their demand for grain both for direct consumption and indirect consumption through livestock products? Hopefully, this is exactly what will occur, and per capita grain use in developing countries will increase over the next quarter century, as has been the case over the last half century. Assuming that per capita grain production and use in the developed countries remain constant or increase slightly, why was there not a projected increase in world per capita production or consumption? The reason is that the world per capita figures are almost meaningless in interpreting the changes in production, consumption, or income. The statement that the world's per capita production of grain is declining contains almost no useful information concerning consumption levels in either developing or developed countries.

The world per capita figure holds little meaning because, over time, it is based on shifting weights—the relative importance of the developing countries in world population has increased and is increasing. Since the developing countries have much lower per capita consumption than the developed countries, when they increase their per capita consumption, the world average may be unchanged or actually decline. For example, in the FAO grain production projections for 1990–1992 to 2010, world per capita production is constant at 326 kilograms. However, per capita production in both developed and developing countries was projected to increase—by 7 percent and 4 percent, respectively. This seeming anomaly

resulted from the projected increase in the percentage of the world's population in the developing countries—from 77 percent in 1990 to 80.7 percent in 2010. Since per capita grain production in the developing
countries in 1990–1992 was 214 kilograms compared with 692 kilograms
in the developed countries, an increase in the relative weight of the developing countries had to have an adverse effect on the world average.
The world average, by itself, tells little or nothing about what has occurred
in individual regions or income groups when the relative importance of
the units is included in the average change.

Much has been made of the decline in the rate of growth of world
grain production and yields since 1990. This concern is largely misplaced.
Much of the slowdown has been concentrated in central and eastern Europe and has occurred without the slightest negative impact on the supply
of grain in the rest of the world. In fact, the demand for grain in that region has fallen by more than the supply and the import of grain by the
countries in the region has declined substantially—by approximately 30
million tons annually since the late 1980s. If the region had maintained
grain production at the 1985–1989 level, world grain production in 1996
would have been more than 100 million tons greater than it was. It would
have increased by 11 percent compared with 1990 and at a compound annual rate of 1.8 percent. This is roughly the same as the annual rate of
grain output growth during the 1980s, though a slower rate than for
1960–1990, but still faster than the less than 1.5 percent rate of world
population growth for the 1990s (FAO).

Thus, it is not obvious that there has been a significant decline in the
rate of growth of world grain production during the 1990s if we account
for the drastic adjustments taking place in central and eastern Europe resulting from the difficulties of moving from a planned to a market economy. I believe that the territory of the former Soviet Union will emerge as
a major grain exporter, though admittedly at a later date than I earlier believed. This possibility should be factored into long-term projections of
the world's supply potential as well as into the trade picture.

Why is it that many believe some reduction in the growth of food output would represent disaster? Given the demand conditions that are likely
to prevail, it would be a disaster for the world's farmers if world output

grew at the 1960–1990 rate. Why is it that the literature on world food supply and demand seldom, if ever, mentions the effects of various outcomes on the welfare of farmers? If I were an agricultural policymaker in a developing country, I would give as much emphasis to the problems associated with low food prices as to food scarcity and high prices over the next quarter century. I believe that grain prices in the early 1990s were at such low levels that they discouraged the expansion of grain production during the first half of the decade. Grain inventories declined, but this was a reasonable economic response to low and possibly falling prices. The 1995 and 1996 increases in grain prices were very short lived, with U.S. export prices of wheat and corn returning to the early 1990 prices by the end of 1997.

CONCLUDING COMMENTS

I am an optimist about future trends in food supply and demand. By that, I mean that there will be continued improvements in productivity, the rate of growth of supply will exceed that of demand, and real international prices of food will decline. Farmers will increase their real income only as they adjust to the changing conditions. The percentage of the world's resources used to produce food will continue to decline, and farmers must adjust to this fact.

This is not a new conclusion for me. I have been an optimist for the last three decades and I have been right. I have long been confident that farmers could expand food production at least as rapidly as demand. However, I must admit that I did not anticipate the large decline in the real prices of grain that has occurred since 1960. The decline in the real price and cost of grain was little short of a miracle, unprecedented in its magnitude. The gain in welfare for hundreds of millions—no, billions—of people was enormous, and the number that could have benefited would have been even greater if more governments had followed appropriate policies with respect to agricultural production, prices, and trade.

I do not foresee such a large decline in costs and prices over the next three decades. But I do anticipate, along with some other researchers, that real grain and food prices will continue to decline in the years ahead. Farmers will continue to contribute to the wealth of nations.

FIGURE 2.3. World Hunger, 1999

The United Nations Food and Agriculture Organization defines adequate nourishment as consumption of at least 2,100 kilocalories (often called calories informally) per day. Countries are shaded to illustrate the proportion of the population that does not have access to enough food to satisfy this requirement.

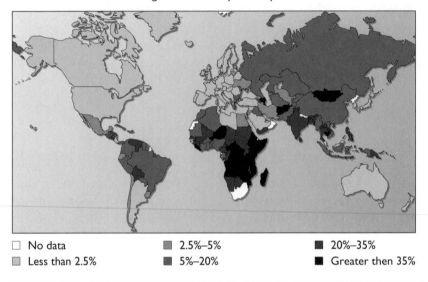

☐ No data   ■ 2.5%–5%   ■ 20%–35%

▨ Less than 2.5%   ■ 5%–20%   ■ Greater then 35%

Source: Population Action International

Chapter Six

LAND

Civilizations of the past have flourished because of the availability of land and the resources that come with it—can this trend continue?

Concern for Land

Anthony Young

This selection was excerpted from "Concern for Land," in *Land Resources: Now and for the Future* (Cambridge: Cambridge University Press, 2000).

With the rise in population placing ever-increasing pressure on scarce land, the governments of developing countries should give high priority to rational land use, improved land management, and avoidance of degradation. At the international level, public concern has been more about pollution aspects of the environment and nature conservation than about land as a productive resource. In developing countries, awareness by governments of the critical importance of land resources is low, and institutions are inadequately funded. Much progress has been made over the past fifty years in approaches and methods for land resource survey, evaluation, and management. What is needed now is the more widespread and effective application of these methods. Sustainability, the combination of production with conservation, is a central concept in land resource management.

Management of land, of its soils, water, forests, pastures, and wildlife, has been central to human society from its earliest times. Land resources provide the basis for more than 95 percent of human food supplies, the greater part of clothing, and all needs for wood, both for fuel and construction. The developments of the industrial age have substituted coal, oil, and minerals to fulfill some of the fuel, construction, and fiber needs but have in no way removed the basic dependency of society on the renewable resources of the land.

There has always been competition for land, sometimes reaching the level of conflict. In prehistoric times, among communities dependent on hunting and gathering, the competition would have shown in the kind of territoriality found among animal populations. From the beginning of recorded history, it is clear that there were great inequalities in land availability. Famine has never been absent, and migrations in search of better resources have extended from biblical times to the great world expansion in the period from the nineteenth to the first half of the twentieth century.

Formerly, the solution to local shortages of food and other basic necessities was to place more land under cultivation. Usually this occurred through clearing the forests, since forested lands are the most fertile. In Europe in medieval times, in North America in the nineteenth century, and in tropical lands until quite recently, forests and woodlands have receded, arable lands have expanded, and land for nature has been constantly reduced. Even in the post-1945 period of planned development, new land settlement schemes were still possible as a solution to the problems of crowding, small farms, and landlessness.

Most parts of the world are now moving into a new era. The early taxation surveys of India recorded "culturable wasteland," which today would be called land that is cultivable but not cultivated. Almost all such land has now been taken up. In 1965, the Malaysian Government, with international agency support, embarked on the Jengka Triangle project, the objective of which was to clear two thousand square kilometers of primary rain forest and plant it with oil palm, to attract settlers from the overcrowded rice-growing deltas. Today, world opinion and the policy of international agencies strongly oppose any such clearance. Malawi, in East Africa, was a crowded country at the time it gained independence in 1964, but cultivation still stopped short at the foot of the hills; ten years later cultivation was widespread on hillsides and on the steeply dissected slopes of the rift valley. In Jamaica, needs for food have led to cultivation of slopes on which one can hardly stand, leading to severe soil erosion.

The massive increase in population that has led to land shortage started with the Industrial Revolution and has been accelerated by improvements in health and by the introduction, since World War II, of international action for famine relief. From 2.5 billion in 1950, world population doubled by 1987 and will pass 6.0 billion in 1998. The current rate of increase is 88 million a year or 240,000 a day. At the present average levels of crop yields, food alone for these extra people calls for an added eighty thousand hectares of land, nearly thirty by thirty kilometers, every day. In much of Asia, the Middle East, and a growing number of countries elsewhere, such extra land is simply not there. The world is becoming a full house.

Barring catastrophe, a further population rise over the next thirty years of at least 2.0 billion, and most probably 2.5 billion, is inevitable. Nearly all of this increase will be in less-developed countries. Much of it will be in families who are already very poor, many of them chronically under-nourished. Because there is little spare land remaining, most of the added production required to provide for the basic needs of these people will have to be achieved by higher productivity in the existing land. Higher crop yields form the largest part, but increased productivity from livestock and forests is also required. The productive potential of the land must be conserved, preventing erosion and other forms of land degradation. Land must be retained for forestry, water supply, and conservation of nature, checking a threatened reduction in the diversity of plants and animals. Lastly, people need land for settlements, not only for housing but for trans-port, industry, and recreation.

In this crowded world of growing population, severely limited land, and strong competition for its use, it is clearly desirable that governments should place high among their priorities:

- rational land use, that is, using different types of land in ways best suited to their potential;
- improved land management in agriculture and forestry, to secure higher productivity;
- avoidance of land degradation—soil erosion, forest clearance, pasture degradation, and the like—to conserve resources for the future;
- good data to guide decisions on the above, and research to advance knowledge on which improvements can be based.

These needs and pressures should therefore mean that land resources and land use lie at the center of national policies, particularly in the de-veloping countries. Regrettably, this is not the case.

AWARENESS AT THE NATIONAL LEVEL

If research and investment into the conservation, management, and de-velopment of land resources are to be made, the initiative has to come from the governments of the countries concerned. In industrialized countries, particularly those in which agriculture contributes only a small percentage to national wealth, it would be understandable if land resources did not play a major role in policy. In fact, many such countries have balanced and responsible policies in these fields. The United States took a lead in soil conservation programs in the 1930s. Australia made surveys of the resources of its northern and central areas from the late 1940s onwards, and a comprehensive land inventory of Canada has been completed. Deforestation was reversed in Europe from the 1920s onward.

In developing countries, the needs are very much more urgent. Many have a high dependence on agriculture for both food needs and exports and supplement their food production with substantial cereal imports. Some have low crop yields, and most encounter problems of land degradation. Many countries have an average farm size of less than one hectare, and populations will rise by at least another 50 percent. One might expect, therefore, that these countries would place land resources at the center of national policies and planning.

The actual position is very different. Natural resource survey organizations and land use planning departments exist, but the information they collect does not weigh strongly in development planning. The information basis for decisions about land is extremely poor. Many countries lack reliable data on even such basic facts as the areas cultivated and under forest. None have yet made systematic efforts to monitor changes in the condition of their soils, nor in the extent of land degradation. The adoption of improved methods of soil management is held back by the weakness of agricultural extension services. National development plans give due attention to agriculture and forestry but rarely make more than passing reference to the land resources on which production in these sectors depends. Most national institutions for agricultural research are poorly funded. The wealth of soils, water resources, forests, and grazing lands is not taken into account in national budgeting. A forest may be cleared or a valley-floor pasture gullied, but these losses of natural capital do not appear in national accounts.

Box 2.4 International Milestones in Awareness of Land, Population, Environment, and Development

1972 U.N. Conference on the Human Environment, Stockholm, leading to establishment of the U.N. Environment Programme (UNEP).

1977 First U.N. Conference on Desertification, Nairobi.

1979 World Conference on Agrarian Reform and Rural Development (WCARRD), directing attention to land tenure reform and social issues.

1980 Report of the Brandt Commission, *North-South: A Programme for Survival*.

1985 Establishment of the International Board for Soils Research and Management (IBSRAM).

1987 Report of the Brundtland Commission, *Our Common Future*.

1990 Four research institutes in land resource management, for forestry, agroforestry, irrigation, and fisheries, are admitted to the international agricultural research system.

1992 U.N. Conference on Environment and Development (UNCED), Rio de Janeiro; *Agenda 21*, programme of action for sustainable development.

1993 Population Summit of the World's Scientific Academies, New Delhi, *Joint Statement*.

1994 Third U.N. Conference on Population and Development, Cairo, *Programme of Action*.

1996 Second World Food Summit, *Rome Declaration and Plan of Action*.

2002 World Summit on Sustainable Development, Johannesburg.

Are We Losing Ground?

Julian Simon

This selection was excerpted from *The Ultimate Resource II* (Princeton, N.J.: Princeton University Press, 1996).

The most important fact about the world's agricultural land is that less and less of it is needed as the decades pass. This idea is utterly counterintuitive. It seems obvious that a growing world population must need larger amounts of farmland. But the title of a remarkably prescient 1951 article by the only economist to win a Nobel Prize for agricultural economics, Theodore Schultz, tells the true story: "The Declining Economic Importance of Land" (*Economic Journal* LXI [December 1951].

Consider these countries, and try to guess which ones are rich and which poor: (1) landlocked, mountainous, almost no oil or metals or other extractive resources, little flat farmland, high population density; (2) flat and low, in constant danger of being flooded by the ocean (which has happened many times in history), high population density, no natural resources; (3) fastest population growth rate and largest rate of immigration in the world in the past half century, very high population density, no natural resources (not even fresh water); (4) low population density, huge stores of natural resources, much fertile farmland.

In order, the first three countries are Switzerland, Holland, and Hong Kong. The fourth country might be most of the countries in Africa or South America. The first three are among the richest and most economically vibrant countries on earth; many of the fourth group are dirt poor.

The reduced economic importance of land is shown by the long-run diminution in the proportion of total tangible assets that farmland has represented in various countries.

Productivity of food per unit of land has grown much faster than has world population in recent decades, and there is sound reason to expect this trend to continue; this implies that there is less and less reason to worry about the supply of land.

The world is not "losing ground" on a net basis. Of course arable land in some places is going out of cultivation because of erosion and other destructive forces, as well as because productivity elsewhere is increasing and the land is no longer needed (for example, in Wisconsin and the southeastern United States). But taken as a whole, the amount of arable land in the world is increasing year by year, in flat contradiction to the clear implications of the statements quoted above.

How can it be that agricultural land is becoming less important? Let us first step back and specify the questions to address, which are never easy to formulate. We should first ask: What is the present trend in the supply of arable land? Next we should ask: what is the effect of increasing affluence on the supply of agricultural land?

As to the meanings of "arable" and "suitable for crops," here again, economics cannot be separated from semantics. At one time most of Europe could not be planted because soils were "too heavy." When a plow was invented that could farm the heavy soil, most of Europe suddenly became "arable" in the eyes of the people who lived there. Most of Ireland and New England originally were too hilly and stony to be farmed, but with backbreaking toil stones were removed and the land became "suitable for crops." In the twentieth century, bulldozers and dynamite have pulled out stumps that kept land from being cropped. And in the future, cheap water transportation and desalination will transform more of what are now deserts into "arable" lands (just as happened with much of California). The definitions change as technology develops and the demand for land changes. Hence any definition of "arable" land should be seen for what it is—a rough temporary assessment that may be useful for a while but has no permanent validity.

"You can even make agricultural land out of Mount Everest, but it would cost a fortune to do so," is a common reply to such optimism by those who worry that we are running out of land. But in many parts of the world, new land can be bought and cleared right now for amounts that are considerably below the purchase price of good developed land. Moreover, the cost of acquiring and clearing is now less than it was in the past, when tree cutting, stump pulling, and irrigation-ditch digging had to be done by hand or with animal power. New areas are made habitable for agriculture as well as for urban activity with air conditioning.

THE TREND OF ARABLE LAND: LOSING GROUND?

The quantity of farmland is not a crucial issue. In fact, some African officials contend that Africa has too much land—at the same time that the U.S. State Department's Agency for International Development (AID) is wringing its hands and pushing policies in Africa intended to reduce the people/land ratio.

Using technology that is in commercial use to raise food in hydroponic artificial-light factories like PhytoFarm, the entire population of the world can be fed using only the land area of Massachusetts and Vermont or the Netherlands and Jamaica. And the area necessary can be reduced to a tenth or a hundredth of that by producing the food in ten- or hundred-story buildings. Nevertheless, doomsters spook the public with fears that we are losing the quantity that now exists. Thus we need to examine the data in order to reassure you.

Joginder Kumar laboriously collected and standardized the first set of data on land supply and use throughout the world. His finding: 9 percent more total arable land in 1960 than in 1950 in the eighty-seven countries for which he could find data; these countries account for 73 percent of the total land area of the world. Some of the places where the quantity of cultivated land is going up may surprise you—India, for example, where the amount of cultivated land rose from 1,261,000 to 1,379,190 square kilometers between 1951 and 1960.

The trend that Kumar found from 1950 to 1960 still continues. The United Nations Food and Agriculture Organization (UNFAO) now has collected data back to the 1960s showing that there was a rise in arable and permanent cropland in the world as a whole during the period 1961–1989 from 10.41 percent to 11.03 percent of earth's dry-land area, which represents an increase of 5 percent in arable area for the roughly twenty-five-year period; the data for agricultural (arable plus pasture land) are comparable. Moreover, the gain in the developing countries is particularly significant and heartening.

We begin, then, by taking notice of the fact that the amount of arable land in the world—and especially in the poor and hungry countries—is increasing, rather than decreasing as the popular press would have it. Nor should we worry about diminishing returns in the long run due to successively poorer land being brought into use, because average yields per acre are increasing.

WHERE IS THE AMOUNT OF CULTIVATED LAND DECLINING?

The amount of cultivated land is certainly going down in some places. But this decline is not necessarily a bad sign. In the United States, the trend is downward. This has happened because both the total agricultural output and average yields per acre have been going up sharply in the United States. This high output is obtained in large part with huge farm machines that require flat land for efficiency. The combination of increased productivity per acre of good land, and the increased use of equipment adapted to flat land, has made it unprofitable to farm some land that formerly was cultivated. For example, in New Hampshire between 1860 and 1950 the tillable area declined from 2,367,000 acres to 451,000 acres.

There are, however, places where, for negative reasons—usually wars or fights about land tenure—good land that was formerly cultivated is no longer farmed. Mexico in the 1970s was a typical example. Frustrated by the slow pace of agrarian reform, Mexican peasants began seizing land. In fear of more seizures, the big estates then cut their investments. Even the people who worry about the "loss" of land acknowledge that it is in our own power to have more land if we will work for it.

Land can be used indefinitely, even on an intensive basis, without loss of fertility. This may be seen in the Morrow Plots at the University of Illinois, the oldest experimental agriculture station in the United States. Starting in 1876, corn has been planted every year without any fertilizer, and the yields are visibly scrawny. But land that has been planted every year and rotated among corn and other crops retains excellent fertility, the corn towering over the no-fertilizer-no-rotation yields, with no observable loss of soil fertility. Crops using commercial and organic fertilizer both do as well as the rotation crops. And crops using both rotation and fertilizer do best of all.

Now we proceed to another question.

IS LAND DIFFERENT FROM OTHER RESOURCES?

Many people consider land to be a special kind of resource. But like other natural resources, land is the result of the human creative process. Though the stock of usable land seems fixed at any moment, it is constantly being increased—at a rapid rate in many cases—by the clearing of new fields or the reclamation of wasteland. Land also is constantly being enhanced by increasing the number of crops grown per year on each unit of land and by increasing the yield per crop with better farming methods and with chemical fertilizer.

Last but not least, land is created anew where there was none. For example, much of Holland originally belonged more to the sea than to the land. According to strict geographical determinism, one would expect to find there nothing but a fever-ridden delta and lagoons, the undisputed domain of sea fowl and migratory birds. Instead, we find a prosperous and densely peopled country, with in fact the highest population density in Europe. The new land was won by diking and draining. This is essentially a triumph of human will: it is the imprint of civilization on the landscape. A hundred years ago someone said of the Netherlands, "This is not soil, it is the flesh and blood and sweat of men."

Modern Japan is applying the lesson of Holland. When land around Tokyo became scarce and extraordinarily expensive, the Japanese built an artificial island in Tokyo Bay and are contemplating building large floating structures, including perhaps an airport. And Hong Kong is planning to build a new airport on reclaimed land just off one of its islands.

Holland was created by muscle power. But the potential for creating new land has increased as new power sources and our knowledge and machinery have developed. In the future, the potential for creating new and better land will be even greater. We will make mountains where there is now water, learn new techniques of changing the nature of soils, and develop our ability to transport fresh water to arid regions.

Extending the process into a third dimension, which Holland demonstrated in two dimensions, the capacity to grow food in multilevel structures using artificial light means that the supply of effective agricultural land can be expanded without limit—that is, it is not finite. This is no pipedream but a demonstrated reality that is economical even at current prices.

The role of landbuilding in population history became clear to Malthus, who said of the Germans in Roman times,

> When the return of famine severely admonished them of the insufficiency of their scanty resources, they accused the sterility of a country which refused to supply the multitude of its inhabitants, but instead of clearing their forests, draining their forests, draining their swamps, and rendering their soil fit to support an extended population, they found it more congenial to their martial habits and impatient dispositions, to go in quest of "food, of plunder, or of glory," into other countries.

The cooperative interrelationship among landbuilding, irrigation, population growth, and prosperity in prehistoric times was also well understood by historians of the ancient Middle East. In the great alluvial valleys of the Nile, the Tigris-Euphrates, and the Indus system, collective effort had created artificial environments, and the organized exploitation of land reclaimed from swamp and desert yielded unprecedented supplies of corn, fish, and other foodstuffs.

But once developed, land can be lost through neglect and depopulation, as happened in the same Tigris-Euphrates area. Many of these districts have not been settled or cultivated in a thousand years or more and have been deeply and cleanly scoured by wind erosion during that interval. One can see, under the sand, traces of the old abandoned ghanats— irrigation systems—when flying over the desert.

Investment in land is as important in the modern world as it was in the ancient world. The key idea is that land is made by people, just like other inputs to farm production. Moreover, whether land deteriorates or improves depends on its treatment by farmers. Land owned in common tends to deteriorate because no one has a property stake in maintaining it; in contrast, private farm owners improve their land because it raises the value of their investment. Reports about increasing soil erosion in various countries should be seen in this context.

The extent of land improvement on subsistence-agriculture farms can be very great, depending on need. Much agricultural investment has always come from the added labor done by farmers during the off-season. For example, in agriculturally primitive Rapitok Parish in New Britain, men of working age invest one-quarter of their manpower per year in the formation of new agricultural assets such as cocoa and coconut trees. This is a long-term agricultural investment.

The United States was blessed with an endowment of land and water that long made irrigation unprofitable. But now, with an increased demand for food and new technological advances, irrigation has become important in creating new land. California's San Joaquin Valley illustrates the miracle: A century ago it was desert, but today a Rhode Island–size tract in California's arid San Joaquin Valley, known as the Westlands Water District, contains some of the richest farmland in the world—the product mainly of multi-billion-dollar federal reclamation projects that irrigated the parched valley floor with water from government dams.

Center-pivot irrigation is a landbuilding innovation so promising that it deserves special mention. (Signs of this irrigation system are the huge circles you see below you as you fly west from Ohio to the West Coast.)

In its natural state, the land along the Columbia River in eastern Washington and Oregon is a forbidding expanse of shifting sand, sage brush, and Russian thistle, and only the hardiest of farmers or ranchers would try to wrest a living from it. The region is so desolate that the Navy uses some of the land as a bombing range. But for all this, the mid-Columbia region is one of the most thriving new agricultural areas in the world. Thanks to a remarkable new system of irrigation, the desert along the river is blooming. With pivot irrigation, the water is pumped from the river to the center of a round field a half mile in diameter. A giant arm of six-inch pipe, a quarter of a mile long, pivots around the center of the field like the hand of a clock, making one revolution every twelve hours. Since much of the land is almost pure sand, it must be continuously fertilized, and here too the sprinkler system is used (by feeding appropriate nutrients into the water).

By the 1970s irrigation had begun to appear even in fertile areas such as Champaign County, Illinois, whose corn-and-soybean land is as rich as any in the world, even without irrigation. And in areas where water is too scarce or saline for ordinary irrigation and where labor is scarce, the Blass system of drip irrigation (also called "trickle irrigation") multiplies yields.

There are vast barren areas of the planet that may be brought into cultivation when energy, together with desalination and irrigation technology, become cheaper. To fly over the Nile River in Egypt is an amazing experience. A beautiful verdant strip surrounds the river. But beyond a few thousand meters from the river, the rest of the country is entirely brown. That narrow green strip supports fifty-six million Egyptians (1990). Irrigation and desalination could make the rest of the country green, too.

Then there is outer space and the planets. Science fiction? Many respected scientists see potential there.

Making plans so bold that they seem almost unbelievable, many of the nation's leading scientists are calling for immediate steps to begin colonizing space. Their goal is to make the vast reaches of space the natural habitat of man with Mother Earth remembered as the "old world." Peering into their crystal balls at the recent meeting of the American Association for the Advancement of Science, the scientists concluded that space colonization is inevitable—and sooner than we think.

As with other resources, the demand for land lessens when new substances are found to substitute for agricultural products. For example, in India in 1897 nearly 2 million acres were used for cultivating indigo plants. Along came the German chemical industry and synthesized an indigo dye that was cheaper than the natural product. The 2 million acres were no longer needed for indigo.

CONCLUSION

I do not preach complacency about the supply of land. I am not suggesting that we cease to care about our agricultural fields, worldwide or regionally. Just as homeowners must take care of their lawns lest they go to ruin, farmers must continually protect and renew their acreage so that the stock of good land is increased and improved.

The message of these land data is that there is no ground for the panic into which anecdotal accounts can throw us when they are not balanced by the longer picture given by accurate figures. And there is no basis in these figures for opposition to continuing economic and population growth.

SNAPSHOT: Forests

Changing Demands on the World's Forests: Meeting Environmental and Institutional Challenges

Roger A. Sedjo

This selection is an excerpt from the *S. J. Hall Lectureship in Industrial Forestry*, delivered on September 28, 2001, at the College of Natural Resources, University of California, Berkeley (Washington, D.C.: Resources for the Future, 2001).

INTRODUCTION

Today there are a number of important demands on the world's forests that are undergoing changes. On the one hand the world's forests continue to be the source of timber and industrial wood used for building materials and paper products. On the other hand the world's forests are increasingly looked at as the source of a variety of recreational, environmental, and ecological services. Increasingly, the provision of timber is being viewed as in conflict with the provision of one or more of these other services.

A number of recent changes are occurring that have implications for the world's forests. While part of the world, the tropics, is continuing to experience deforestation, net reforestation is occurring in the temperate zone of the world. The deforestation of the tropics is driven primarily by land use conversion for other purposes, primarily agriculture. The reforestation of the world is also driven by changes in the agriculture sector, but in this case the abandonment of agricultural crop and pasture lands in temperate regions.

A second important change relates to the nature of the way society provides for wood supply. Today we see the continuation of the gradual transition of wood production from a foraging operation, where the bounty provided by natural forests is collected, to a cropping operation akin to agriculture. Food production experienced most of its transition from hunting and gathering to livestock raising and cropping many centuries ago. For forestry, however, most of this transition began in the twentieth century, and the transition is far from complete. However, the process has been accelerating and trees are increasingly being planted, cared for, and harvested in a cropping mode. The benefit of direct tree planting, as in agriculture, is to provide an approach that leads to increases in yields and productivity, and the effect of which is to substitute a supply of wood from intensively managed plantations for wood that had traditionally been obtained from natural forests through an extensively managed process. Planted forests also provide an opportunity for embodying technology in the planted forest. Superior trees are being developed through traditional breeding techniques and, perhaps in the future, through biotechnological innovations. As in agriculture, planting allows the selection of seed stock and provides the opportunity to capture the financial benefits of investments in improved germ plasm. Hence the transition to planted forests is accelerated by the opportunities that plantations provide for the application of modern technology. High productivity from planted forests opens the promise of relieving logging pressures on natural forests and thereby allowing many of them to be used for other, nontimber, purposes.

However, although the specialization inherent in this approach suggests that less forest land will ultimately be required to meet society's timber needs, some areas with particularly favorable tree-growing conditions may expect to further increase their specialization in timber production. Thus, just as Iowa tends to specialize in the production of corn, other regions may be expected to specialize in wood production from planted forests. This appears to be happening now in the southern United States.

Additionally, there are important changes occurring on the demand side for industrial wood. Even as planted forests have been replacing natural forests, very recent decades have seen the relative stabilization of global demand for industrial wood. This stabilization reflects a relative decline in the importance of the marketed commodities of the forest and particularly of industrial wood as a material. Whether this trend is temporary or permanent remains to be seen. However, there are a number of factors that suggest the stabilized demand could well be a permanent feature.

Even as demand growth is ebbing, the forests are increasingly being looked at as a source of noncommodity values, including recreation, environmental and ecological services, carbon sequestration, and biodiversity. Until recent decades, there was little serious concern about the loss of overall biodiversity or about the function of forests as a storehouse of carbon, which decreases the amount of the carbon dioxide greenhouse gas in the atmosphere. However, this perspective has changed dramatically over the past decade or two, and programs are increasingly being designed to protect biodiversity and promote forest carbon sequestration.

Moreover, it should be noted that all of these changes are occurring in the context of a global population that, while it is becoming progressively richer, may also be well on its way to stabilization, or even decline. A world with a stable and perhaps largely wealthy population is likely to place different demands on its forests than were experienced in the twentieth century.

SUMMARY AND CONCLUSIONS: THE FOREST OF 2050

The world consumption of industrial wood has stabilized over the past two decades. This stabilization has not been due to the lack of supply choking off production, as might be reflected in dramatically higher prices. Rather, there appears to be a lack of increase in basic demand worldwide, probably due largely to the substitution of other materials for wood.

Recent assessments by a variety of organizations have suggested the likelihood of only modest increases in consumption and demand over the next several decades. Simultaneously, in the latter part of the twentieth century, there has been a burgeoning of investment and activity in fast-growing planted forests. This has been especially true in North and South America, Oceania, and parts of Asia and Europe. The production of these forests has affected worldwide markets, and greater portions of world industrial wood output come from these forests. The world has seen a shift in the source of industrial wood away from old-growth and second-growth forests to planted and intensively managed forests. Moreover, the rate of planted forest expansion and the potential for additional expansion are both great. This basic trend is being promoted by technological improvements, particularly related to tree breeding, which enhance the economics of tree growing. Furthermore, biotechnology offers the potential to further accelerate this process. As this process continues, the portion of the world's natural forest free from serious commercial logging pressure will increase.

As the world moves through the first half of the twenty-first century, it is likely to move toward a global forest that is largely in some broad global balance. Industrial wood production will be increasingly confined to high productivity sites, where very intensive management is practiced. The total area involved in industrial plantation forests, although large in an aggregate sense, will be small on a global scale—perhaps consisting of a couple of hundred million hectares, or perhaps about 5 percent of the 3.4 billion hectares of land area currently in the global forest. Some natural forests will continue to be harvested for specialized types of industrial wood, but as of today, specialized wood types will constitute only a small fraction of total industrial wood requirements. This will leave about 90 percent of the world's forest for other purposes. Under a host of conditions, these forests will be providing environmental and ecological services, ranging from watershed protection to biodiversity reserves.

The major threat to the natural forest over the next fifty years is the continuation of high levels of deforestation in the tropics as land continues to be converted from forest to other uses, particularly agricultural uses. The appropriate remedial actions for this problem, however, have relatively little to do with industrial wood and commercial logging directly, and probably more to do with the spatial distribution of infrastructure and roads.

164

FIGURE 2.4. Changes in Land Use and Population

Historical and Projected Changes in Land Use and Population

Over the span of human history, the greatest cause of forest loss has been the development of sedentary agriculture, driven by the need to feed an increasing human population. This figure reveals the dramatic declines in forested land that occurred during the nineteenth and early twentieth centuries. The pace of this decline slowed somewhat with the introduction of agricultural technologies such as synthetic fertilizers and high-yield crop strains. (Time series is not drawn to scale)

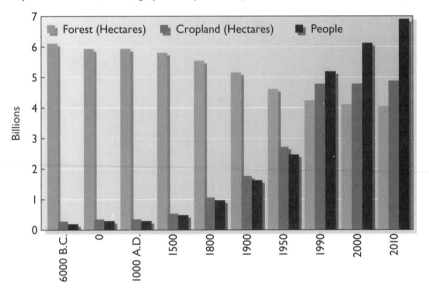

Source: Population Action International

Chapter Seven

ENERGY

Are renewable energy sources a viable option?

The Case for Renewables

This selection was excerpted from "The Case for Renewables," in *State of the World 2003* (Washington, D.C.: Worldwatch Institute, 2003).

New renewable resources provide only a small share of global energy production today. Yet the advantages of shifting away from fossil fuels and nuclear energy and toward greater reliance on renewables are numerous and enormous. Several countries have begun this transition in response to the rising demand for energy, increasing concern about fuel supplies and global security, the growing threat of climate change and other environmental crises, and significant advances in renewable technologies and the benefits they offer.

Global oil production is expected to peak early in this century. "In 20–25 years the reserves of liquid hydrocarbons are beginning to go down so we have this window of time to convert over to renewables," according to Harry Shimp, president and chief executive officer of BP's solar division. But of greater concern to many is not when or if economically recoverable fossil fuel reserves will be depleted but the fact that the world cannot afford to use all the conventional energy resources that remain.

The Intergovernmental Panel on Climate Change, a body of approximately two thousand scientists and economists who advise the United Nations on climate change, has concluded that global carbon dioxide (CO_2) emissions must be reduced by at least 70 percent over the next hundred years to stabilize atmospheric CO_2 concentrations at 450 parts per million (ppm), which would be 60 percent higher than preindustrial levels. The sooner societies begin to make these reductions, the lower the impacts and the associated costs—of both climate change and emissions reductions—will be. (See box 2.5.) Because more than 80 percent of human-made CO_2 emissions are due to the burning of fossil fuels, such reductions are not possible without significant and rapid improvements in energy efficiency and a shift to renewable energy.

Box 2.5 Climate Change and the Kyoto Protocol

In its 2001 report, the Intergovernmental Panel on Climate Change found that "there is new and stronger evidence that most of the warming observed over the last fifty years is attributable to human activities" that have increased atmospheric concentrations of CO_2. Preindustrial concentrations were 280 ppm; today they are 371 ppm. Between 1990 and 2100, global temperatures are projected to increase between 1.4 and 5.8 degrees Celsius, and land areas will most likely warm faster than the global average. To stabilize CO_2 "at 450 ppm would require global anthropogenic [human-made] emissions to drop below 1990 levels, within a few decades." Even if greenhouse gas emissions were to stabilize at present levels, it is expected that average temperatures and sea level would continue rising for centuries, but the rate of change would slow once stabilization is achieved.

Under provisions of the Kyoto Protocol to the U.N. Framework Convention on Climate Change, industrial countries must reduce their CO_2 emissions on average 5.2 percent below their 1990 levels by the end of the first "commitment period" (2008–2012). The protocol will enter into force ninety days after ratification by fifty-five countries accounting for at least 55 percent of industrial-country 1990 CO_2 emissions. As of mid-October 2002, ninety-six nations had ratified Kyoto, including the European Union and Japan, representing 37.4 percent of industrial-country emissions. Russia (17.4 percent) and Poland (3 percent) have officially declared their intention to ratify it soon—which would raise the total to 57.8 percent and thus bring the protocol into effect.

The United States represents 25 percent of current global emissions and 36.4 percent of industrial-country 1990 emissions. Its March 2001 withdrawal from negotiations on the protocol dealt a blow to international efforts to battle climate change, but it also pushed the rest of the world to move forward and reach final agreement on the treaty in July 2001.

The added environmental costs of conventional energy production and use include destruction wrought through resource extraction; air, soil, and water pollution; acid rain; and biodiversity loss. Conventional energy requires vast quantities of fresh water. Mining and drilling affect the way of life and the very existence of indigenous peoples worldwide. In China, the environmental and health costs of air pollution, caused mainly by coal burning, totaled approximately 7 percent of gross domestic product (GDP) in 1995. The World Bank estimates that under business as usual, these costs could rise to 13 percent of China's GDP by 2020. After a decade-long study, U.S. and European researchers calculated that the environmental and health costs associated with conventional energy are equivalent to 1–2 percent of the European Union's annual GDP, and that the price paid for conventional energy is significantly lower than its total costs (see table 2.1). These estimates do not include the costs of climate change—potentially the most expensive consequence. Global economic losses caused by natural disasters, which are in line with events anticipated as a result of global warming, appear to be doubling with each decade, and annual losses from such events are expected to approach $150 billion over the next ten years.

The direct economic and security costs associated with conventional energy are also substantial. Nuclear power is one of the most expensive means of generating electricity, even without accounting for the risks of nuclear accidents, weapons proliferation, and problems associated with nuclear waste. Political, economic, and military conflicts over limited resources such as oil will become more significant as demand increases worldwide. Similarly, the price of fossil fuels will become increasingly erratic as demand rises and conflicts rage in oil-rich regions, which in turn would affect the stability of economies around the world. The economic

TABLE 2.1   Costs of Electricity with and without External Costs

Electricity Source	Generating Costs[1]	External Costs[2]	Total Costs
	(Cents per Kilowatt-hour)		
Coal/Lignite	4.3–4.8	2–15	6.3–19.8
Natural Gas (New)	3.4–5.0	1–4	4.4–9.0
Nuclear	10–14	0.2–0.7	10.2–14.7
Biomass	7–9	1–3	8–12
Hydropower	2.4–7.7	0–1	2.4–8.7
Photovoltaics	25–50	0.6	25.6–50.6
Wind	4–6	0.05–0.25	4.05–6.25

[1]For the United States and Europe.
[2]Environmental and health costs for 15 countries in Europe.

costs of relying on imported fuels are extremely high—it is estimated that African countries spend 80 percent of their export earnings on imported oil. Likewise, the benefits of reducing imports can be significant. If not for Brazil's twenty-five-year ethanol program, which now displaces 220,000 barrels of oil a day, the country's foreign debt would be about $140 billion higher, according to one estimate.

Renewable resources are generally domestic, pose no fuel or transport hazards, and are much less vulnerable to terrorist attack. They can be installed rapidly and in dispersed small- or large-scale applications—getting power quickly to areas where it is urgently needed, delaying investment in expensive new electric plants or power lines, and reducing investment risk. All renewables except biomass energy avoid fuel costs and the risks associated with future fuel price fluctuations. They pose significantly lower social, environmental, and health costs than conventional energy fuels and technologies do.

Further, "renewables is not just about energy and the environment but also about manufacturing and jobs." This ringing endorsement came from United Kingdom Energy Minister Brian Wilson in July 2002, after the commissioning of a new thirty-megawatt wind farm atop Beinn and Tuirc, a hill in the northern reaches of Argylle, Scotland. The Kintyre Peninsula of Argylle once thrived on its fisheries, whiskey production, and textile manufacture. These traditional sources of employment are in decline, and now wind power is breathing new life into the region's economy, generating enough electricity to supply twenty-five thousand homes. A new turbine manufacturing plant on the peninsula will provide steady jobs and produce the first large-scale wind turbines ever built in Britain.

Using renewables stimulates local economies by attracting investment and tourist money and by creating employment not only in northern Scotland but elsewhere around the world. Renewable energy provides more jobs per unit of capacity of output and per dollar spent than conventional energies do. Many of the jobs are high-wage and high-tech and require a range of skills, often in areas that are rural or economically depressed. Economic woes and high unemployment rates influenced Spain's 1994 decision to invest in renewable energy. In Germany, the wind industry has created forty thousand jobs, compared with thirty-eight thousand in nuclear power—an industry that generates 30 percent of Germany's electricity.

A recent study in California concluded that increasing renewable energy technologies in that state would create four times more jobs than continued operation of natural gas plants, while keeping billions of dollars in California that would otherwise go to out-of-state power purchases. According to Governor Gray Davis, over a five-year period the net benefits of renewable energy, compared with business as usual, include $11 billion in economic development benefits for California because of associated job creation and in-state investments.

In developing countries such as Brazil and India, where millions of people lack access to power, renewables can provide electricity more cheaply and quickly than the extension of power lines and construction of new plants could, and can aid in economic development. Renewables are also sources of reliable power for business in countries such as India, where power cuts are common. M. Kannappan, India's minister of non-conventional energy sources, has stated that renewables have "enormous potential to meet the growing requirements of the increasing populations of the developing world, whilst offering sustainable solutions to the threat of global climate change."

The energy services delivered by renewables provide communities with access to education, clean water, improved health care, communications, and entertainment. These resources, in turn, improve the quality of life (particularly for women), raise living standards, increase productivity, and reduce the potential for economic and political instability. In Inner Mongolia, thousands of people now have access to education, information, and other benefits for the first time, thanks to the use of television and radio powered by small wind and solar systems. As a result, they have become more productive and increased their monthly household incomes by as much as $150. (The average per capita annual net income in Inner Mongolia ranges from about $120 to $240.)

Many components if not the entire systems for solar homes, wind farms, and other renewable technologies are now manufactured or assembled in developing countries, creating local jobs, reducing costs, and keeping capital investments at home. China and India have both developed domestic wind turbine industries. Brazil's ethanol program, begun in 1975, has created more than 1 million jobs while also bringing the nation's CO_2 emissions 20 percent below what they would have been otherwise. Brazil now exports ethanol fuel and will soon begin exporting its technologies as well. And in Kenya, more than one hundred firms (six of them domestic) provide photovoltaic (PV) systems or service, with numerous companies selling solar home systems in almost every town.

Developing countries that invest in renewables will discover that they are energy-rich—that they can leapfrog over dirty technologies relied on earlier in industrial countries and can develop their economies with clean, domestic, secure sources of energy that avoid long-term and costly imports.

In light of the many advantages of renewables, the Task Force on Renewable Energy of the Group of Eight industrial countries concluded in 2001 that "though there will be a higher cost in the first decades, measured solely in terms of the costs so far reflected in the market, successfully promoting renewables over the period to 2030 will prove less expensive than taking a 'business as usual' approach within any realistic range of discount rates" ("G8 Renewable Energy Task Force—Final Report" [London: World Energy Council, 2001]).

STATE OF THE TECHNOLOGIES 2003

Since the 1970s and 1980s, renewable technologies have improved significantly in both performance and cost. Some are experiencing rates of growth and technology advancement comparable only to the electronics industry. Global clean energy markets exceeded $10 billion in 2001 and are expected to surpass $82 billion by 2010, and major corporations are entering the renewables marketplace—including Royal Dutch/Shell, BP, and General Electric. Technical progress of many renewables—particularly wind power—has been faster than was anticipated even a few years ago, and this trend is expected to continue. While costs are still a concern with some technologies, these are falling rapidly because of technological advances, learning by doing, automated manufacturing, and economies of scale through increased production volumes.

Solar and wind are the most commonly known renewables, but inexhaustible energy supplies are also offered by biomass; geothermal; hydropower; ocean energy from the tides, currents, and waves; and ocean thermal energy. This chapter principally focuses on wind power and solar photovoltaics—which produce electricity from sunlight—because they

are the fastest-growing renewables and have the greatest potential for helping all countries achieve more sustainable development.

During the past fifteen to twenty years, wind energy technology has
evolved to the point where it competes with most conventional forms of
power generation. In many instances, wind is now the cheapest option on
a per-kilowatt-hour (kWh) basis. The main trends in wind energy development are toward lighter, more flexible blades, variable speed operation,
direct-drive generators, and taller machines with greater capacity. The average turbine size has increased from 100–200 kilowatts (kW) in the early
1990s to more than 900 kW today, making it possible to produce more
power with fewer machines. (One 900 kW machine can provide the electricity needed for about 540 European homes.) Turbines with capacity ratings of 2,000–5,000 kW (2–5 megawatts [MW]) are being manufactured
for use offshore. At the same time, small wind machines that can be installed close to the point of demand—atop buildings, for example—are
also under development (see box 2.6). Advances in turbine technology
and power electronics, along with a better understanding of siting
needs and wind energy resources, have combined to extend the lifetime of
today's wind turbines, improve performance, and reduce costs.

Box 2.6 Examples of Advances in Wind Technology

- At the Rocky Flats test site in Colorado, the U.S. Department of Energy is
testing a lightweight turbine with two blades rather than the usual three. It is
expected to be 40 percent lighter than today's standard turbines, require less
material, and thus be 20 to 25 percent cheaper.

- Vestas is now equipping offshore turbines with sensors to detect wear and
tear on components, along with backup systems in case of power electronic
system failures.

- A turbine developed in Germany can desalinate water, generate electricity, or
make hydrogen by electrolysis.

- Mathematical climatic models have been developed in Germany and Denmark
to predict wind resources twenty-four to thirty-six hours in advance with reasonable accuracy. This will be important for managing wind power as it
reaches a high percentage of the total electric system.

Since the early 1980s, the average cost of wind-generated electricity has fallen from about 44 cents per kilowatt-hour (in 2001 dollars) to 4–6 cents at good wind sites. Costs vary from one location to the next due primarily to variations in wind speed and also different institutional frameworks and interest rates. Globally, wind costs have declined by some 20 percent over just the past five years, and the Danish turbine manufacturer Vestas predicts that the generating costs of wind energy will continue to drop annually by 3–5 percent. As this happens, it will become economical to site turbines in regions with lower wind speeds, increasing the global potential for wind-generated electricity.

Global wind capacity has grown at an average annual rate over 30 percent during the past decade. An estimated 6,824 MW of wind capacity were added worldwide in 2001, bringing the total to more than 24,900 MW—enough to provide power to approximately 14 million households. While Europe accounts for more than 70 percent of total capacity, wind is now generating electricity in at least forty-five countries. Sales in 2001 surpassed $6 billion, nearly double the total two years earlier, and it is estimated that more than one hundred thousand people are now employed in the wind industry worldwide.

The majority of turbines operating today are on land, but wind power is now moving offshore. This is due to the shortage of sites on land, particularly in Europe, and the fact that wind speeds offshore are significantly higher and more consistent. Stronger winds generate more electricity, while consistency reduces wear and tear on machines. More than 80 MW of turbines are now spinning offshore, all of them in Europe, with an added 5,000 MW in the pipeline worldwide and more than 20,000 MW proposed for areas surrounding northern Europe.

Experts estimate that onshore wind resources could provide more than four times global electricity consumption. Offshore resources are substantial as well. While some of that potential is too costly to exploit over the near term, the promise of large amounts of wind power at competitive prices is enormous.

As with all energy technologies, there are disadvantages associated with wind power. The environmental factor that has caused the most controversy and concern is bird mortality. This is a site-specific problem, however, and it is relatively low compared with other threats to birds, such as vehicles, buildings, and cell phone towers. Further, such problems have been mitigated in recent years through the use of painted blades, slower rotational speeds, tubular turbine towers, and careful siting of projects.

Both wind and sun are intermittent resources, meaning they cannot be turned on and off as needed. But there is no guarantee that any resource will be available when it is required, and utilities must have backup power for generation every day. Assessments in Europe and the United States have concluded that intermittent sources can account for up to 20 percent of an electric system without posing technical problems; higher levels might demand minor changes in operational practices. The wind already provides electricity to the grid (transmission lines) that greatly exceeds 20 percent in regions of Germany, Denmark, and Spain, and distributed generation—for example, the use of solar panels on rooftops, or clusters of turbines along the path of a power line—can improve electric system reliability.

The challenges posed by intermittency are not of immediate concern in most countries and will be overcome with hybrid systems, improvements in wind-forecasting technology, and further development of storage technologies. New storage technologies could also help tap renewable resources that are far from demand centers. Moreover, what is most significant is the per-kilowatt-hour cost of electricity generated. Wind power is already cost-competitive with most conventional technologies. Solar PVs are likely to see dramatic cost reductions, and they produce power in the middle of hot summer days when demand is greatest and electricity costs are highest.

According to the U.S. National Renewable Energy Laboratory (NREL), PVs have the "potential to become one of the world's most important industries." The potential PV market is huge, ranging from consumer products (such as calculators and watches) and remote standalone systems for electricity and water pumping to grid-connected systems on buildings and large-scale power plants.

Each year the sun delivers to earth more than ten thousand times the energy that humans currently use. While PVs account for a small share of global electricity generation, they have experienced dramatic growth over the past decade. Since 1996, global PV shipments have increased at an average annual rate of 33 percent. It took nearly thirty years, up until 1999, for the world to produce its first gigawatt (GW) of solar PVs, but some experts expect a doubling as soon as 2003. The PV industry generates business worth more than $2 billion annually and provides tens of thousands of jobs. More than a million households in the developing world now have electricity for the first time from solar PVs, while more than one hundred thousand households in industrial countries supplement their utility power with PV systems.

The production of solar cells is concentrated in Japan, Europe, and the United States, but there are growing markets and manufacturing bases in developing countries as well, including China and India. Global PV output is expected to increase at annual rates of 40–50 percent over the next few years. As larger factories come into operation, manufacturers can increase the degree of automation.

Such evolving industrial processes, along with technological advances in PVs and economies of scale, have led already to significant cost reductions. Since 1976, costs have dropped 20 percent for every doubling of installed PV capacity, or about 5 percent annually. PVs are now the cheapest option for many remote or off-grid functions. When used for facades of buildings, PVs can be cheaper than other materials such as marble or granite, with the added advantage of producing electricity. Currently, generating costs range from 25 cents to $1 per kWh, which is still extremely high, and cost remains the primary barrier to more widespread use of solar PVs. But companies around the world are in a race to create future generations of products to make PVs cost-competitive even for on-grid use (see box 2.7).

In addition to cost, one of the primary concerns regarding the ability of PVs to meet a major portion of the global electricity demand is the length of time they must operate to produce as much energy as was used to manufacture them. The energy "payback" period for today's cells in rooftop systems is one to four years, with expected lifetimes of up to thirty years, depending on the technology. The manufacture of PVs also requires a number of hazardous materials, including many of the chemicals and heavy metals used in the semiconductor electronics industry. There are techniques and equipment to reduce environmental and safety risks, however, and these problems are minimal compared with those associated with conventional energy technologies.

Box 2.7 The Solar Race

- An Australian company is the first to manufacture solar PVs that can be incorporated into glass walls of buildings. When light falls on the glass from any angle, it will generate electricity.

- The U.S. National Renewable Energy Laboratory and Spectrolabs have developed a Triple-Junction Terrestrial Concentrator Solar Cell that is 34 percent efficient and that can be manufactured for less than $1 per watt, according to NREL. (The maximum recorded laboratory efficiency is 24.7 percent, while the average cost of today's PVs is $5–12 per watt.)

- Spheral solar technology, being developed in Canada, will bond tiny silicon beads into an aluminum foil. While mass market application could take decades, this technology could halve the cost of power generation.

Global markets for renewables such as solar and wind power are only just beginning a dramatic expansion, starting from relatively low levels. It is useful to point out, however, that despite high costs and growing concerns regarding safety, nuclear power took less than thirty years to develop into an industry that provides 16–17 percent of global electricity. The same can happen with renewable technologies. In fact, during 2001 the nuclear industry added only 25 percent as much capacity to the grid as wind did. If the average growth rates of wind and solar PV over the past decade were to continue to 2020, the world would have about 48,000 MW of installed solar PV capacity and more than 2.6 million MW of wind—equivalent to 78 percent of global electric capacity in 2000, or about 45 percent of projected 2020 capacity. Such continued growth is unlikely, but recent industry reports have concluded that if the necessary institutional framework is put in place, it is feasible for wind to meet 12 percent of the global electricity demand by 2020 and for PVs to meet 26 percent by 2040.

Energy in the Twenty-First Century

Dave Gorak

This selection originally appeared in *Environment News* (Chicago: Heartland Institute, September 1999).

As technology improves and world energy markets liberalize, conventional energy sources—fossil fuels and nuclear power—promise to be both economically and environmentally sustainable for decades, centuries, and even millennia to come.

Fossil fuels, once thought by many to be nearing depletion, are in fact becoming more abundant and environmentally sustainable, according to a recent Cato Institute policy analysis.

"Fossil-fuel resources are becoming more abundant, not scarcer, and they promise to continue expanding as technology improves, world markets liberalize, and investment capital expands," writes Robert L. Bradley Jr. in "The Increasing Sustainability of Conventional Energy" (Washington, D.C.: Cato Institute, 1999). Bradley is president of the Institute for Energy Research in Houston, Texas, and a Cato Institute adjunct scholar.

By contrast, according to Bradley, "unconventional energy technologies by definition are not currently competitive with conventional energy technologies." In order for alternative energy sources to achieve any degree of success in an increasingly competitive energy marketplace, writes Bradley, their technologies will have to be substantially improved, and they will have to be successfully weaned from the government subsidies and tax preferences that now sustain them.

THE AMAZING DISAPPEARING FOSSIL-FUEL SHORTAGE

"Fossil-fuel availability has been increasing even in the face of record consumption," Bradley reports. "World oil reserves today are more than 15 times greater than they were when record-keeping began in 1948."

According to Bradley, "proven world reserves of oil, gas, and coal are officially estimated to be 46, 63, and 230 years of current consumption, respectively. Probable resources of oil, gas, and coal are officially forecast to be 114, 200, and 1,884 years of present usage, respectively." But even probable resources estimates can expand over time.

Oil shortages like those experienced in the 1970s are highly improbable because of the "market learning" that has led to increased energy efficiency; greater diversity of supply; enlarged spot-market trading, futures trading, and risk management; and greater integration and alignment of producer interests with consumer interests, Bradley writes.

The real threat to energy sustainability in the twenty-first century, he argues, is the environmentalist movement: antiprogress activists who seek to "stabilize the climate" by replacing affordable and reliable energy sources used by a global economy with inferior and costlier substitutes. But even that threat is waning. The most recent setback came this spring, when the NASA scientist who started the public debate on climate change reversed his position.

"The weakening scientific case for dangerous climate change makes the global warming issue a transient political problem for fossil fuels, rather than a death warrant," Bradley predicts.

And if anti-auto activists were to fall back on air quality concerns to justify their attacks on fossil fuels, Bradley predicts, that effort would also fail. The quality of the nation's outdoor air has improved markedly, due in part to cleaner-running automobiles and unleaded gasoline. That trend, Bradley writes, will eventually include the rest of the world.

"The clean transportation movement is an international phenomenon, not just a U.S. initiative," he notes. Already, twenty countries worldwide have banned the use of leaded gasoline.

MOST ALTERNATIVES DON'T MEASURE UP

Alternative energy sources—wind, solar, ethanol, and methanol, for example—have benefited from government subsidies but remain economically unfeasible. Such alternatives as synthetic fuels to convert coal and other solids into oil and gas have met with a similar fate. Indeed, the much-touted federal Synthetic Fuels Corporation, created in 1980 as "the cornerstone of U.S. energy policy," ceased operations after only five years, with most of its funding unused.

Among the alternative fuels that remain in regular production is ethanol, a high-octane motor fuel made from grain and corn. Although its burning reduces nitrous oxide emissions, ethanol produces higher evaporative emissions of smog-producing volatile organic compounds. Nevertheless, the federal government recently saw fit to extend ethanol's tax breaks, scheduled to expire in the year 2000, for an additional seven years. The move according to Bradley, "was more a victory for agricultural interests than the environmental community, which has traditionally been ambivalent if not hostile toward this motor-fuel alternative."

NUCLEAR POWER: A LONG-RUN BACKSTOP ENERGY

Nuclear power, in addition to hydroelectricity, says Bradley, qualifies as a sustainable alternative to fossil fuels. "The size of the world's nuclear power industry," he writes, "qualifies uranium as a conventional energy source that complements fossil fuels. . . . For large-scale needs in future centuries, nuclear technologies may be the leading backstop to fossil fuels for primary electricity generation."

Currently, the industry's 103 operating reactors in the United States supply 20 percent of the nation's electricity needs. In remarks to the Nuclear Energy Institute's annual meeting in May, Vice Chairman Christian H. Poindexter predicted a bright future for the industry.

"This optimism is not based on a starry-eyed attraction to a new technology, but on the environmental contributions and the economic potential of well-run nuclear power plants in a competitive marketplace. . . . Our improved performance now has policy makers considering seriously a revival of nuclear energy," he observed.

Bradley would qualify this assessment. "Because of relative economies," he writes, "nuclear power is already a backstop technology for new capacity in the United States and other areas of the world." Obstacles both political and market-related remain to be hurdled by the industry to get back in the new-capacity picture.

"Regulatory streamlining and a political resolution of the nuclear waste problem are necessary but not sufficient conditions for the United

States to join Asian countries in installing a new generation of nuclear re-actors. The other hurdles for market power are market-related." Gas- and coal-fired plants, Bradley notes, remain less expensive than nuclear plants and can be more flexibly sized.

Moreover, writes Bradley, "Nuclear power will also need to outgrow its federal insurance subsidy (the Price-Anderson Act) as the U.S. court system moves toward more rational liability laws." The Act indemnifies power plants against legal liability resulting from a nuclear incident in connection with contractual activity for the Department of Energy. The Department of Energy has noted that, without the Act, "the nuclear power industry would not have developed or grown."

WORLD'S ENERGY FUTURE IS BRIGHT

Confident in the power of what economist Julian Simon deemed the "ul-timate resource," human ingenuity, Bradley predicts a bright future for all energy technologies, conventional and unconventional alike, if energy markets are kept relatively free of government intervention.

"If the 'ultimate resource' of human ingenuity is allowed free rein," he concludes, "energy in its many and changing forms will be more plen-tiful and affordable for future generations than it is now. . . . For the nearer and more foreseeable term, all signs point toward conventional en-ergies' continuing to ride the technological wave, increasing the prospects that when energy substitutions occur, the winning technologies will be different from what is imagined (and subsidized by government) today. Such discontinuities will occur not because conventional energies failed, but because their substitutes blossomed."

FIGURE 2.5.   World Energy Consumption by Energy Source

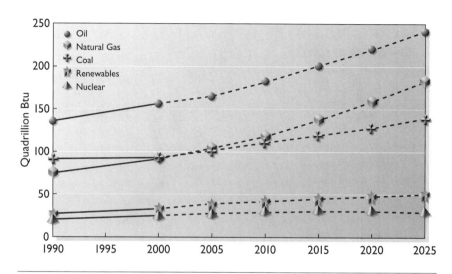

Sources: History: Energy Information Administration (EIA), *International Energy Annual 2001*, DOE/EIA-0219 (2001) (Washington, D.C., February 2003), website www.eia.doe.gov/iea//. Projections: EIA, *Annual Energy Outlook 2003*, DOE/EIA-0383 (2003) (Washington, D.C., January 2003), Table A1; and Systems for the Analysis of Global Energy Markets (2003).

FIGURE 2.6.   World Energy Production by Energy Source

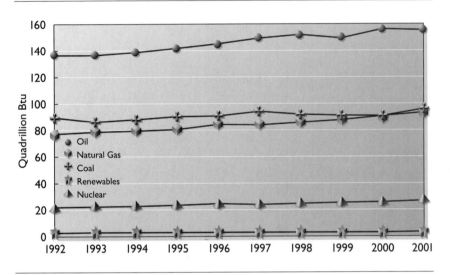

Sources: Energy Information Administration (EIA), *International Energy Annual 2001*, DOE/EIA-0219 (2001) (Washington, D.C., February 2003), Table 29, website www.eia.doe.gov.iea/.

POPULATION AND QUALITY OF LIFE

PART III: QUICK FACTS

"When every province of the world so teems with inhabitants that they can neither subsist where they are nor remove themselves elsewhere, every region being equally crowded and over-peopled, . . . it must come about that the world will purge itself in one or another of these three ways (floods, plagues, or famines)."

Niccolo Machiavelli, in From Malthus to the Club of Rome and Back (1994)

"This hysterical clamor that population increase leads to poverty, hunger, and uncontrolled ecological destruction is not only false—it also carries with it a certain danger: it effectively diverts attention from political questions, which are the real problems of this world."

Colin Clark, in From Malthus to the Club of Rome and Back (1994)

- In 2002, the total fertility rate (TFR) across the globe was 2.8. The past fifty years witnessed a remarkable reduction of fertility levels in the less-developed regions, with total fertility falling from six to three children per woman. In 2002, the TFR of more-developed countries was 1.6.

Population Reference Bureau (2002),
United Nations World Population Prospects (2002 Revision)
(See figure 3.1, figure 3.2, and table 3.1 for further information.)

- In 2000, life expectancy for the least-developed countries in the world was 48.7 years of age; in 1950, it was 35.5. In 2000, life expectancy for the more-developed regions of the world was 74.8; in 1950, it was 66.2.

United Nations Development Programme (2003),
United Nations World Population Prospects (2002 Revision)
(See figure 3.3.)

- In addition to the 20 million people who have already died of AIDS (2003), the 42 million now living with HIV/AIDS are likely to die a decade or more prematurely. Each day, fourteen thousand people—twelve thousand adults and two thousand children—become infected with HIV. At least 95 percent of these new infections occur in less-developed countries; more than 50 percent afflict women and young adults.

Joint United Nations Programme on HIV/AIDS (2003)
(See figure 3.4, figure 3.5, and table 3.3 for further information.)

- Nearly seventy thousand foreigners arrive in the United States every day. More than sixty thousand are tourists, business people, students, or foreign workers. About five thousand enter illegally; four thousand of them are apprehended, and about one thousand elude detection. Immigration accounted for approximately 30 percent of the total U.S. population increase from 1990 to 2000.

  Population Reference Bureau (1999), U.S. Census Bureau (2000),
  U.S. Office of Immigration Statistics (2003)
  (See figure 3.6 for number of U.S. immigrants from 1900 to 2000.)

- The number of wars worldwide stood at twenty-eight in 2002, down from thirty-five in 2000. In addition, there were seventeen "armed conflicts" in 2002 that were not of sufficient severity to meet the criteria for war.

  Worldwatch Institute (2002)
  (See table 3.4.)

INTRODUCTION

Population and Quality of Life

Do more people on the earth improve our quality of life? And, how do we determine whether or not the quality of the human experience has been enhanced? Quality of life is often determined by demographics; rising and falling birth and death rates, disease and public health, violent conflict and war. Part 3 explores these very questions and related issues.

According to an extensive national survey by RAND, a public policy research institution, the general population is divided in regard to the effect of population size on quality of life. In 1998, for example, 51 percent of those surveyed agreed that rapid population growth causes civil war and regional conflicts.

What are the recent trends in population? Moreover, what are their long-term implications? Chapter 8 explores the implications of recent demographic shifts. John Caldwell argues that we must not let up on the battle against overpopulation. Below-replacement fertility is a clear sign that we are well on our way to circumventing what many considered an impending crisis caused by overpopulation. Ben Wattenberg, author of *The Birth Dearth*, argues that we should not be fearful of a population explosion, but rather, a population implosion. His premise: "never before have birthrates fallen so far, so fast, so low, for so long all around the world." Wattenberg suggests that the implications are colossal.

In chapter 9, Richard Robbins exposes the relationship between culture, capitalism, and disease. He concludes that along with the disparity between rich and poor, "increases in population density clearly relate to the emergence and frequency of disease" (for further information on global mortality by disease, see table 3.2). In contrast, Nicholas Eberstadt explores the unexpected decline or stagnation of life expectancy. Despite the extraordinary advancement in health throughout the twentieth century, he concludes that this decline must be addressed if we desire a "distinctly more humane" future.

Chapter 10 delves into immigration and its relationship to population growth. How should the United States handle the influx of immigration? Stuart Anderson and Alvin Powell present differing views and conclusions.

To what degree do demographic factors affect international security? In chapter 11 Michael Renner explores the changing nature of conflict shaped by a new globalism. He argues for a cooperative approach to security challenges that focuses on root problems, such as poverty and the unequal distribution of land, rather than on military stockpiling. In contrast, Brian Nichiporuk proposes that while population pressures influence international security, "it is clear from an even cursory analysis of the national security literature on demographic effects that [they] do not cause armed conflict. . . ."

Part 3 allows the reader to engage in much-debated policy issues in the broader context of the population challenge.

Chapter Eight

FERTILITY

*Is there cause for concern over decreasing
fertility rates?*

The Contemporary Population Challenge

John C. Caldwell

This selection was excerpted from *Completing the Fertility Transition* (Canberra, Australia: Australian National University, 2002). (Available online at http://www.un.org/esa.population/publications/completingfertility/RevisedCaldwellpaper.PDF.)

The present is unexpectedly a critical time for population change and policy. We are little more than halfway through the great population growth spurt that began in the middle of the twentieth century, but developed-country governments seem to be losing interest in the issue. This loss of interest may have a significant demographic impact. The probable reasons for the declining interest are a vague belief that the present demographic change has a momentum of its own, a reaction to the International Conference on Population and Development (ICPD) in Cairo in 1994 which may misinterpret the complex document that came out of that meeting, and a preoccupation with below-replacement-level fertility in the developed world.

Huge population growth is not now past history. The United Nations's estimates and medium projections (United Nations, 2001a) show a world population numbering 2.5 billion in 1950, 6.1 billion in 2000, and 9.3 billion in 2050. The next half-century will see almost as many people added to the world's population as the last half-century, and thereafter there may be 1 or 2 billion more people before growth comes to a halt. The global fertility decline is believed to have traversed over four-fifths of the journey from a total fertility rate of 5.0 in 1950 to 2.1 in 2050. But because of population growth momentum and an ever-expanding base population, the additions to world population did not peak until the 1990s at around 80 million per year and are only a little below that now.

There are two main messages for future-gazers and policymakers. The first is that projections are far from certain. The second is that projections are necessarily based on past experience—including past policy experience—and if this changes, then the projections must do so too.

The lack of certainty is shown by the fact that for 2050 the United Nations provides, in addition to the medium projection of 9.322 billion, a low projection of 7.866 billion and a high projection of 10.934 billion. The high projection is over 3 billion or almost 40 percent above the low projection. Another recent projection, by Lutz and others (Wolfgang Lutz, Warren Sanderson, and Sergei Scherbov, "The End of World Population Growth," *Nature* 412, no. 2 [2001]), provides a 2050 medium figure of 8.797 billion, with an 80 percent probability of it falling between 7.347 and 10.443 billion. The latter projection's "most likely" figure for 2050 is about half a billion below that of the United Nations but still implies huge growth and great uncertainty about its magnitude.

Most analysts have preferred during recent years to employ the United Nations medium projection because it has proved in these years to be remarkably accurate. This period of near-certainty may be passing. Two years after its release in 1999 of the 1998 projections, the United Nations produced revised figures raising the 2050 medium estimate by 413 million people, 96 percent of the difference being attributable to new figures for Africa and Asia, mostly in sub-Saharan Africa and South Asia. The United Nations Population Division said that 59 percent of the upward adjustment was explained by countries (mostly in sub-Saharan Africa) failing to begin fertility declines as early as expected, and 32 percent was because of greater sluggishness than anticipated in fertility decline in such large countries as Bangladesh, India, and Nigeria.

Will the whole world move toward below-replacement fertility? The experience of such non-Western societies as Japan and South Korea suggest that this will be so. Nearly the whole world is heading toward agreement that ever-higher educational levels are needed, that females should be educated as much as males, and that educated women should be in the workforce if they wish to be; and it seems that most wish to be. Both China and India are likely to keep national family planning programs in position even with below-replacement fertility, and each would probably be sanguine about some decline in population size. Such movements will not stop the world's population reaching 8, 9, or 10 billion, but they will help achieve an ultimate stationary or declining total.

The most painful aspect of the world's future demographic behavior is likely to be international migration. International migration has until now been restricted by the fact that much of the world's population was illiterate and rural and practiced subsistence farming. Such people usually do not want to leave home, especially for societies very different from theirs, and know that they would find it hard to cope with the inevitable social and psychological transitions. Economic and social globalization and the spread of education have changed this position dramatically, and until such time as the developing world is developed, we face the distressing situation where the pressure from both legal and illegal migrants to enter rich countries will be far greater than the numbers these countries are willing to admit. The efforts made by rich countries to restrict the flow threaten to change the nature of these societies and to increase racism. The settlement countries will certainly take enough immigrants to sustain population growth. The reaction in Europe is less certain. In European countries where the indigenous population is declining, a considerable immigrant stream would certainly sustain numbers, but the faster the indigenous numbers declined, the greater would be the ethnic diluting effect of immigration.

Demographers will also have more routine work to do in important but less politically fraught areas such as morbidity and mortality change, internal migration, and urbanization. The two are not totally independent, for the growth of huge cities in poor countries raises questions about the health levels of the poor that must be answered by quantitative inquiry in order to give direction to remedial measures. Even in developed countries there is a growing interest in health differentials by social class, extent of education, and residential environment; and the demand for such information will certainly rise. Specialized work will also be needed for specific crises, such as delineating and measuring the impact of the AIDS epidemic. The urbanization of the world is an extraordinary phenomenon, from little more than one-third of the human race living in towns in 1970, to about two-thirds in 2025, and perhaps 80 percent not long after the middle of the twenty-first century. We are monitoring this growth but are doing little about elucidating its nature or its effects.

The immediate challenge is to maintain some of the attitudes, policies, and expenditure patterns that have so far sustained the developing world's fertility decline. If this does not happen, then slow or stationary population growth may be attained, not with 8 billion people but with 9,

10, 11, or 12 billion. The differences in long-term environmental sustainability could be huge. The lower figures are likely to be attained if the West does not become too fixated on population decline over the next two or three decades. The minor concern is that technical aid for developing-country family planning programs will continue to fall if declining population becomes an all-absorbing policy concern. The major concern is that the whole world is likely to follow the new policies and strategies for stabilizing population numbers in low-fertility countries, even in those countries with moderately high fertility.

We once thought of the end of demographic transition being a stationary population, around 10 billion. More recently we have thought in terms of a maximum population, followed by a long period of perhaps accelerating decline. This might not be a bad outcome. There is now a real possibility that measures to halt population decline will have a global effect in the second half of the twenty-first century, leading either to continuing modest population growth or to an oscillating global population as ideologies and policies replace each other. In the long run much depends on environmental evidence and ideologies.

The Population Explosion Is Over

Ben Wattenberg

This selection originally appeared in the *New York Times Magazine* (New York: The New York Times Company, November 23, 1997).

The prediction that spawned a generation of alarmists has now been turned on its head. But the prospect of an emptier planet is creating its own set of problems.

For thirty years, one notion has shaped much of modern social thought: that the human species is reproducing itself uncontrollably, and ominously. In his best-selling book of 1968, *The Population Bomb*, Paul Ehrlich warned that "the cancer of population growth must be cut out" or "we will breed ourselves into oblivion." He appeared on the Johnny Carson show twenty-five times to sell this idea. Lester Brown's "29th Day" compared people to geometrically multiplying waterlilies; on the 30th day, the world would end. A study by the Club of Rome (which it later renounced) described how rapacious humans would soon "run out of resources."

Several generations of schoolchildren have been taught these lessons; the State Department endorses them. A 1992 documentary on Ted Turner's CNN described the impending global chaos "as the planet's population grows exponentially." Turner and Jane Fonda were honored at a gala for Zero Population Growth, which preaches the mantra of out-of-control overpopulation. The issue of global warming, linked to soaring population growth deep into the next century, is front-page news.

Thirty years of persistent alarm. But now, mounting evidence, from rich nations and poor, strongly suggests that the population explosion is fizzling. Earlier this month, for the first time ever, the United Nations Population Division convened expert demographers to consider aspects of low and tumbling fertility rates. That discussion is a step toward a near-Copernican shift in the way our species looks at itself. Never before have birthrates fallen so far, so fast, so low, for so long all around the world. The potential implications—environmental, economic, geopolitical, and personal—are both unclear and clearly monumental, for good and for ill.

THE PLOT THINS

The free fall in fertility can best be seen in *World Population Prospects: The 1996 Revision*, an eye-opening reference book published by the United Nations, from which most data used here are drawn. From 1950 to 1955, the global "total fertility rate" (roughly speaking, the average number of children born per woman per lifetime) was 5. That was explosively above the so-called replacement rate of 2.1 children, the rate needed to keep a population from falling over time, absent immigration. This scary growth continued for about fifteen years until, by 1975 to 1980, fertility had fallen to 4 children per woman. Fifteen years after that, the rate had fallen to just below 3. Today the total fertility rate is estimated at 2.8, and sinking.

Five children per woman. Then 4. Then 3. Then less than 3. In estimating the population for the year 2050, demographers were caught with their projections up. Suddenly, worldwide, 650 million people were "missing." Many more will be missing soon. They will never be born.

But what about women in those teeming less-developed countries (LDCs)—those swarming places where the population bomb was allegedly ticking most loudly? Even there, the fuse is sputtering. The LDC fertility rate in 1965 to 1970 was 6 children per woman. Now it's 3, and falling more quickly than ever before in demographic history.

Those are broad numbers. Consider some specific nations. Italy, a Catholic country, has a fertility rate of 1.2 children per woman, the world's lowest rate—and the lowest national rate ever recorded (absent famines, plagues, wars, or economic catastrophes). India's fertility rate is lower than American rates in the 1950s. The rate in Bangladesh has fallen from 6.2 to 3.4—in just ten years.

The European birthrates of the 1980s, already at record-breaking lows, fell another 20 percent in the 1990s, to about 1.4 children per woman. The demographer Antonio Golini says such rates are "unsustainable." Samuel Preston, director of the University of Pennsylvania's Population Studies Center, recently calculated what will happen if European fertility changes and moves back toward a rate of 2.1. Even then, by the year 2060, when its population levels off, Europe will have lost 24 percent of its people. Japanese and Russian rates are also at about 1.4 children.

In Muslim Tunisia, over three decades the rate has fallen from 7.2 to 2.9. Rates are higher, but way down, in Iran and Syria. Fertility rates are plunging in many (though not all) sub-Saharan African nations, including Kenya, once regarded as the premier demographic horror show. Mexico has moved 80 percent of the way toward replacement level.

In the United States, birthrates have been below replacement for twenty-five straight years. There was an uptick in the late 1980s, but rates have fallen for five of the last six years. The National Center for Health Statistics reports solidly lower levels for early 1997, which will "continue the generally downward trend observed since early 1991" and will soon be reflected in U.S. Census Bureau projections.

This sounds strange. After all, we have gone through a half-century of the greatest population growth in history, and such growth has not quite ended. What's happening is that two powerful trends—the population explosion and the baby bust—are now at war. They can coexist, but only for a while. The recent evidence makes it clear which of these trends will prevail: the baby bust.

The population explosion is a long-distance runner. From 1750 to 1950, global population increased from 1 billion to 2.5 billion. From 1950 to 2000, it will increase to 6 billion. Remarkable. But the baby bust is also a marathon player. In America in 1790, women bore an average of 7.7 children. Benjamin Franklin saw children "swarming across the countryside like locusts." But for two centuries, except for a bump during the baby boom, American fertility has fallen steadily. Since 1972, the fertility rate has averaged 1.9. (Among the lowest rates are those experienced by Jewish women and black women with college degrees.)

An explosion and a bust? It sounds contradictory. But the number of potential mothers today was set two and three decades ago, when they were born, and when birthrates were much higher. And the rates in most less-developed countries, though falling rapidly, are still above replacement. Life expectancy has been climbing. These factors create "population momentum," which automatically yields more people—for a while.

Soon, however, reflecting the recent sharp reduction in fertility, the number of potential mothers will be much lower than previously anticipated. Fertility will most likely drop below replacement level in many less-developed countries. It already has in nineteen of them, including Cuba, China, Thailand, and, probably soon, Brazil. The momentum then turns the other way. (A bust, like an explosion, moves in geometric progression.)

What next? There are arguments, as well there should be, when dealing with the future. The United Nations's "medium variant" projection shows a global population of 9.4 billion people in 2050. Because of its "medium" designation, this Mama Bear projection is cited most often. But its central assumption is questionable: that all nations will move to a fertility rate of about 2.1 children per woman by 2050. Based on current data, this scenario seems implausible. Indeed, the experts met at the United Nations to change some assumptions in the medium-variant projections—downward.

The United Nations's "low variant" projection estimates that there will be fewer people: 7.7 billion in 2050, and shrinking. The central assumption behind this projection is that the global fertility rate will drop to 1.6 children per woman. Unlike the 2.1 figure, that is not an abstract construct. It is the current rate in the developed nations. The assumption is that as nations modernize, they will behave like modern nations.

When the U.N. demographers revise their medium variant downward next year, they will not go that far. For now, they are concentrating on the fifty-one nations with 44 percent of the world's people that are already at or below replacement. At the same time, they project that by 2010 to 2015, there will be eighty-eight such nations, with 67 percent of the population. The U.N. Population Division is cautious—some say too cautious, even while acknowledging the tricky nature of their task. All four revisions in the 1990s will be downward. What is going on is a process, not an event.

If one splits the difference between the low- and medium-variant projections, that would yield a global fertility rate of about 1.85 children per woman in 2050. Global population would then top out at about 8.5 billion people and start declining. Samuel Preston and many other leading demographers think that is near the range of what is most likely to happen.

How valid are such demographic calculations? Far from perfect, and sometimes controversial, but quite a bit better than simplistic straight-line-to-the-future projections. After all, medium-range demographic forecasts deal with girls who have already been born. A girl born today will be twenty in 2017. Knowing what the potential pool of mothers will be—far smaller than previously expected—forms a solid basis for projections.

What about the unpredicted baby boom? Birthrates soared in America from 1945 to 1965. Could this happen again? Yes. But that boom followed two unusual circumstances that had artificially depressed fertility: a harsh economic depression and a blistering world war. In part, the boomer kids made up for kids not born earlier.

In the past, demographers drew neat charts with rates falling to the 2.1 replacement level and staying there. But young adults conceiving children, or not, aren't thinking about an invisible line called "replacement." There're thinking about a good life for themselves and the children they elect to have, in new and modern circumstances. Their recent individual actions have collectively sliced through the invisible line like a laser.

WHERE DID EVERYBODY GO?

What is causing this birth dearth? Paul Demeny, the editor of *Population and Development Review*, points to the famous "demographic transition" theory, which he describes as the move "from high fertility and high mortality to low fertility and low mortality, with lots of complicated and contradictory things going on in the middle."

One of the main factors pushing this transition is urbanization—reflecting the shift from wanting more children to help on the farm to wanting fewer mouths to feed in the city. Among the many other factors are more education for women, legal abortion, higher incomes, unemployment yielding lower incomes, greater acceptance of homosexuality, new aspirations for women, better contraception (including "morning-after pills," endorsed by new Food and Drug Administration guidelines), later marriage, difficulty conceiving at an older age, more divorce, and vastly lower infant-mortality rates. When parents know their children will survive, fertility rates plummet.

These trends toward modernization are continuing, along with some new ones. For example, the black American fertility rate is down to about the national average; black teenage birthrates have declined by 20 percent since 1991. (On the other hand, advances in infertility treatment and a small increase in births among women in their later thirties slightly mitigate the trend toward lower fertility.)

Demographic transition theory explains, or at least describes, the downward arc of high fertility rates. But there is not a theory (yet) that explains why, when, or how long-term below-replacement fertility rates would ever go back up.

THEREFORE WHAT?

First the population was growing too fast. Now in many places it has sunk too low too quickly, with more to come. Is there cause for concern? Certainly, but not for despair. The demographers at the U.N. conference were not talking about a world where people can't control their destiny. Quite the opposite. We are in control and are changing how we see ourselves and our world.

SNAPSHOT: Aging

Grey Dawn: The Global Aging Crisis

Peter G. Peterson

This selection was excerpted from *Foreign Affairs* (Washington, D.C.: Council on Foreign Relations, Inc., January/February 1999).

INTRODUCTION: DAUNTING DEMOGRAPHICS

The list of major global hazards in the twenty-first century has grown long and familiar. It includes the proliferation of nuclear, biological, and chemical weapons; other types of high-tech terrorism; deadly super-viruses; extreme climate change; the financial, economic, and political aftershocks of globalization; and the violent ethnic explosions waiting to be detonated in today's unsteady new democracies. Yet there is a less-understood challenge—the greying of the developed world's population—that may actually do more to reshape our collective future than any of the above.

Over the next several decades, countries in the developed world will experience an unprecedented growth in the number of their elderly and an unprecedented decline in the number of their youth. The timing and magnitude of this demographic transformation have already been determined. Next century's elderly have already been born and can be counted—and their cost to retirement benefit systems can be projected.

Unlike with global warming, there can be little debate over whether or when global aging will manifest itself. And unlike with other challenges, even the struggle to preserve and strengthen unsteady new democracies, the costs of global aging will be far beyond the means of even the world's wealthiest nations—unless retirement benefit systems are radically reformed. Failure to do so, to prepare early and boldly enough, will spark economic crises that will dwarf the recent meltdowns in Asia and Russia.

How we confront global aging will have vast economic consequences costing quadrillions of dollars over the twenty-first century. Indeed, it will greatly influence how we manage, and can afford to manage, the other major challenges that will face us in the future.

For this and other reasons, global aging will become not just the transcendent economic issue of the twenty-first century but the transcendent political issue as well. It will dominate and daunt the public-policy agendas of developed countries and force the renegotiation of their social contracts. It will also reshape foreign policy strategies and the geopolitical order.

The United States has a massive challenge ahead of it. The broad outlines can already be seen in the emerging debate over Social Security and Medicare reform. But ominous as the fiscal stakes are in the United States, they loom even larger in Japan and Europe, where populations are aging even faster, birthrates are lower, the influx of young immigrants from developing countries is smaller, public pension benefits are more generous, and private pension systems are weaker.

Aging has become a truly global challenge and must therefore be given high priority on the global policy agenda. A grey dawn fast approaches. It is time to take an unflinching look at the shape of things to come.

GREYING MEANS PAYING

Official projections suggest that within thirty years, developed countries will have to spend at least an extra 9 to 16 per cent of their gross domestic product (GDP) simply to meet their old-age benefit promises. The unfunded liabilities for pensions (that is, benefits already earned by today's workers for which nothing has been saved) are already almost $35 trillion. Add in health care, and the total jumps to at least twice as much. At minimum, the global aging issue thus represents, to paraphrase the old quiz show, a $64 trillion question hanging over the developed world's future.

To pay for promised benefits through increased taxation is unfeasible. Doing so would raise the total tax burden by an unthinkable 35 to 40 percent of every worker's taxable wages — in countries where payroll tax rates sometimes already exceed 40 percent. To finance the costs of these benefits by borrowing would be just as disastrous. Governments would run unprecedented deficits that would quickly consume the savings of the developed world.

And the $64 trillion estimate is probably low. It likely underestimates future growth in longevity and health care costs and ignores the negative effects on the economy of more borrowing and higher interest rates. Moreover, every developed nation will soon reach a point where 18.5 percent of its population is age sixty-five or over. Italy will hit the mark as early as 2003, followed by Japan in 2005 and Germany in 2006. France and Britain will pass present-day Florida around 2016; the United States and Canada, in 2023 and 2021.

- *Societies much older than any we have ever known.* Global life expectancy has grown more in the last fifty years than over the previous five thousand. Until the Industrial Revolution, people age sixty-five and over never amounted to more than 2 or 3 percent of the population. In today's developed world, they amount to 14 percent. By the year 2030, they will reach 25 percent and be closing in on 30 percent in some countries.

- *An unprecedented economic burden on working-age people.* Early in the twenty-first century, working-age populations in most developed countries will shrink. Between 2000 and 2010, Japan, for example, will suffer a 25 percent drop in the number of workers under age thirty. Today the ratio of working taxpayers to nonworking pensioners in the developed world is around 3:1. By 2030, absent reform, this ratio will fall to 1.5:1, and in some countries, such as Germany and Italy, it will drop all the way down to 1:1 or even lower. While the longevity revolution represents a miraculous triumph of modern medicine, and the extra years of life will surely be treasured by the elderly and their families, pension plans and other retirement benefit programs were not designed to provide these billions of extra years of payouts.

- *The aging of the aged: the number of "old old" will grow much faster than the number of "young old."* The United Nations projects that by 2050, the number of people age sixty-five to eighty-four worldwide will grow from 400 million to 1.3 billion (a threefold increase), while the number of people age eighty-five and over will grow from 26 million to 175 million (a sixfold increase)—and the number age one hundred and over from 135,000 to 2.2 million (a sixteenfold increase). The "old old" consume far more health care than the "young old"—about two to three times as much. For nursing-home care, the ratio is roughly 20:1. Yet little of this cost is figured in the official projections of future public expenditures.

■ *Falling birthrates will intensify the global aging trend.* As life spans increase, fewer babies are being born.

Global aging could trigger a crisis that engulfs the world economy. This crisis may even threaten democracy itself. By making tough choices now world leaders would demonstrate that they genuinely care about the future, that they understand this unique opportunity for young and old nations to work together, and that they comprehend the price of freedom. The grey dawn approaches. We must establish new ways of thinking and new institutions to help us prepare for a much older world.

FIGURE 3.1.   Estimated and Projected Total Fertility for the World and Major Development Areas

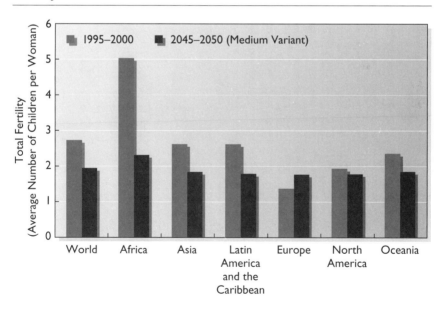

Source: Population Division of the Department of Economic and Social Affairs of the United Nations Secretariat (2003). *World Population Prospects: The 2002 Revision. Highlights.* New York: United Nations. Available over the Internet at http://esa.un.org/unpp/p2k0data.asp.

FIGURE 3.2.   Fertility Rates at or below Replacement Level

1975—Total world population 4.08 billion

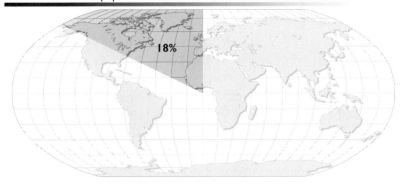

2000—Total world population 6.07 billion

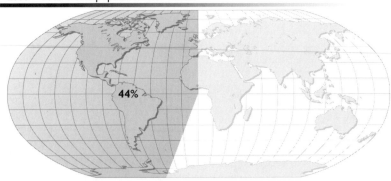

2025—Total world population 7.20 billion

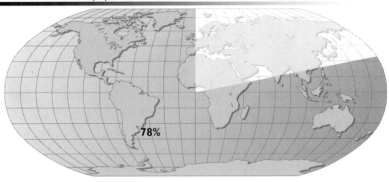

Source: United Nations

TABLE 3.1.   Highest and Lowest Total Fertility Rates by Country

Total Fertility Rate (Bottom 10)		
Rank	*Country*	*Children Born/Woman*
1	Bulgaria	1.13
2	Spain	1.16
3	Czech Republic	1.18
4	Latvia	1.18
5	Italy	1.19
6	Singapore	1.23
7	Estonia	1.24
8	Hungary	1.25
9	Slovakia	1.25
10	Andorra	1.26
Total Fertility Rate (Top 10)		
Rank	*Country*	*Children Born/Woman*
1	Somalia	7.05
2	Niger	7
3	Ethiopia	6.94
4	Yemen	6.9
5	Uganda	6.8
6	Congo	6.77
7	Mali	6.73
8	Chad	6.5
9	Marshall Islands	6.49
10	Angola	6.43

Source: Geography IQ. World Atlas. Available via the Internet:
http://www.geographyiq.com/ranking/ranking_Total_Fertility_Rate_top25.htm;
http://www.geographyiq.com/ranking/ranking_Total_Fertility_Rate_bottom25.htm.

Chapter Nine

MORTALITY AND DISEASE

What is the correlation between population size and disease?

Disease

Richard H. Robbins

This selection originally appeared in "Disease," in *Global Problems and the Culture of Capitalism* (Boston: Allyn and Bacon, 2002).

> Cities . . . were microbe heavens, or, as British microbiologist John Cairns put it, "graveyards of mankind." The most devastating scourges of the past attained horrific proportions only when the microbes reached urban centers, where population density instantaneously magnified any minor contagion that might have originated in the provinces. Any microbes successfully exploited the new urban ecologies to create altogether novel disease threats.
>
> Laurie Garrett, *The Coming Plague*

> A thorough understanding of the AIDS pandemic demands a commitment to the concerns of history and political economy: HIV . . . has run along the fault lines of economic structures long in the making.
>
> Paul Farmer, *AIDS and Accusation*

In the halcyon days after World War II, when everything seemed possible and the advance of science and economic prosperity inspired government leaders and leading academics to predict a coming era of worldwide peace and prosperity, medical professionals were predicting the end of infectious disease. Universal health was set as a realistic and achievable goal. The U.S. Surgeon General in 1967 said it was time to close the door on infectious disease. There was some reason for this optimism. As a result of a worldwide vaccination campaign, smallpox had been completely eliminated, the last case in the world being diagnosed in 1979. Malaria, one of the world's major killers, had been reduced worldwide and even eliminated in some areas by controlling the vector—the mosquito—which spread the disease, and through the development and massive distribution of curative drugs. Tuberculosis, the major killer of the nineteenth century, was disappearing. The U.S. Surgeon General declared that measles would be eliminated by 1982 with an aggressive immunization campaign. Jonas Salk had discovered a cure for poliomyelitis, the scourge of childhood; and the development of antibiotics promised to rid us of every infirmity from pneumonia to bad breath. Then, in the space of a decade, everything changed.

AIDS was one of the shocks that changed universal optimism to what Marc Lapp in 1994 called "therapeutic nihilism," an attitude common today among hospital personnel, who think that nothing will work to cure patients. But there were other reasons for the change: the emergence of antibiotic-resistant strains of disease; the reemergence of malaria, cholera, and tuberculosis in even deadlier forms; the emergence of other new diseases, particularly Lyme disease, dengue-2, and hemorrhagic fevers such as eboli that result in massive internal bleeding and have mortality rates of up to 90 percent. Measles, supposed to be eradicated from the United States in 1982, was ten times more prevalent in 1993 than in 1983. These developments and others have required medical researchers in biology, epidemiology, and anthropology, among others, to reexamine the relationship between human beings and the microbial world, particularly those pathogens that cause disease. It is clear that we underestimated the ingenuity of microbes to adapt to our adaptations to them and failed to appreciate how our patterns of social, political, and economic relations affect the emergence and transmission of disease.

Each age, it seems, has its signature disease. Bubonic plague in the fourteenth and fifteenth centuries emerged because of the opening of Asian trade routes and was carried by merchants and warriors from the middle of the then world system west to Europe and east to China. Syphilis spread in the sixteenth and seventeenth centuries through increased sexual contact of people in towns and cities. Tuberculosis, the disease of the nineteenth century, spread through the air in the densely packed cities and slums of Europe and the United States.

As we shall see, AIDS is very much the signature disease of the latter quarter of the twentieth century, serving as a marker for the increasing disparity in wealth between core (first world nations) and periphery (third world nations) and for the accompanying disparity in susceptibility to disease. More than 98 percent of deaths from communicable disease (16.3 million a year) occur in the periphery. Worldwide 32 percent of all deaths are caused by infectious disease, but in the periphery infectious disease is responsible for 42 percent of all deaths, compared with 1.2 percent in industrial countries.

The fact that each historical epoch has its characteristic illness reveals clearly that how we live—the social and cultural patterns at any point in time and space—largely define the kind and frequency of disease to which human beings are susceptible. The questions we need to ask are: *What do we do that exposes us to disease?* What do we do that exposes others to disease? How do we create the conditions for unique interactions between pathogens, their environments, and their hosts? Moreover, what features of human societies make pathogens more or less lethal?

For example, *increases in population density clearly relate to the emergence and frequency of disease,* as does the division of the world into rich and poor. The crowding into cities of rural workers and peasants, as agricultural land becomes concentrated in the hands of a few, influences disease susceptibility. Public policy that makes economic growth a priority and neglects health programs encourages the spread of disease, as do International Monetary Fund structural adjustment programs in peripheral countries that demand the cutting of health, sanitation, and education programs. The alteration of the environment has enormous consequences for the spread and emergence of disease.

Infectious disease, of course, is not the only health problem we face. Environmental pollutants, often a direct outgrowth of industrialization, cause sickness. For example, asthma, often aggravated by industrial pollutants, is on the rise. Millions of people face malnutrition and starvation, conditions that further expose them to disease. Commercially promoted products such as alcoholic beverages and tobacco endanger health. Of the estimated 1.1 billion smokers in the world today, 800 million are in the periphery. The World Health Organization reports that smoking-related deaths in the periphery will rise from 1 million per year in the early 1990s to 2 million by the year 2000 (World Health Organization: *The Tobacco Epidemic*, 1995). Moreover, as cigarette sales continue to fall in the core in response to antismoking campaigns and state legislation, cigarette companies, with the support of core governments, have intensified their efforts to sell their products to people in other countries, particularly to women and the young. For example, the United States has used free trade arguments to pressure other nations—Thailand, Taiwan, and South Korea—with economic sanctions to open their markets to American cigarettes. In such cases it is easy to see a direct connection between the capitalist world system and the onset of disease. However, the relation that exists between the culture of capitalism and infectious pathogens is often more subtle and hidden.

Death Makes a Comeback

Nicholas Eberstadt

This selection was excerpted from "The Population Implosion," in *Foreign Policy* (Washington, D.C.: Council on Foreign Relations, March/April 2001).

Given the extraordinary impact of the twentieth century's global health revolution, well-informed citizens around the world have come to expect steady and progressive improvement in life expectancy and health conditions during times of peace. Unfortunately, troubling new trends challenge these happy presumptions. A growing fraction of the world's population is coming under the grip of peacetime retrogressions in health conditions and mortality levels. Long-term stagnation or even decline in life expectancy is now a real possibility for urbanized, educated countries not at war. Severe and prolonged collapses of local health conditions during peacetime, moreover, is no longer a purely theoretical eventuality. As we look toward 2025, we must consider the unpleasant likelihood that a large and growing fraction of humanity may be separated from the planetary march toward better health and subjected instead to brutal mortality crises of indeterminate duration.

In the early post–World War II era, the upsurge in life expectancy was a worldwide phenomenon. By the reckoning of the U.N. Population Division, in fact, not a single spot on the globe had a lower life expectancy in the early 1970s than in the early 1950s. And in the late 1970s only two places on earth—Khmer Rouge–ravaged Cambodia and brutally occupied East Timor—had lower levels of life expectancy than twenty years earlier. In subsequent years, however, a number of countries unaffected by domestic disturbance and upheaval began to report lower levels of life expectancy than they had known two decades earlier. Today that list is long and growing. U.S. Census Bureau projections list thirty-nine countries in which life expectancy at birth is anticipated to be at least slightly lower in 2010 than it was in 1990. With populations today totaling three quarters of a billion people and accounting for one eighth of the world's population, these countries are strikingly diverse in terms of location, history, and material attainment.

This grouping includes the South American countries of Brazil and Guyana; the Caribbean islands of Grenada and the Bahamas; the Micronesian state of Nauru; ten of the fifteen republics of the former Soviet Union; and twenty-three sub-Saharan African nations. As might be surmised from the heterogeneity of these societies, health decline and mortality shocks in the contemporary world are not explained by a single set of factors but by several syndromes working simultaneously in different parts of the world to subvert health progress.

Russia has experienced a prolonged stagnation and even decline in life expectancy, and its condition illuminates the problems facing some of the other former Soviet republics. After recording rapid postwar reductions in mortality in the 1950s, Russian mortality levels stopped falling in the 1960s and began rising for broad groups of the population. By 1990, overall life expectancy at birth in Russia was barely as high as it had been twenty-five years earlier. With the end of communist rule in 1991, Russia suffered sudden and severe increases in mortality, from which it has not yet fully recovered. By 1999, overall life expectancy at birth in Russia had regressed to the point where it had been four decades earlier.

Although many aspects of Russia's continuing health crisis remain puzzling, it appears that lifestyle and behavioral risks—including heavy smoking and extremely heavy drinking—figure centrally in the shortening of Russian lives. A weak and rudderless public health system, combined with apparent indifference in Moscow to the nation's ongoing mortality crisis, also compromises health progress. Although Russia is an industrialized society with an educated population and a large indigenous scientific-technical cadre, such characteristics do not automatically protect a country from the kinds of health woes that have befallen the Russian Federation.

In sub-Saharan Africa, a different dynamic drives mortality crises: the explosive spread of the HIV/AIDS epidemic. In its most recent report, the Joint United Nations Programme on HIV/AIDS (UNAIDS) estimated that 2.8 million died of AIDS in 1999, 2.2 million in sub-Saharan Africa alone. UNAIDS also reported that almost 9 percent of the region's adult population is already infected with the disease. By all indications, the epidemic is still spreading in sub-Saharan Africa. As of 2000, UNAIDS projected that in several sub-Saharan countries, a fifteen-year-old boy today faces a greater than 50 percent chance of ultimately dying from AIDS — even if the risk of becoming infected were reduced to half of current levels.

Given sub-Saharan Africa's disappointing developmental performance and conspicuously poor record of governance over the postindependence period, the pervasive failure in this low-income area to contain a deadly but preventable contagion may seem tragic but unsurprising. Yet it is worth noting that the AIDS epidemic appears to have been especially devastating in one of Africa's most highly developed and best-governed countries: Botswana.

Unlike most of the region, Botswana is predominantly urbanized; its rate of adult illiteracy is among the subcontinent's very lowest; and over a generation in which sub-Saharan economic growth rates were typically negative, Botswana's was consistently positive. Yet despite such promising statistics, Botswana's population has been decimated by HIV/AIDS over the last decade. Between 1990 and 2000, life expectancy in Botswana plummeted from about sixty-four years to about thirty-nine years, that is to say, by almost a quarter century. Recent projections for 2025 envision a life expectancy of a mere thirty-three years. If this projection proves accurate, Botswana will have a much lower life expectancy twenty-five years from now than it had nearly half a century ago.

One of the disturbing facets of the Botswanan case is the speed and severity with which life expectancy projections have been revised downward. Assuming most recent figures are accurate, as recently as 1994 expert demographers were overestimating Botswana's life expectancy for 2000 by about thirty years. Such abrupt and radical revisions raise the question of whether similar brutal adjustments await other sub-Saharan countries—or, for that matter, countries in other regions of the world. This question cannot be answered with any degree of certainty today, but we would be unwise to dismiss it from consideration. HIV/AIDS may not be the only plague capable of wrenching down national levels of life expectancy over the coming quarter century. Twenty-five years ago, HIV/AIDS had not even been identified and diagnosed.

Surprisingly, sub-Saharan Africa's AIDS catastrophe is not projected to alter the region's population totals dramatically. That speaks to the extraordinary power of high fertility levels. Given the region's current and prospective patterns of childbearing, the subcontinent's population totals in 2025 may prove to be unexpectedly insensitive to the scope or scale of the disasters looming ahead. Yet it is the mortality patterns that will do much to define the quality of life for those human numbers—and to circumscribe their economic and social potential.

THE SHAPE OF THINGS TO COME

Looking toward 2025, we must remember that many twentieth-century population forecasts and demographic assessments proved famously wrong. Depression-era demographers, for example, incorrectly predicted depopulation for Europe by the 1960s and completely missed the baby boom. The 1960s and 1970s saw dire warnings that the population explosion would result in worldwide famine and misery, whereas today we live in the most prosperous era humanity has ever known. In any assessment of future world population trends and consequences, a measure of humility is clearly in order.

Given today's historically low death rates and birthrates, however, the arithmetic fact is that the great majority of people who will inhabit the world in 2025 are already alive. Only an apocalyptic disaster can change that. Consequently, this reality provides considerable insight into the shape of things to come. By these indications, indeed, we must now adapt our collective mind-set to face new demographic challenges.

A host of contradictory demographic trends and pressures will likely reshape the world during the next quarter century. Lower fertility levels, for example, will simultaneously alter the logic of international migration flows and accelerate the aging of the global population. Social aging sets in motion an array of profound changes and challenges and demands far-reaching adjustments if those challenges are to be met successfully. But social aging is primarily a consequence of the longer lives that modern populations enjoy. And the longevity revolution, with its attendant enhancements of health conditions and individual capabilities, constitutes an unambiguous improvement in the human condition. Pronounced and prolonged mortality setbacks portend just the opposite: a diminution of human well-being, capabilities, and choices.

It is unlikely that our understanding of the determinants of fertility or of the long-range prospects for fertility will advance palpably in the decades immediately ahead. But if we wish to inhabit a world twenty-five years from now that is distinctly more humane than the one we know today, we would be well advised to marshal our attention to understanding, arresting, and overcoming the forces that are all too successfully pressing for higher levels of human mortality today.

SNAPSHOT: AIDS

HIV/AIDS Pandemic Spreads Further

Radhika Sarin

This selection originally appeared in *Vital Signs 2003* (Washington, D.C.: Worldwatch Institute, 2003).

The number of people living with HIV/AIDS rose to 42 million at the end of 2002. Five million people became infected with HIV in 2002 (figure 3.4), and another 3.1 million died of AIDS-related causes (figure 3.5).

For the first time, women account for half the people living with HIV/AIDS. Heterosexual transmission, particularly in Africa and the Caribbean, is the primary cause of infection among women, who are two to four times more likely than men to become infected during unprotected vaginal sex.

Women's biological vulnerability—due to a large surface area of reproductive tissue and high virus concentrations in infected semen—is compounded by economic and social inequities. Women who are economically dependent on husbands or sexual partners have little control over sexual relations and condom use. Social taboos prevent women from learning about reproductive health, while the stigma associated with sexually transmitted infections is a barrier against seeking care. Young women risk contracting HIV from older partners, which explains large differences in HIV prevalence between teenaged males and females in many countries.

In sub-Saharan Africa, home to 70 percent of the world's HIV-positive people, AIDS is the leading cause of death. In 2002, average life expectancy in sixteen African nations was at least ten years lower than it would have been without AIDS. HIV/AIDS is also exacerbating Africa's food crisis, threatening about 38 million people with starvation. The epidemic has reduced the number of agricultural workers and has unraveled social safety nets as families sell off assets to pay for medical or funeral expenses. For the poor without access to antiretroviral therapies, good nutrition is all that can ward off illness and early death. When this is also lost, weakened immune systems become susceptible to tuberculosis, malaria, and other infections.

Though Africa carries the greatest burden of disease, the epidemic is growing fastest in eastern Europe and central Asia, where it is linked to intravenous drug use, high unemployment, and crumbling public health facilities. In Russia, up to 90 percent of registered infections are due to drug use. High rates of sexually transmitted infections in the region indicate that heterosexual transmission could spread HIV into the wider popula-

FIGURE 3.3. Expectation of Life at Birth for the World and Major Development Areas

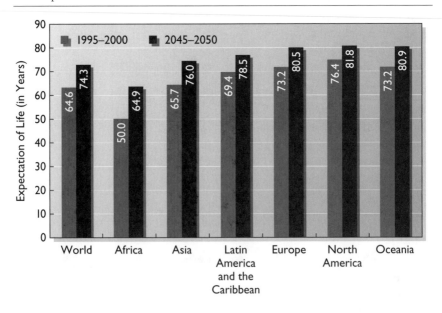

Source: Population Division of the Department of Economic and Social Affairs of the United Nations Secretariat (2003). *World Population Prospects: The 2002 Revision. Highlights.* New York: United Nations. Available via the Internet at http://esa.un.org/unpp/p2k0data.asp.

tion, as seen in the Ukraine and Belarus. In the Baltic states, overcrowded prisons and juvenile justice institutions serve as breeding grounds for the virus.

Another emerging AIDS hotspot is Asia, where low national prevalence levels in populous nations mask the magnitude of localized infection. Nearly 4 million people are infected in India, and the epidemic has hit the general population in several states. In China, people in poor rural communities who participated in blood-selling programs in the 1990s have become concentrated pockets of HIV-positive villagers with limited access to any kind of care. In all, China reports an estimated 1 million infections, with drug use and heterosexual transmission continuing the spread.

Although AIDS-related mortality has fallen dramatically in high-income countries since antiretroviral treatment became widespread in 1996, only 4 percent of those who need treatment in low- and middle-income countries receive it. The price of antiretrovirals has fallen dramatically,

FIGURE 3.4. Estimates of Cumulative HIV Infection Worldwide

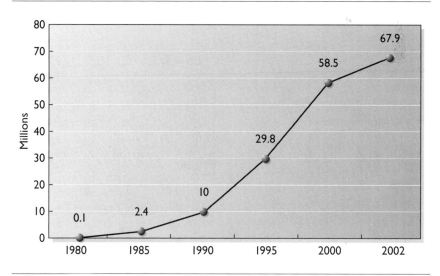

Source: Joint United Nations Programme on HIV/AIDS.

FIGURE 3.5.   Estimates of Cumulative AIDS Deaths Worldwide

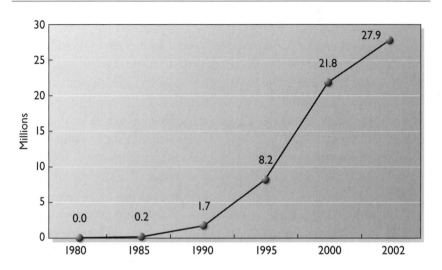

Source: Joint United Nations Programme on HIV/AIDS.

from $10,000 to $12,000 a year per person in early 2000 to $350 by December 2001. The world's poorest, however, cannot afford even this.

Yet some progress has been made in making access to treatment more equitable. In 2002, Botswana became the first African nation to adopt a policy of universal access to treatment. The biggest strides have been made in Latin America and the Caribbean: Brazil, Argentina, Costa Rica, Cuba, Uruguay, Honduras, and Panama are among the countries providing free or subsidized treatment.

Even so, a huge gap persists between needed and available resources. In 2002, $3 billion was spent on efforts to stem the epidemic in low- and middle-income countries. The Joint United Nations Programme on HIV/AIDS (UNAIDS) estimates that funding will have to more than double, to $6.5 billion, in 2003—with two thirds of the resources coming from international sources.

TABLE 3.2. Global Mortality by Cause (2000)

Cause of Death	Number (Thousands)	Share of Total (Percent)
Cardiovascular diseases	16,701	30
Infectious and parasitic diseases	14,398	25.9
Cancers	6,930	12.4
Maternal and perinatal conditions and congenital abnormalities	3,591	6.4
Chronic respiratory diseases	3,542	6.4
Unintentional injuries (such as auto accidents)	3,403	6.1
Digestive diseases	1,923	3.5
Neuropsychiatric disorders	948	1.7
Violence and war	830	1.5
Genitourinary diseases	825	1.5
Suicide	815	1.5
Diabetes	810	1.5
Nutritional deficiencies and disorders	669	1.2
Other	309	0.6
Total	55,694	100

Source: World Health Organization.

TABLE 3.3. Cumulative HIV Infection and AIDS Deaths Worldwide

Year	HIV Infection (Millions)	AIDS Deaths (Millions)	Year	HIV Infection (Millions)	AIDS Deaths (Millions)
1980	0.1	0.0	1992	16.1	3.3
1981	0.3	0.0	1993	20.1	4.7
1982	0.7	0.0	1994	24.5	6.2
1983	1.2	0.0	1995	29.8	8.2
1984	1.7	0.1	1996	35.3	10.6
1985	2.4	0.2	1997	40.9	13.2
1986	3.4	0.3	1998	46.6	15.9
1987	4.5	0.5	1999	52.6	18.8
1988	5.9	0.8	2000	58.5	21.8
1989	7.8	1.2	2001	62.9	24.8
1990	10.0	1.7	2002		
1991	12.8	2.4	(prelim.)	67.9	27.9

Source: Joint United Nations Programme on HIV/AIDS.

Chapter Ten

IMMIGRATION

Immigration: a population boom or bust?

Migration Washes Over Ambivalent America

Alvin Powell

This selection originally appeared in the *Harvard University Gazette* (Boston: Harvard University, February 24, 2000).

Make up your mind, America.

That's the message of Kennedy School of Government economist George Borjas, a specialist in immigration who believes the United States is of two minds about which immigrants—and how many of them—to let into the country.

In his own estimation, Borjas believes the country is admitting too many immigrants—about a million a year—and too many of them are low-skilled workers. He believes the United States should let in about half as many immigrants as it does now and should create a point system to screen for skills needed in the nation's economy.

Borjas, an immigrant himself, came to the United States as a boy from Cuba in the early 1960s. Before coming to Harvard, he taught at the University of California at San Diego and served as an adviser on immigration to former Governor Pete Wilson.

Borjas, Pforzheimer Professor of Public Policy at the Kennedy School, acknowledges that the policies he espouses would have barred him and his mother from settling here. In addition, the policies he recommends would effectively bar many immigrants from third world nations where education standards are lower than they are here.

Still, he maintains, a country should consider its national interests when setting policy.

Borjas acknowledges that he's looking at the problem from the standpoint of an economist and said he understands that immigration policy is not set according to economic data alone. Other considerations, such as political and humanitarian concerns, are also important driving forces in crafting immigration guidelines.

"All the data is meaningless unless the country first decides what it wants to get out of immigration," Borjas said. "If one thinks immigration should help native workers, then current policies are bad. If immigration is to help those who are less well off [in the world], then it is more of a humanitarian program."

One symptom of America's two minds about immigration is the recent public and bitter debate over whether to send six-year-old Elian Gonzales back to Cuba or keep him here, "safe" from Cuban communism, Borjas said. Borjas penned a *New York Times* op-ed piece comparing the Gonzales case with the more clear-cut case of a young girl from Togo facing culturally mandated genital mutilation if she returns to her native land. While this girl's case seems clear, he wrote, our ambivalence over immigration is what becomes clear in Elian's case.

"We have to decide at this point what a refugee is. It used to be easy. If the person came from a communist country, they were a refugee," Borjas said.

Borjas said the op-ed piece, which supported keeping Gonzales here, gained him more feedback, mostly favorable, than any of his other books or publications.

The economics of immigration, asserts Borjas, clearly indicate that a radical change in immigration policy is needed, one that moves away from a system, based on family ties, that he says annually admits more than 1 million legal and illegal immigrants, many of them unskilled, to a more selective policy that allows half that many and that selects much more closely for those who would better fit into the increasingly highly skilled workplace of the United States.

His argument is detailed in his most recent book, *Heaven's Door: Immigration Policy and the American Economy*, published by Princeton University Press. In it, Borjas argues that immigration has a small net effect on the U.S. economy, adding roughly $8 billion to $10 billion in a national economy that was $8 trillion in 1998. Even that small beneficial effect, he argues, may be outweighed by the increased use of social services by immigrants, who, he argues, have a higher usage of welfare programs than native-born Americans.

The largest effect of today's immigration policy, he says, is a redistribution of America's economic pie. He estimates that immigration has caused the shift of roughly $160 billion from the paychecks of low-skilled

Americans into the profits of the business owners they work for by increasing the supply of low-skilled workers and allowing business owners to lower wages.

All this happens even though today's immigrants are better educated than those of decades past because the average American has even more education and the U.S. workplace places a high premium on skilled work.

Heaven's Door has put Borjas squarely in the midst of the contentious, emotional debate about U.S. immigration policy. The book garnered a wide variety of reviews, ranging from "impressively researched, brightly written and tightly argued" by the *New York Times*, which characterized Borjas as "one of the nation's leading—and certainly gloomiest—experts on immigration," to "critically flawed" and an "alarmist analysis," by the *Wall Street Journal*.

Borjas said the purpose of his book was to reframe the debate away from arguing about numbers and shift it instead toward a discussion of the nation's goal for its immigration policy: to benefit workers, to benefit the country as a whole, to reunite families, or to provide a new start to workers from disadvantaged countries.

Borjas terms the immigration that has taken place since the immigration reforms of the mid-1960s "The Second Great Migration," noting that the number of immigrants entering the country today surpasses even the peak years of the Great Migration, which lasted from 1880 until 1924.

Further, he says, though Great Migration immigrants were also unskilled, they came at a time when the Industrial Revolution was demanding a large supply of unskilled workers, unlike today, when American jobs increasingly require advanced skills.

Borjas's point system would assign a certain number of points to things like age, education, and field of expertise and would be designed to admit workers skilled in fields policymakers deem important.

Immigration guidelines, Borjas said, should be designed based on more than the Statue of Liberty's invitation to "Give me your tired, your poor, your huddled masses yearning to breathe free."

"At that time [1886, when the Statue of Liberty was given to the United States by France], the country wanted the tired and poor because it wanted to build an industrial infrastructure," Borjas said. "One shouldn't make policy based on mythic history."

Muddled Masses

Stuart Anderson

This selection originally appeared in *Reason* (Los Angeles: The Reason Foundation, February 2000).

Throughout the history of American immigration, critics have viewed each new generation of arrivals as a threat to the nation's prosperity and culture. George Borjas, an economist and professor of public policy at the John F. Kennedy School of Government at Harvard University, sounds that warning yet again in his new study, *Heaven's Door: Immigration Policy and the American Economy*. Borjas is no nativist know-nothing: He is the author or co-author of many peer-reviewed articles on immigration and a major voice in the ongoing debate on the subject, so his book demands careful attention. So, too, does his life: Borjas is a Cuban-born refugee, yet the immigration policies he proposes would have precluded his own family's arrival in this country. That irony undercuts his anti-immigrant prescriptions as fully as the inconvenient facts he ignores.

The central argument of *Heaven's Door* is that America is being harmed economically because it allows citizens and permanent residents (green card holders) to sponsor close family members for immigration. Borjas writes that such immigration patterns are a direct result of the 1965 amendments to the Immigration and Nationality Act, and that we should change the law.

His argument is flawed. First, the book is ahistorical, suffering from a lack of understanding of—or an unwillingness to acknowledge—the discriminatory treatment that the 1965 legislation sought to address. Second, Borjas uses inappropriate data to support his conclusions, failing to distinguish between legal and illegal immigrants, and using information on illegal immigrants to advocate reducing legal immigration. Third, he assumes immigrants remain economically static, ignoring much evidence that they adapt to America by acquiring skills or training unavailable in their home countries. Finally, Borjas writes as if his conclusions are generally accepted—which they are not—and neither engages nor refutes criticisms of his earlier work.

Some history is necessary to understand the changes in immigration policy that occurred in 1965. In the 1920s, Congress replaced what had been a policy of nearly open immigration with "national origins" quotas that, in effect, barred Asians, Italians, Greeks, and Jews. These quota laws, passed after lobbying by the Ku Klux Klan and others, codified the eugenics theories of Madison Grant, whose work focused on the supposedly inferior skull sizes of Jews and other immigrants.

The 1965 amendments eliminated these quotas and carried forward almost intact the family immigration categories put in place by the 1959 amendments to the Immigration and Nationality Act. Although on paper half of the available immigration slots under the quotas were reserved for skill-based immigration, 86 percent of the visas issued between 1952 and 1965 went to family immigration, according to the Immigration and Naturalization Service.

Borjas is simply wrong when he states that the 1965 act "enshrined a new objective for awarding visas . . . the reunification of families." The historical records at Ellis Island make clear that most immigration prior to the 1920s was also family-based, and such unification never entirely lost its role. In fact, a report of the House Judiciary Committee on the 1959 legislation states, "The recognized principle of avoiding separation of families could be furthered if certain categories of such relatives were reclassified in the various preference portions of the immigration quotas." Joyce Vialet of the Congressional Research Service analyzed the 1965 Immigration Act and concluded, "In response to the demand for admission of family members, Congress enacted a series of amendments to the Immigration and Nationality Act (INA), beginning in 1957, which gave increasing priority to family relationship. The family preference categories included in the 1965 Act evolved directly from this series of amendments. Arguably, the 1965 Act represented an acceptance of the status quo rather than a shift to a new policy of favoring family members."

Under current law, a U.S. citizen can sponsor a spouse, child, parent, brother, or sister, while a green card holder can sponsor a spouse or child. We also accept refugees and employer-sponsored immigrants. Approximately 75 percent of family immigrants are spouses or children. Borjas argues that such immigration practices have caused numerous problems:

Education. Using U.S. census data, Borjas concludes that immigrants today are less skilled than natives. But the census includes data about many *illegal* immigrants. If one measures only legal immigrants, as the New Immigrant Survey (1998) does in a sophisticated research project led by RAND economist Jim Smith, one arrives at quite different conclusions. The New Immigrant Survey's findings directly contradict Borjas. "The median years of schooling for the legal immigrants, thirteen years, is a full one year higher than that of the U.S. native-born," the survey concludes. It would seem that, on balance, legal immigrants are not less skilled than natives. Legal immigrants do congregate at the top and bottom of the education scale, but less so than census data imply. Besides, economists agree that immigrants increase America's labor productivity most when they fill niches at the top and bottom.

Earnings Growth. Based on his study of the census data, Borjas finds that the earnings of immigrants never catch up with those of natives. But other researchers using the same census data, including refugees and illegal immigrants, have questioned that finding. Writing in the May 1999 *American Economic Review*, economists Harriet Duleep, a senior research associate at the Urban Institute, and Mark Regets, a senior analyst at the National Science Foundation, found that the gap in earnings between new immigrants and natives largely disappears after ten years in the United States, with immigrant wage growth faster than native (6.7 percent vs. 4.4 percent).

Borjas misses this point because he excludes the self-employed, a major statistical blind spot when looking at immigrants. If, out of one hundred thousand immigrants, sixty thousand started restaurants and software firms, and forty thousand worked as waiters, Borjas would count only the earnings of the forty thousand waiters. Moreover, if ten thousand of the waiters later started their own successful restaurants, Borjas would remove them from the calculations of immigrant earnings growth, thus further biasing the results downward.

A July 1998 study by Stephen Moore of the Cato Institute supports the Duleep-Regets findings. It shows a direct correlation between time spent in America and economic well-being, finding that after two decades immigrants' home ownership rates exceed 60 percent, while their poverty rates fall below those of natives.

Fiscal Impact. Borjas portrays immigrants as fiscal liabilities by citing information on the annual costs of immigrant households from a 1997 National Academy of Sciences (NAS) study. Yet economist Ronald Lee of the University of California, Berkeley, who performed the principal fiscal analysis in the NAS report, testified before the Senate Immigration Subcommittee in 1997 that such data are highly misleading. "These numbers do not best represent the panel's findings and should not be used for assessing the consequences of immigration policies," Lee testified. The problem, Lee found, was that calculating annual numbers requires using a model that counts the native-born children of immigrants as "costs" created by immigrant households when those children are in school but fails to include the taxes those children pay once they grow up and enter the work force.

According to Lee, the entry of a typical immigrant into the United States has a positive cumulative effect within the immigrant's lifetime: Taxpayers save $80,000 as a result of that entry, most of it during the lifetime of the immigrant and his offspring. "Most immigrants arrive at young working ages, with their education already paid for," testified Lee, and they "help pay for government activities such as defense for which they impose no additional costs." Borjas asserts incorrectly that any benefits come only after the passage of hundreds of years. As for the fiscal effect of *legal* immigration on the states, Berkeley's Lee said that, with the appropriate assumptions, a dynamic analysis would likely show forty-nine of the states coming out ahead, with the fiftieth, California, a close call.

Overall Immigrant Contributions. Borjas argues that the economic contribution of immigrants to the economy is only $8 billion a year. Cato's Stephen Moore and others have called that assertion absurd, noting that Borjas's methodology depends on immigrants being identical to natives and with no benefits accruing to Americans from immigrant entrepreneurs, immigrants with abilities different from natives, a larger economic pie, or a greater selection of goods and services. Borjas asserts immigrants save Americans money—and thereby benefit the economy—only if they lower native wages. That would mean that Hungarian-born Intel founder Andy Grove has provided no economic benefit to America, even though Intel today employs over sixty-five thousand people and has net revenues of $26 billion a year.

In the San Francisco area alone, 2,775 companies led by Chinese and Indian immigrants have annual sales of nearly $17 billion and employ more than fifty-eight thousand people, according to Anna Lee Saxenian of the Public Policy Institute of California. Economies of scale, immigrant-induced productivity improvements, and other factors that Borjas concedes would exponentially increase the immigrant benefit to the economy are not included in his book because, he says, they are difficult to quantify. Even if that's the case, he should at least concede that his $8 billion figure tells us very little.

Borjas further asserts that immigrants who succeed in the United States would likely succeed in their own country. But if this is true, then Borjas should provide a list of all the great semiconductor firms started in communist Hungary after Andy Grove fled in 1956. In fact, immigrants come here precisely because oppressive political or economic policies block them from succeeding in their own countries.

Labor Market Impact. Borjas argues that native high school dropouts nationally experience lower wages because of immigrants. This rests on the assumption that low-skill natives leave states in response to increased immigration, thus perhaps explaining why numerous studies have not detected negative wage effects from immigrants. However, 1997 research by Columbia University economist Francisco L. Rivera-Batiz demonstrates that Borjas's theory cannot be correct. To the extent that any native out-migration is measurable in states that receive a lot of immigrants, it's actually college-educated natives who have left (and possibly for reasons that have nothing to do with immigration).

Borjas does not appear to have researched the out-migration question himself, nor does he refute Rivera-Batiz's conclusions. Instead, he writes, "The few studies that attempt to determine if native migration decisions are correlated with immigration have yielded a confusing set of results."

Borjas's labor-market analysis has other problems. For example, he sets up a model that guarantees that immigrants have a negative effect by assuming they fill all the same jobs as natives, rather than allowing for the more likely scenario found by many other economists that immigrants are complements to natives in the labor market.

Also, Borjas's assertion that we have too many workers appears mistaken to anyone monitoring today's economy or long-term labor trends. Under current immigration levels, the U.S. labor force will grow by a (possibly inadequate) 40 percent between 1995 and 2050, according to the National Academy of Sciences. Under Borjas's immigration proposals, the U.S. labor force would grow by perhaps half that much.

The restrictionist argument that lower-skilled jobs have almost all disappeared is contradicted by an August 1997 study by economist Linda Levine of the Congressional Research Service. Levine concludes that "many occupations with limited educational requirements are experiencing above-average rates of job growth or substantial increases in employment levels." In 2005, writes Levine, "about one-half of all jobs" in America will require "no more than a high school diploma."

To solve problems that better research indicates do not exist, Borjas recommends the adoption of a Canadian-style point system, in which a government body assigns points to such characteristics as education level and admits only those who achieve a designated score. In practice, Borjas's plan would transfer power to federal bureaucrats at the expense of individuals, families, and employers. "A point system has many imperfections," concedes Borjas. "A few hapless government bureaucrats have to sit down and decide which characteristics will enter the admissions formula, which occupations are the ones that are most beneficial, which age groups are to be favored, how many points to grant each desired characteristic and so on."

After noting that the list of occupations, each assigned points, takes up ten pages in the Canadian system, Borjas writes, "Most of these decisions are bound to be arbitrary and clearly stretch the ability of bureaucrats to determine labor market needs well beyond their limit." As if bureaucrats are well suited to handle *any* labor market decisions. In any case, it's clear that no government test can ever measure life's most important intangibles: drive, individual initiative, and a commitment to family.

Borjas concedes that keeping out Mexicans is a goal of the point system. "Most likely," he writes, "the predominance of Mexican immigrants and of immigrants from some other developing countries will decline substantially." In other words it's not just bad policy but bad politics.

It's important to understand that those who advocate a more "skill-based" immigration system are also among the most vociferous opponents of skilled immigrants. In 1998, anti-immigrant groups and their congressional allies fought the expansion of H-1B temporary visas for high-skilled, foreign-born engineers, computer scientists, and others, as if adding fifty thousand more professionals to a 130-million-person work force would mean the end of Western civilization. Borjas himself derisively refers to these scientists and engineers as "high-tech braceros," equating them with migrant farm workers.

Borjas undermines any pretense of rigorous analysis when he writes, "I suspect that an annual flow of one million immigrants is probably too large." We should reduce this number, he thinks, to five hundred thousand (the average annual immigration level in the 1970s, he later notes). This is a breathtaking denial of opportunity to a half million people on the basis of unsupported suspicions.

But that's not the end of Borjas's proposal. Noting that establishing a point system would be useless if those excluded entered illegally, he argues that we should subtract the number of illegal immigrants each year from the number of legal immigrants. Based on the Immigration and Naturalization Service (INS) estimates, that would further reduce legal immigration to two hundred thousand persons a year.

What would such a limit mean? If so restrictive a proposal had been the law in 1997, nearly 50,000 citizens would have been unable to sponsor their own spouse or minor children for immigration (there were 248,326 spouses and minor children of U.S. citizens who immigrated legally in 1997). In addition, the government would have prohibited citizens from sponsoring parents, adult children, or siblings, while green card holders would have been forbidden from sponsoring spouses or children. No refugees would have entered. And not one "skilled" immigrant would have been admitted, either through a point system or through high-tech company sponsorship, because no slots would have been available. Thankfully, there's little chance Congress would adopt such a proposal. In

1996, it turned back, by decisive margins, efforts to reduce legal immigration.

As for what to do about illegal immigration, Borjas advocates stiffer employer sanctions and improved identification documents, though he does not appear convinced those will do the trick. Illegal immigration is a legitimate concern. In places such as Douglas, Arizona, where illegal immigrants are literally trampling on ranchers' property rights, the interesting policy question raised by Governor Jane Hull is whether illegal entry can be curtailed or prevented by a combination of law enforcement and market forces, such as by providing temporary visas to willing workers in hospitality and other service industries. But Borjas merely adopts the view of many restrictionists: We're not sure we can stop people who are entering illegally, so let's go after the people who immigrate legally. That's not an acceptable policy.

In 1962, George Borjas's widowed mother, with the help of Catholic priests, came with George to America on one of the last "freedom flights" from Cuba. With little money or education, his mother worked hard to raise George, and he obviously worked hard, too. Borjas writes, "Although my family and I entered the country as refugees, my family would have been unable to 'pass the test' implicit" in the policy he now advocates.

Critics of immigration can't explain why, if legal immigration is supposed to be so harmful, America remains a society rich in opportunities. George Borjas can't explain it either. "To this day, I continue to be amazed by the courage and boldness that my mother and millions of others exhibited in picking up the little they had, and starting life again in a foreign country—without knowing the language, the culture, or almost anything about it," he writes. "They all relied on their unshakable belief that the United States was a far better place, and that even if they themselves could not share in those opportunities, their children surely would." This is the same dream that brings so many to America. We benefit and they benefit.

We should admire his mother's courage and all that Borjas has accomplished. And by all means, we should read and ponder his book. But in the end it is George Borjas's life, not his book, that teaches us the most about the right immigration policy for America.

SNAPSHOT: Migration

Global Shifts in Population

RAND

This selection originally appeared in *Population Matters*, Policy Brief RB-5044 (Santa Monica, Calif.: RAND Corporation, 2000).

THE U.S. IMMIGRATION DEBATE

Given the complexity of these issues and the fact that most developed countries have no history of immigration, it is instructive to look at the debate about immigration policy in the United States, where immigrants are currently responsible (directly and indirectly) for about two-thirds of total population growth. The debate centers around three key policy questions—how many to admit, whom to admit, and under what conditions to admit them—and focuses on the economic and social effects of immigration.

One important question concerns the distributional effects of immigration—that is, who wins and who loses. Typically, the winners are employers of immigrants and those who consume services produced by immigrants, while the losers are those who must compete with immigrants in the labor market. A related question concerns the effects of immigration on the public sector: do immigrants contribute more to the public coffers than they draw in services? Other questions pertain to the integration and assimilation of immigrants into the economy and into American society. Various studies show that immigration clearly has both costs and benefits, depending on the skill level of immigrants and the state of the economy. However, the public debate about these effects is complicated by interest groups that speak on every conceivable side of the issues and make it difficult to distinguish between public and private interests.

TWO WILD CARDS: ATTITUDES TOWARD GROWTH AND TECHNOLOGICAL CHANGE

Further complicating the public deliberations on immigration are evolving views of technological change and economic and population growth. One view, concerned about the effects of technological change on the environment, questions traditional assumptions about the benefits of technological progress. Proponents of this view suggest that technological innovations driven by the need to sustain population growth may be doing more harm than good. A related view holds that population growth and economic development should be rejected because environmental degradation is too high a price to pay for them. These emerging attitudes are wild cards because it is not clear how they will influence the immigration debate. If technological change comes to be widely viewed as more of a problem than a solution, and if population growth is increasingly seen as a threat to the environment, the West will find it more difficult to embrace immigration.

BEYOND DEMOGRAPHICS

The growing pressure on the developed world to admit immigrants will be difficult to resolve. It raises issues that go well beyond demographics. Ultimately, the debate will push the United States and other parts of the West to address central questions about what their societies value most. Moreover, given today's growing global interdependence, neither the United States nor the other developed countries can solve immigration problems unilaterally. They must consider the consequences of their policies on the larger system of exchange in which they have a central stake. Finally, because social and economic realities change so quickly, it would be wise to promote greater flexibility in immigration policies, allowing them to be adapted to changing conditions. At present, public opinion on all aspects of immigration is poorly informed and volatile. Leadership is needed to frame the issue and clarify the benefits and costs so that informed public opinion can direct the political process toward ends that will ultimately prove useful.

FIGURE 3.6.   Immigration to the United States

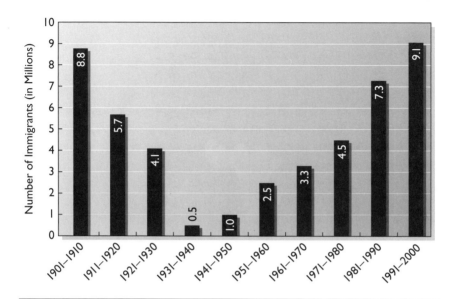

Source: Population Reference Bureau (1999). *Reports on America. America's Diversity: On the Edge of Two Centuries.* Washington, D.C.: Population Reference Bureau. Available over the Internet at http://www.prb.org/Content/NavigationMenu/PRB/AboutPRB/Reports_on_America/ReportonAmer icaTwoCenturies.pdf. U.S. Department of Justice, 2000.

Chapter Eleven

WAR AND VIOLENCE

What is the relationship between population and national security?

The Transformation of Security

Michael Renner

This selection was excerpted from *Fighting for Survival: Environmental Decline, Social Conflict, and the New Age of Insecurity* (Washington, D.C.: Worldwatch Institute, 1996).

The phenomena of globalization and fragmentation and the nature of the social, economic, and environmental pressures worldwide call for a fundamentally different understanding of the meaning of security—who is to be secure and by what means?—and hence for a new set of priorities.

Conditioned by a worldview that largely equates security with military strength, traditional analysts tend to regard emerging issues simply as new "threats" to be deterred. By subsuming these new issues under the old thinking of national military security, efforts to address them in effect become militarized. Hence, weapons proliferation is countered by developing new weapons for preemptive raids on foreign arms facilities instead of by promoting disarmament; refugees are seen as menacing hordes to be intercepted on the high seas instead of as people forced from their homes by poverty; environmental degradation is seen as simply another item in which national interests are to be protected against those of other nations instead of acknowledging the common challenge; and the proliferation of drugs is tackled through the military eradicating cocaine crops instead of through efforts to provide alternative livelihoods for desperate peasants.

But many sources of conflict are simply not amenable to any military "solution." Poverty, unequal distribution of land, and the degradation of ecosystems are among the most real and pressing issues undermining people's security. Soldiers, tanks, or warplanes are at best irrelevant in this context, and more likely an obstacle. The military absorbs substantial resources that could help reduce the potential for violent conflict if invested in health, housing, education, poverty eradication, and environmental sustainability.

The past two decades have witnessed a series of efforts to reconceptualize the meaning of security. Recognizing that competitive national security policies had yielded international insecurity, in the early 1980s the Independent Commission on Disarmament and Security, chaired by Swedish Prime Minister Olof Palme, embraced the concept of "common security"—the argument that for a state to be secure, its opponents must feel secure. In the 1980s and 1990s, additional reconceptualizations questioned whether state security was the proper focus and argued that environmental and other nonmilitary factors were at least as important as military ones. The *Human Development Report* produced by the U.N. Development Programme has woven together the different strands of these redefinition efforts and coined the term human security, which is used throughout *Fighting for Survival.*

The twentieth century has seen the pursuit of national security elevated to near theological levels; modern military technology has dramatically increased the destructive power of weaponry, the range and speed of delivery vehicles, and the sophistication of targeting technologies. Yet arms ostensibly designed to enhance security increasingly imperil humanity's survival. We live in what is the most violent time in human history: the twentieth century accounts for 75 percent of all war deaths inflicted since the rise of the Roman Empire.

As we approach the twenty-first century, the key question is whether we will see a continuation of the current era or a departure in security policies that focuses less on the symptoms and more on the root causes of conflict and insecurity, less on the dangers from abroad and more on the perils from within.

An understanding of security consonant with the realities of today's world requires a shift from conflict-laden to cooperative approaches, from national to global security. Rather than defense of the status quo, human security calls for change and adaptation; rather than a fine-tuning of arms and recalibration of military strategies, it calls for demilitarization, conversion of war-making institutions, and new priorities for sustainable development.

The Security Dynamics of Demographic Factors

Brian Nichiporuk

This selection was excerpted from *The Security Dynamics of Demographic Factors* (Santa Monica, Calif.: RAND Corporation, 2000).

As American policymakers stand at the beginning of the twenty-first century, they tend to view weapons proliferation, hypernationalism, ethnic and tribal conflict, political repression, and protectionism as the principal threats to the open, liberal international order they are trying to create. All these factors are indeed dangerous and worthy of attention, but the risk posed to U.S. security interests around the world by demographic factors must not be neglected either. The dynamics of population growth, settlement patterns, and movement across borders will have an effect on international security in the upcoming decades, and Washington can do much to solidify its geopolitical position in critical regions by anticipating demographic shifts that have security implications and by working with allies, friends, and international organizations to deal effectively with the causes and consequences of these shifts.

The nature of the future international security environment will be determined by complex interactions between geopolitical alignments, technological advances, economic developments, demographic factors, and environmental trends. It is not the intention of this report to explain or even map out these interactions, as that would be far beyond our scope. *However, it is clear from even a cursory analysis of the national security literature on demographic effects that population pressures and movements by themselves do not cause armed conflict*; rather, demographic shifts occurring in political environments that are already tense because of territorial disputes, ethnic rivalries, ideological divides, environmental stresses, and so on, can very often be just the spark needed to transform a tense situation into a violent conflict or perhaps even outright war. Demographic factors therefore need to be viewed by the analyst as a potentially important contributor to armed conflict, one that interacts with other variables in a complex series of linkages and feedback loops to cause the tensions that are often precursors to political violence.

Clearly, demographic issues and concerns have weighed on the minds of policymakers and scholars throughout the modern era, so it is legitimate to pose the following question: why do the security dynamics of demographic factors merit consideration now, at the outset of the twenty-first century? The simple answer to this question is that there are a number of current trends that heighten the importance of the demographic–national security nexus. The end of the Cold War has forced security analysts to widen their scope of thinking both functionally and geographically as broadened notions of the threat to U.S. interests have come to the fore. Moreover, increasing globalization in the form of rapidly multiplying mass communications links (satellite TV, Internet, etc.) has made it more difficult for American leaders to ignore demographic-induced instability in even remote regions of the world. Accompanying these broadened notions of threat has been an increasing focus within the U.S. military on such nontraditional missions as peacekeeping and humanitarian assistance, missions that are sometimes required because of demographic factors such as sudden refugee movements. Finally, one sees increasingly stark differences between the demographic profiles of high- and low-fertility nations, the implications of which have yet to be fully explored. However, one can hypothesize that these diverging trends will have some effect on the views of both developing and developed nations toward different options for achieving security.

SNAPSHOT: Conflict

Violent Conflicts Continue to Decline

Michael Renner

This selection originally appeared in *Vital Signs 2003* (Washington, D.C.: Worldwatch Institute, 2003).

According to Arbeitsgemeinschaft Kriegsursachenforschung (AKUF), a conflict research group at the University of Hamburg, the number of wars worldwide stood at twenty-eight in 2002, down from thirty-one the previous year. In addition, there were seventeen "armed conflicts" in 2002 that were not of sufficient severity to meet AKUF's criteria for war. Combining both categories, the total number of violent clashes declined slightly—from forty-eight in 2001 to forty-five. (See table 3.4.)

The overall number declined because the number of conflicts ending—those in the Kurdish areas of eastern Turkey, the Democratic Republic of the Congo, Guinea, Kosovo, Iran, Tajikistan, and Uzbekistan—surpassed those newly erupting—in Côte d'Ivoire, Madagascar, Congo-Brazzaville, and the Central African Republic.

Meanwhile, the U.S.-led "war on terror," initially focused on the Afghan Taliban regime, more and more has the makings of an open-ended campaign of worldwide scope. The Bush administration's words and actions made it seem all but inevitable that an invasion of Iraq would occur in 2003. Other countries, including Russia, China, India, Indonesia, and Israel, have also cited antiterrorism as an excuse for wars or acts of internal repression.

The armed forces of countries on whose territory fighting is taking place number in the millions, but it is unclear how many of their soldiers are actually engaged in combat. Nonstate armed groups worldwide have at least some 350,000 fighters. Of these, about 140,000 were with groups that observed ceasefires or were otherwise inactive in 2002. Some 300,000 children are among government or opposition forces involved in fighting.

TABLE 3.4. Wars and Armed Conflicts

Year	Wars	Wars and Armed Conflicts (number)	Year	Wars	Wars and Armed Conflicts (number)
1950	13	—	1985	41	—
1955	15	—	1986	43	—
1960	12	—	1987	44	—
1965	28	—	1988	45	—
1970	31	—	1989	43	—
1971	31	—	1990	50	—
1972	30	—	1991	54	—
1973	30	—	1992	55	—
1974	30	—	1993	48	65
1975	36	—	1994	44	61
1976	34	—	1995	34	49
1977	36	—	1996	30	48
1978	37	—	1997	29	47
1979	38	—	1998	33	50
1980	37	—	1999	35	49
1981	38	—	2000	35	47
1982	40	—	2001	31	48
1983	40	—	2002		
1984	41	—	(prelim.)	28	45

Source: AKUF and the Institute for Political Science at the University of Hamburg.

Measuring whether the world is becoming more or less violent is not an easy task. Information is often incomplete or contradictory. And definitional and methodological problems confound efforts to establish unambiguous categories and thresholds to tally the number of armed conflicts.

Researchers at the Heidelberg Institute for International Conflict Research in Germany are assessing political conflict trends from a broader perspective. The total number of conflicts has increased from 108 in 1992 to 173 in 2002. Of these, violent conflicts have recently accounted for a fairly steady one-quarter share. The seventeen conflicts that escalated during 2002 were more than outweighed by thirty-one de-escalated cases.

The majority of conflicts are resolved by nonviolent means, including negotiations and other diplomatic efforts. In addition to various peace-keeping efforts, negotiations took place in forty-three conflicts in 2002, resulting in three peace treaties (in Chad, the Moluccas, and Aceh) and seven cease-fire agreements (which were successful in Angola, Sri Lanka, and Somalia). U.N. arms embargoes and other sanctions were maintained in eight cases.

Researchers at the Interdisciplinary Research Project on Root Causes of Human Rights Violations (PIOOM) in the Netherlands have made an even more extensive effort to capture a broader multitude of conflicts, including intercommunal conflicts not recorded elsewhere. PIOOM finds that there are more than three hundred "political tension situations"—hard-to-monitor cases that typically either predate violent conflict or follow it, possibly giving rise to renewed violence ("The PIOOM Experience with Mapping Dimensions of Contemporary Conflicts and Human Rights Violations" [Amsterdam, 2000]). These findings underscore the fact that today's human rights violations, inequalities, and environmental destruction often end up as tomorrow's wars.

The number of wars alone cannot of course convey the severity of warfare in terms of human suffering, political instability, or social, economic, and environmental damage inflicted. AKUF estimates that more than 7 million people, most of them civilians, have died in the course of the forty-five wars and armed conflicts currently active. Cumulatively, these conflicts have cost at least $250 billion—imposing a heavy toll on countries that for the most part are already desperately poor. And the cost of reconstruction could be much higher.

POPULATION AND PROSPERITY

PART IV: QUICK FACTS

"Just as we have laws compelling death control, so we must have laws requiring birth control—the purpose being to ensure a zero rate of population increase. We must come to see that it is the duty of government to protect women against pregnancy as it protects them against job discrimination and smallpox, and for the same reason—the public good. No longer can we tolerate the doctrinaire position that the number of children a couple has is a strictly private decision carrying no social consequences."

Dr. Edward Chasteen, *The Ultimate Resource II* (1998)

"It is coming to be widely believed that the results of allowing parents freely to decide how many children they have must, in the long run, be catastrophic under any tolerable social institutions. It is already widely believed that the results of allowing parents freely to decide how many children they have, in the United States, have already proved catastrophic, or soon will. I can find no justification in economic theory for the first belief. I can find no justification in either economic theory or the present circumstances of this country for the second."

David Friedman, *Laissez Faire in Population: The Least Bad Solution* (1972)

- An estimated 38 percent of all pregnancies occurring around the world every year are unintended, and about six out of ten such unplanned pregnancies result in induced abortion.

World Health Organization, *Family Planning* (2003)

- One hundred thirteen million school-age children (ages six to eleven) are not in school—97 percent of them in developing nations.

United Nations Educational, Scientific, and Cultural Organization, *The Millennium Development Goals: Progress, Reversals, and Challenge* (2000)
(See figure 4.1 and table 4.1 for more information on educational attainment.)

- Since 1990, fifty-four countries are poorer, as measured by per capita gross domestic product (GDP). Per capita GDP fell in twenty sub-Saharan African nations, seventeen nations in eastern Europe, six in Latin America, and six in east Asia and the Pacific.

United Nations, *Human Development Report* (2003)
(See figure 4.2 for further information.)

- Since 1980, eighty-one countries have taken significant steps towards democracy, with thirty-three military regimes replaced by civilian governments.

  United Nations, *Human Development Report* (2002)

- The twentieth century saw unparalleled economic growth, with global per capita GDP increasing almost fivefold.

  International Monetary Agency, *Globalization: Threat or Opportunity?* (2000)

  (See figure 4.3.)

INTRODUCTION

Population and Prosperity

Experts have debated the impact of population growth on human prosperity for decades. The population pessimists (neo-Malthusians) assert that rapid population growth will inhibit development. The push for family planning programs and other policies designed to limit growth can be credited to this viewpoint. Population optimists (neoinstitutionalists) have taken the opposite stance: population growth has a net positive effect because it promotes economic prosperity by creating more human capital and increasing market size. The purpose of part 4 is to explore these differing perspectives and how they play out in the real world.

For many people, the population problem equates to a fear that global population growth will overwhelm the capacity of economic systems and of the global ecosystem. A few possible solutions to this problem include (1) a reproductive health approach with an emphasis on women's health and basic rights, (2) focus on the power of education to influence the pace of population growth, and (3) redistribution of wealth to third world nations to help eliminate poverty—the root cause of overpopulation (according to the United Nations Population Fund). These types of approaches require decisive government action at the local, national, and international level.

On the other hand, human welfare advanced more during the twentieth century than it did throughout the rest of humankind's tenure on earth—thanks in part to the largest population pool in human history. This progress in human well-being is often credited to institutions that promote economic growth, technological advances, and free trade. A substantial amount of evidence suggests that growth based on institutions such as the rule of law and property rights, rapid diffusion of new technologies, and liberalization of trade offer the best hope for prosperity over the long run.

Worries about population growth and the state of humanity have come full circle: from the Malthusian concern over natural resources such as land, to the focus on physical capital, to a more recent spotlight on human capital, and back again to natural constraints with an emphasis on renewable resources. Should policies be designed to limit population growth, or would a laissez faire approach lead to greater prosperity over time?

Population and Economic Growth: Theory

Richard Easterlin

This selection was excerpted from "Malthus Revisited," in *Growth Triumphant: The Twenty-First Century in Historical Perspective* (Ann Arbor, Mich.: University of Michigan, 1998).

As I have shown, the central feature of modern economic growth is an immense and continuous rise in productivity. The fundamental basis for such productivity growth has been technological innovation on a widespread and continuous scale. This has required a marked rise in schooling and capital investment per worker.

The question of the effect of population growth on economic development thus centers on the issue of its productivity impact, either directly via increasing the labor supply or indirectly through its concurrent influence on other productivity determinants such as technological change, education, and capital investment. In the following I take up, first, arguments for negative effects, then those for positive effects.

The most common reasoning regarding negative effects, the Malthusian analysis, is rooted in the law of diminishing returns. If total output were unaffected by the growth of population, then a rise in the rate of population growth would entail a corresponding reduction in the growth of output per head of the population. But such a simplified view overlooks the fact that, with due allowance for the lag between birth and labor force entry, population growth implies growth in the labor supply and thus in productive capacity. Thus, population growth should raise total output. The Malthusian view, however, stresses that the growth in output would not be proportionate to the increase in labor supply. Labor is but one of the inputs in the production process, and only if other inputs were increased in the same proportion as labor might one expect output to grow correspondingly. If nonlabor inputs do not increase proportionately with labor, and if production methods remain unchanged, then one would expect output to grow less than proportionately to labor, reducing output per worker. To put it differently, if technology is assumed to be fixed, then population growth coupled with slower or zero growth in one or more other productive inputs implies that, on average, there will be progressively less materials, equipment, or natural resources for each worker to use and, hence, that output per worker will tend to diminish.

Traditionally, in this reasoning the fixity of natural resources, particularly land, is most often emphasized, and the inference is drawn that agricultural productivity, and thus food supplies per capita, will progressively diminish. Of course, if the new workers provided by population growth simply increase the under- or unemployed and do not add to the actual labor input in the economy, then the productivity of employed labor would be unaffected. However, since the same total output must be shared among progressively greater numbers, output per head of the total population would decline.

Historically, the Malthusian theory was the dominant antipopulation-growth argument. In the 1950s, however, a highly influential variant known as the Coale-Hoover analysis moved to the forefront. This approach concerns itself with the relation to population not of natural resources but of reproducible capital—structures, equipment, and inventories. In this analysis, the stock of reproducible capital is taken as normally growing rather than constant, at a rate varying with the proportion of national income invested. If population and labor force were constant, then capital per worker and, hence, output per worker would normally grow over time. Population and labor force growth, however, imply a reduction in the increase of capital per worker—part of the addition to capital being required simply to keep the stock of capital per worker constant—and the consequent slowing down of the growth of output per worker. This analysis thus sees high population growth not necessarily as reducing the *level* of output per head but as lowering the rate of increase—the higher the rate of population increase, the greater the reduction in the *growth* of output per head. This reasoning has often been used in discussions of development plans in developing countries, where the proportion of national income invested is a strategic planning variable, usually taken as determined by the plan. High population growth is seen as using up limited additions to capital resources on "unproductive" investment such as housing as well as diverting government revenues that might have been used for capital formation to "current" expenditures on items such as education and health.

The proportion of national income invested depends not only on government capital formation but also on private saving and investing decisions. The question arises whether population growth may affect private decisions and thereby influence the growth of capital, both total and per worker. The Coale-Hoover analysis addresses this issue, stressing the adverse consequences of high fertility on the age structure of the population and through this on personal savings rates. High fertility tends to produce a population with a relatively large proportion of people below working age and thus a situation in which the number of dependents per worker is relatively high. This dependency burden creates pressures on the household to spend currently for consumption rather than save. The lower rate of private saving in turn keeps down private investment.

Putting these arguments—Malthusian and Coale-Hoover—together, rapid population growth in developing nations is seen as creating pressures on limited natural resources, as reducing private and public capital formation, and as diverting additions to capital resources toward merely maintaining rather than increasing the stock of capital per worker. In consequence, the growth of output per employed worker is retarded, or underemployment and unemployment grow. Output per head of the total population grows at a reduced rate or actually declines in absolute levels. The concern with such problems is manifest in past governmental statements in response to United Nations inquiries on problems resulting from the interaction of economic development and population change. An excerpt from Sri Lanka's reply provides an illustration:

> Unless there is some prospect of a slowing down in the rate of population growth and relative stability in at least the long run, it is difficult to envisage substantial benefits from planning and development. It is not so much the size of the population in an absolute sense; but rather the rate of increase that tends to frustrate attempts to step up the rate of investment and to increase income per head. Apart from the difficult process of cutting present levels of consumption, the source for increasing the volume of investment is the "ploughing back" of portions of future increase in incomes. This task

is handicapped if these increases have instead to be devoted each year to sustaining a large population.

Turning to favorable effects, the most common argument for the positive effect of population growth on economic development, harking back to Adam Smith, relates to economies of scale and specialization. Within a productive establishment there tends at any given time to be an optimum scale of operation, large in some industries, small in others. If the population is small, then the domestic market may not be able to support the most efficient level of operation in large industries. Extending one's view from an establishment in a given industry to the economy as a whole brings into view added productivity gains associated with increased size. Nobel laureate George Stigler has pointed out some of the specific gains:

> The large economy can practice specialization in innumerable ways not open to the small (closed) economy. The labor force can specialize in more sharply defined functions. . . . The business sector can have enterprises specializing in collecting oil prices, in repairing old machinery, in printing calendars, in advertising industrial equipment. The transport system can be large enough to allow innumerable specialized forms of transport, such as pipelines, particular types of chemical containers, and the like.

It does not follow, however, that any given nation must have a population large enough to realize all or even most of such gains if it is willing to participate in international trade. Through specialization in particular branches of economic activity and exchange with other nations, it is possible for a nation using modern technology to achieve high levels of economic development. This is one important argument for customs unions and free trade areas among nations. It helps explain how among the richest nations today there are some with small populations; for example, Norway, Finland, Denmark, Israel, and New Zealand all have populations around five million or less.

An argument put forward by perhaps the leading opponent of the doomsday theorists, Julian Simon, stresses the positive effect of population on the growth of knowledge and thus technological change. Building on a suggestion of Simon Kuznets, Simon argues that more children create new knowledge because of both the extra demand for output and the additional supply of minds as well as the larger number of possible fruitful interactions thereby made possible.

Another argument for the positive effect of population growth on economic growth centers on the impact of the pressure of increased family size on individual motivation. It may be illustrated by comparison with the Malthusian approach. Assume, in a population with initially a zero growth rate, that a substantial cut occurs in the infant mortality rate owing, say, to a new public health measure. The effect will be to raise dependency and, with a lag, the labor supply. The Malthusian view reasons that, with no change in production methods or other productive factors, the employment of this extra labor will reduce output per worker and consumption per head of the population.

At this point one might ask, if consumption levels were, indeed, so threatened, would human beings be oblivious to the effect on their well-being of the growth in dependency? If a rise in dependency creates a threat either to maintaining existing consumption levels or to future improvements in them, will individuals passively accept this consequence? Or will the threat posed by this "population pressure" motivate changes in behavior? At least two broad alternatives to passive acceptance of declining living levels come to mind. One, first stressed in sociologist Kingsley Davis's presidential address to the Population Association of America, is a change in demographic behavior, a reduction in fertility, or a rise in out-migration. Looking back at western European experience over the last century and a half, Davis asserts:

> The fact is that every country in northwest Europe reacted to its persistent excess of births over deaths with virtually the entire range of possible responses. Regardless of nationality, language, and religion, each industrializing nation tended to postpone marriage, to increase celibacy, to resort to abortion, to practice contraception in some form, and to emigrate overseas.

The stimulus to this, in Davis's view, was the Mortality Revolution and sustained natural increase to which it gave rise:

> Mortality decline impinged on the individual by enlarging his family. Unless something were done to offset this effect, it gave him, as a child, more siblings with whom to share whatever derived from his parents as well as more

likelihood of reckoning with his parents for a longer period of life; and, as an adult, it gave him a more fragmented and more delayed share of this patrimony with which to get married and found his own family, while at the same time it saddled him, in founding that family, with the task of providing for more children—for rearing them, educating them, endowing their marriages, and so on—in a manner assuring them a status no lower than his.

Another alternative to passive acceptance of lower living levels is a change in productive rather than demographic behavior, such as the adoption of new production methods or an increase in saving to use more capital in production. A leading exponent of such positive effects of population pressure has been Ester Boserup. She argues that what are typically regarded as more advanced agricultural techniques have actually required more labor time per unit output, that is, the sacrifice of leisure. Historically, therefore, populations that have been aware of the availability of more advanced methods have often resisted their adoption until population growth raised population density to a point that compelled the adoption of such methods in order to maintain consumption levels. With this shift to more advanced methods may come better work habits and other changes facilitating sustained economic growth (although leisure time would decline, according to this theory). Some support for a positive association between population density and more advanced techniques has been found in empirical work on tropical agriculture.

It is clear that this line of reasoning does not lead inexorably to the conclusion that economic growth is promoted by the pressure arising from accelerated population growth (nor need population growth be the only threat to income levels inducing such change). Whether there is a change in production behavior depends on many conditions, including the education of those involved, the supply of information, and institutional conditions that may impede change along some lines or favor it in other directions. But the Davis and Boserup arguments do raise a valid issue that is often neglected in discussions of the effects of population growth: the effect of population pressure on individual motivation. To the proponent of the view that population pressure induces favorable behavioral change, government planners who bewail population growth as excessive are perhaps assuming for themselves undue responsibility and influence in the promotion of economic growth and are failing to allow for the possible significance for the growth process of the increased individual initiative, enterprise, and saving that population growth may spur.

Chapter Twelve

PROSPERITY BY DESIGN

Does solving the "population problem" require institutional management?

Women and Fertility

Population Control and Women's Health: Balancing the Scales

Adrienne Germain and Jane Ordway

This selection was excerpted from "Population Control and Women's Health: Balancing the Scales" (New York: International Women's Health Coalition, 1989).

To most people, the "population problem" means "overpopulation"— primarily in the third world, where three-quarters of the world's 5 billion people live. Overpopulation conjures up images of malnourished and dying children, burgeoning slums, deforestation and desertification, an unending cycle of poverty, disease, illiteracy, and social and political chaos. Population growth, along with poorly planned industrialization and environmental destruction, are seen as threats to sustaining life at acceptable levels in the future.

Hoping to change this devastating prospect, family planning and related programs have supplied millions of women in the third world with contraceptives that would otherwise be unavailable to them. Most such programs have viewed women as producers of too many babies and as potential contraceptive "acceptors." The tendency to neglect other aspects of women's reproductive health has often undermined or negated the achievement of effective and widespread contraceptive use, however. For example, inappropriate contraceptive use because of poor counseling, and high discontinuation rates because of side effects or infection, among other causes, are common in the third world.

The population problem and possible solutions need careful review and redefinition. A "reproductive health" approach, with women at its center, could considerably strengthen the achievements of existing family planning and health programs, while helping women to attain health, dignity, and basic rights.

A reproductive health approach requires

- Reallocation of resources among existing programs;
- Attention to currently neglected reproductive health issues;
- Changes in training and reward systems to enable and encourage service providers to offer choices and to treat women with respect;
- Services for girls and women currently excluded from programs;
- Commitment not only to improving contraceptive understanding and use but also to empowering women to manage their overall health and sexuality; and
- Increased participation by women in reproductive health policy and program decisions to build political will and institutional impetus for program changes.

USE OF CONTRACEPTION GLOBALLY

Of 800 million couples of reproductive age in the world (most of them in the third world), only 40 percent are today estimated to use modern contraception. Approximately 2.5–5.0 percent say they use abstinence, withdrawal, or other traditional methods. In China, as well as most developed countries, 70 percent or more of couples use contraception.

Surveys suggest that in Latin America and the Caribbean, some 50–60 percent of fertile couples do not use contraception on average; in most developing Asian countries (except China), about 60–80 percent do not; in the Middle East and North Africa, about 75 percent do not; and in Africa south of the Sahara, 90 percent do not use any form of contraception.

WHY BIRTHRATES ARE HIGH

Populations grow rapidly for many reasons. First, because of declining mortality and rapid population growth in the past twenty years, the number of women entering the reproductive ages (fifteen to forty-nine years) is increasing in the third world. This produces a built-in "demographic momentum" for rapid future growth.

Second, from the perspective of individual couples in the third world, high fertility is often beneficial. Children can be important sources of labor and income, old age security, social status, and enjoyment. Many couples know that some of their children are likely to die before the age of five, as infant mortality rates in many countries remain tragically high. People therefore have many children to ensure that some survive.

Third, the means of reproductive choice are often not available to women and men who want them. The lack of sex education and contraceptive services, together with tradition and the wider social environment, mean that many women in the third world spend most of their lives pregnant or lactating, recovering from pregnancy and birth, or coping with the effects of clandestine abortion.

Even when services are available, women often do not have a choice in the matter. The preference for sons over daughters, pressures from men and in-laws, and male dominance of sexual relations may force women to have more pregnancies than they otherwise would.

MORE THAN A PROBLEM OF CONTRACEPTION

Solving the "population problem" requires more than simply the provision of contraceptives. Fertility control involves the most intimate of human relations, complex behavior, and substantial risk. To control their own reproduction, therefore, women must also be able to achieve social status and dignity, to manage their own health and sexuality, and to exercise their basic rights in society and in partnerships with men.

Early sexual relations and pregnancy, however, curtail education, employment, and other social and political opportunities for millions of young women in the third world, just as they do for 1 million teenage women in the United States every year. The prevention of adolescent pregnancy will require social acceptance of sex education and contraceptive services for teens, wide-ranging support for the development of young women's self-esteem, and other interventions that are politically or otherwise challenging.

Third world women who become pregnant face a risk of death due to pregnancy that is fifty to two hundred times higher than that of women in industrial countries. Pregnant adolescents frequently face obstructed labor that culminates in death or serious physical damage. Sixty percent of pregnant women in the third world are anemic, which makes them especially vulnerable to problems in pregnancy and labor that result in death. Over half, in some countries 80–90 percent, of pregnant women give birth without trained assistance or emergency care. As many as 250,000 to 375,000 women are estimated to die annually when giving birth. This tragedy is intensified many-fold by its effect on the families left behind.

Fears about the safety of modern contraceptives are strong deterrents to contraceptive use. Women must bear most of the social and health risks of modern contraception, partly because contraceptive methods available to men are extremely limited in number and appeal. Condoms have no side effects and can be very useful in preventing the spread of disease, but men are often reluctant to use them and women are not in a position to persuade them to. Similarly, vasectomy, safer and simpler than female sterilization, is practiced far less in the third world. Thus, population control requires the development of new and improved contraceptive methods.

Increasingly, women in the third world who do not want to be pregnant avoid pregnancy by using contraception effectively. But millions of women have unwanted pregnancies. Many of these carry their pregnancies to term and end up with one to three more children than they want. Every year an estimated 30–45 million pregnant third world women who cannot accept a birth resort to abortion And every year, at least 125,000 of them—and quite possibly at least twice that many—die in the process. Uncounted others are rendered sterile or suffer severe chronic health consequences. Those who survive abortion often face greatly increased risk of death in subsequent pregnancies.

Sexuality and sexual relationships are fraught with other dangers for girls and women that also affect their views about fertility and contraception. First, millions suffer sexually transmitted diseases (STDs), including AIDS, transmitted by men. As a result of STDs, botched abortion, harmful surgical practices, or their partners' infertility, among other causes, millions of women are subfertile or infertile. They live in dread of divorce and social ostracism because they cannot bear children. Second, millions are subject to violence because of their gender—rape, incest, and emotional and physical battering by husbands or relatives.

"Population" is a fundamentally human problem. The solutions must be both humane and responsive to the complexities of people's behavior. For both humanitarian and political reasons, those concerned about population growth need also to reaffirm their commitment to individual well-being. That commitment can be enacted by making reproductive choices possible, by modifying program approaches to emphasize quality of care, and by recognizing and seeking to meet women's multiple reproductive health needs. The potential scope for innovation is broad. In setting program priorities, it is essential to recognize that the woman is important in her own right, as well as the key actor in fertility regulation and in infant and child health. Her needs, not just those of her children, family, and society, must be central. Alliances for this purpose will be to the benefit of all.

SNAPSHOT: China

Family Planning in China: A Strategic Policy That Suits National Conditions

This selection was excerpted from "White Paper on Family Planning in China 1995" (Beijing: Information Office of the State Council of the People's Republic of China, 1995).

The population problem is an important question that touches on the survival and development of the Chinese nation, the success or failure of China's modernization drive, as well as the sustained and coordinated development of the population on the one hand, and the economy, society, resources, and environment on the other. It is a natural choice that the Chinese government has made to implement family planning, control population growth, and improve the quality of life—a state policy based on the wish to make the state strong and powerful, the nation prosperous, and the people happy.

After the founding of the People's Republic of China, because of the stable society, developing production, and improved medical and health care conditions, people lived and worked in peace and happiness. The death rate was reduced markedly while population increased rapidly; thus the period was characterized by more births, fewer deaths, and higher growth. It should be pointed out that this was an inevitable phenomenon at the time. But, just as the international community did not respond promptly to the question of swelling global population, China lost the chance to solve the problem of overly rapid population growth in the first birth peak period after the founding of New China.

In the 1960s, China's population entered its second peak birth period. From 1962 to 1972, the annual number of births in China averaged 26.69

million, totaling 300 million. In 1969, China's population exceeded 800 million. Beginning in the 1960s, the contradiction between the population on the one hand, and the economy, society, resources, and environment on the other, became gradually apparent. In view of the situation, the Chinese government issued a call for family planning and advocated the use of contraceptives. However, as there was still little understanding of the seriousness of the population problem and the government still had not worked out a clear population policy, family planning was not effectively carried out throughout the country.

In the early 1970s, the Chinese government became increasingly aware that the overly rapid growth of population was unfavorable to economic and social development. The government decided to carry out family planning energetically in both urban and rural areas and to integrate the plan for population development into the plan for economic and social development. Consequently, family planning work entered a new phase of development.

At the end of the 1970s, Deng Xiaoping, the chief architect of China's reform and opening to the outside world, made an in-depth analysis of China's national conditions based on the experience and lessons of socialist construction since the founding of the People's Republic. He pointed out that, to accomplish the goal of the four modernizations in China, it was imperative to take into consideration the basic features of the Chinese environment, that is, the vast scale of the country, its weak foundation, its massive population, and the low ratio of cultivated land, all of which demonstrated an objective need for coordinating the development of population with the development of the economy, society, resources, and environment. Deng Xiaoping's major contribution to the solution of China's population problem was to advocate the study and treatment of the population problem in the larger context of national economic and social development and to clearly point out the importance and strategic significance of China's population policy. In accord with Deng Xiaoping's thinking, the Chinese government has made it a basic state policy to carry out family planning and population control and to improve the quality of life and has clearly incorporated this policy in the

Constitution of the People's Republic of China, thus establishing the importance of family planning in China's overall task of economic and social development. By February 15, 1995, China's population had reached 1.2 billion. Over the past few years, annual births have averaged about 21 million, with a net annual increase of 14 million. Such massive total population and annual population growth constitute a heavy burden for China, a country that has a weak foundation and little cultivated land, whose economic development is rather low, and where development is regionally imbalanced. The negative effect of China's overabundant population has permeated all aspects of social and economic life; in fact, many difficulties China has encountered in its economic and social development are directly related to the problem of population.

"Food is the first necessity of the people"; and solving the problem of feeding a population of 1.2 billion is a big challenge to China. Cultivated land in China accounts for only one-tenth of its territory. In contrast, cultivated land in India accounts for 55 percent of its territory, with a per capita average twice that of China. Although cultivated land in the United States makes up only 20 percent of its territory, still its per capita average is nine times that of China. The greatest pressure on China's agriculture, particularly grain production, is the continuous growth of population and incessant shrinkage of cultivated land. The United States and India, as well as China, are all major grain-producing nations. Though its cultivated land is less than that of the United States or India, China ranks first in the world in grain output; its per-unit grain yield is much higher than the world average. But, as China's population is almost five times that of the United States, its per capita share of grain is less than one-fourth of the latter's. In 1993, despite a bumper harvest in China's grain production, the per capita share of grain was only 387.3 kilograms. Forecasts show that China's per capita share of grain will remain at the low level of less than 400 kilograms of crude grain for an extended period because of the continued growth of population in the future. If China fails to effectively check the overly rapid growth of population and alleviate the great pressure wrought by population growth on cultivated land, forests, and water resources, an ecological and environmental deterioration will be inevitable in the coming decades, profoundly endangering the minimum living conditions of the overwhelming majority of Chinese people as well as the sustainable development of their society and economy.

Although China's abundant labor force is of course conducive to development, it will be difficult to tackle the employment problem of a continuously growing labor force under the shortage of funds and relative insufficiency of resources. Nearly 20 million young people reach working age in China every year, and most of them need jobs. The surplus labor force in China's rural areas has reached 120 million, and by the year 2000 the rural surplus labor force will exceed the 200 million mark. Although the state has adopted various measures to open up channels for employment and satisfactory results have been achieved, there are still large numbers of people in the plight of job-waiting or recessive unemployment. Only by resolutely controlling population growth while making energetic efforts to develop the economy and create new employment opportunities will it be possible to make the growth of the work force fall in step with the demand of economic development for the work force. Despite the rapid pace of economic development, the continuous improvements in China's national strength, and the leap of China to the world's front rank in gross national product since the adoption of reform and the opening to the outside world, the country's per capita gross national product still lags behind and remains lower than average for developing countries because of China's huge population. Owing to excessively rapid population growth, the state's accumulation has become relatively less; funds that can be invested in educational, medical and health care, and other social services are limited; and there are significant difficulties in further improving cultural quality and health, particularly in the massive rural population and the population living in areas haunted by poverty.

It is precisely to bring about sustained economic growth and sustainable development, to satisfy the daily increasing material and cultural demands, and to guarantee the fundamental and long-term interests of the current generation and their posterity, that the Chinese government has chosen the strategic policy of family planning. Facts have proved and will continue to prove that, together with energetic efforts to develop the economy, the comprehensive promotion of family planning in China since the latter half of the twentieth century has been the correct policy decision, bringing benefits to the present and constituting a meritorious service for the future.

Current Situation and Prospect

This selection was excerpted from "White Paper on Family Planning in China 2000" (Beijing: Information Office of the State Council of the People's Republic of China, 2000).

After nearly thirty years of effort, China has found a successful method for dealing with the population issue in a comprehensive manner, a path suited to the country's unique conditions. A system of regulating and adjusting population growth with a proper management mechanism through a family planning program has gradually been developed. This system is in keeping with the demands of the market economy and has achieved universally acknowledged success. The citizens' rights to subsistence and development and their rights socially, economically, and culturally have been substantially improved.

China's excessive population growth has been brought under effective control. The birthrate and natural growth rate decreased from 33.43 and 25.83 in 1970 to 15.23 and 8.77 in 1999, respectively. The total fertility rate fell below the replacement level, making China a country with one of the lower fertility rates in the world. Though economically underdeveloped, China has accomplished a historic transition in population reproductive pattern from a pattern featuring high birthrate, low death rate, and high growth rate to one featuring low birthrate, low death rate, and low growth rate in a relatively short period of time, a change that has taken decades or even as much as a hundred years for developed countries to realize in the past.

China's national economy has developed at a fast pace, with national strength notably increased and people's living standards greatly improved. Since the implementation of the family planning program, over 300 million births have been averted nationally, thus saving society a great amount in the cost of raising children. This has alleviated the pressure of excessive population growth on natural resources and the environment, thus contributing to economic development and better living standards.

With the gross national product (GNP) quadrupled over that of 1980 ahead of schedule, the Chinese people now live a relatively comfortable life. By the end of 1999, the population under the poverty line in rural areas had decreased from over 250 million in the late 1970s to 34 million, down from 33 percent to around 3 percent of the total rural population. Impoverished people in rural areas have basically achieved adequate nourishment and clothing.

Great achievements have been made in various social undertakings such as education and public health. By the end of 2000, a nine-year compulsory education program will be made universal, and illiteracy among young and middle-aged people will be basically eliminated. On average, the number of college students for every ten thousand people increased from 8.9 in 1978 to 32.8 in 1999. Nearly everyone has access to primary health care service. The maternal mortality rate has plummeted from 94.7 per one hundred thousand in 1990 to 56.2 per one hundred thousand in 1998. The hospitalized delivery rate reached over 66.8 percent in 1999. The average life expectancy increased to seventy-one years, the same as in medium-level developed countries.

Women's status has been raised substantially, children's rights protected, and the living standard of the elderly consistently improved. Currently, women account for more than one-third of all government functionaries, managerial personnel in state-owned enterprises and institutions, and professionals of all trades. In 1999, employed women composed 46.5 percent of the work force in China, compared with the world level of 34.5 percent, and women's income was 80.4 percent of men's. The mortality rate for children under five was forty-two per one hundred thousand in 1998, a decrease of 31.8 percent from that of 1991.

In 1999, the enrollment rate of school-age children reached 99.1 percent, and the rate of primary school graduates entering middle schools reached 94.4 percent. Also in 1999, the rate of one-year-old children inoculated with the bacillus Calmette-Guerin (BCG) vaccine was 97.8 percent, the polio vaccine 97.4 percent, the diphtheria-pertussis-tetanus (DPT) vaccine 97.8 percent, and the measles vaccine 97.5 percent. In the same year, nearly 30 million retired people throughout the country were covered in the basic retirement insurance scheme, and there were some one thousand social welfare institutions run by the government and around forty thousand community-run senior citizens' homes.

The whole society has gained a better understanding of the issue of population. It is agreed that population control is beneficial to the coordinated and sustainable development of population, economy, society, resources, and environment; that birth control should be stepped up and a laissez faire attitude should be guarded against; while slowing down population growth, efforts should be made to improve the reproductive health, quality of life, and well-being of the population to realize human development in an all-round way. The issue of population is essentially a problem of development and can only be solved through economic, social, and cultural development. The same period saw impressive changes in public attitudes toward marriage, childbearing, and supporting the elderly. The traditional concepts of "early marriage, early childbirth," "the more sons, the more happiness," and "men are superior to women" have been gradually replaced by the scientific and advanced concepts of "late marriage and later childbearing, fewer and healthier births" and "men and women are equal." More and more people are voluntarily practicing family planning. The marriage age for women of childbearing age averaged 23.57 years in 1998, compared with 20.8 years in 1970. The contraceptive prevalence rate of married women of childbearing age reached 83 percent, and the average family size decreased from 4.84 members in 1971 to 3.63 members in 1998.

International cooperation and exchange in the area of population and development have been expanded. China is fully aware that the solution of its own population and development problem is important to stabilizing global population and promoting world peace and development. In the light of its own specific conditions, China has followed the basic principles laid down at all international population conferences and has actively carried out relevant resolutions. Since the 1994 International Conference on Population and Development (ICPD), the Chinese government has adopted a series of measures to carry out the ICPD Program of Action. In recent years, China has worked in effective cooperation with international institutions and governmental and nongovernmental organizations of related countries in areas such as reproductive health, adolescent education, emergency contraception, male participation in family planning, and so on. The successful implementation of China's population and family planning program has provided useful experience and lessons for many others.

Education

Overall Impact of Education on Population Dynamics

This selection originally appeared in *Population and Education Policies as Part of an Integrated Sustainable Development* (Paris: United Nations Educational, Scientific, and Cultural Organization, 2001).

During the last decades the need for population policies as a component of overall development policies has been widely recognized, especially in developing countries. Population policies are increasingly seen as an essential element in a broader vision of development aimed at improving the quality of life of present and future generations. The aim is to establish a sustainable balance between demographic rates and social, economic, and environmental goals. In seeking this balance, education is expected to play a double role: contributing to economic growth and accelerating the demographic transition in developing countries.

Although the effect of population on education systems is direct and evident, the reciprocal effect of education on population is subtle, complex, and longer-term. Usually, education works, not alone, but in combination with other variables to affect population-related preferences and practices. Yet, both historical experience and empirical evidence suggest the power of education to influence the process and pace of demographic change.

Even if education is only one of the factors involved in the demographic transition, it is usually the factor most amenable to change through public policies. Public authorities can, for example, mandate school attendance, invest in school buildings, libraries, public television and radio, and indeed make a whole range of decisions aimed at extending the reach and improving the quality of education.

INFLUENCE OF EDUCATION IN THE EVOLUTION
OF DEMOGRAPHIC BEHAVIOR

Education shapes the attitudes, expectations, and self-image of individuals as well as the way they are perceived and regarded by others. It influences many fundamental aspects of one's life: the kind of work, place of residence, network of friends and acquaintances, level of aspirations and expectations.

What is it about education that accounts for its power to transform individual behavior and social realities? Is it the cognitive changes that count, the new and different ways of thinking and understanding, including the development of awareness concerning the critical issues of one's life and society? Is it the institutional effect, the break with tradition that school attendance represents? Or is it the "seepage" of more reasoned and less traditional attitudes into the minds of individuals that occurs as the education levels in society rise and exposure to the media increases?

Certainly, all these factors—and many more—are involved. The mix of ingredients is probably very different from one society to another, depending on a wide range of cultural and contextual factors.

Rising education levels—especially among women—have been statistically shown to be closely associated with declining birthrates, an essential step in slowing population growth. Does this, however, imply that education is responsible for the reduction in fertility? The question is difficult to answer unambiguously because the increase in education does not occur in isolation. It is usually part of a complex change in lifestyle.

Quality education is related to fertility behaviors just as it is known to be related to income, employment, and socioeconomic status. Indeed, education is essentially a qualitative pursuit. A small dose of inspiring learning is probably more effective in nearly every respect than many years of dull routine. What is surprising is the power and impact of even limited amounts of education of very questionable quality on reproductive and social behavior. The reestablishment of population balance requires changes in the preferences and behaviors of millions of individuals.

Education, in the broadest sense of the term, plays an evident role in the rethinking of individual values and ways of life that, taken collectively, completes the demographic transition.

Box 4.1 "Missing Girls"

In nearly all societies, particularly where the hold of tradition remains strong, there is a pervasive tendency for women to be disadvantaged relative to men. In many societies, these disadvantages involve the subordination and oppression of women and girls. Such abuse is often presented and justified as part of time-honored traditions deriving from particular systems of values or religious codes. At early ages, when children are dependent for their survival on the care and attention of others, this discrimination can prove fatal. The most brutal contributing factors are infanticide and the selective abortion of female fetuses. Negligence in the care of girls and greater efforts to protect boys from malnutrition, disease, and other consequences of poverty also play their part.

Education is essential in correcting this tragic situation. The strong links between the education of mothers and the survival of their children suggests that female education must be given even greater priority in the future. Education is a means for eroding traditional sex-biased attitudes and encouraging more egalitarian views and more equal treatment of boys and girls. The effect of education in limiting family size and improving the socioeconomic conditions of life are other factors that can reduce the excess fatality rates experienced by girls. While many measures could improve the situation, the heart of the problem is a cultural tendency to devalue women and girls. Until this is overcome—and education is usually the most effective means to that end—the problem will remain.

SNAPSHOT: Education

Is Mass Schooling Essential for Fertility Decline to Begin?

This selection originally appeared in *Population Briefs*, vol. 5, no. 3 (New York: Population Council, September 1999).

The noted demographer John Caldwell hypothesized twenty years ago that transitions from high to low fertility would begin as countries achieved universal primary schooling. Surprisingly, few researchers have explored this relationship. Council researchers Cynthia B. Lloyd, Carol E. Kaufman, and Paul Hewett have investigated links between mass schooling and fertility decline in seventeen sub-Saharan African countries ("The Spread of Primary Schooling in Sub-Saharan Africa: Implications for Fertility Change," *Policy Research Division Working Paper No. 127* [New York: Population Council, 1999]). "Most countries in sub-Saharan Africa are far from universal enrollment at the primary level," says Lloyd. "The countries that achieved mass schooling did so by the late 1970s and early 1980s. These include all the countries that are on the leading edge of the fertility decline." The researchers, however, also found signs of fertility decline more recently in a few countries in which much less formal schooling exists.

Africa's colonial past informs current schooling patterns on the continent. Various aspects of colonial education for Africans were tightly bound to the ideology of each colonial power and were ultimately designed to serve their interests. At independence, each new African state faced the daunting task of using limited resources to transform segregated educational structures into national systems. Economic and political conditions in the 1980s, in turn, sharply curtailed early postindependence educational gains in many countries.

Using data from the Demographic and Health Surveys (DHS) for the seventeen countries studied—Botswana, Burkina Faso, Cameroon, Côte d'Ivoire, Ghana, Kenya, Madagascar, Malawi, Mali, Namibia, Nigeria, Senegal, South Africa, Tanzania, Uganda, Zambia, and Zimbabwe—Lloyd, Kaufman, and Hewett investigated trends in three indicators of the extent of mass schooling for fifteen- to nineteen-year-olds: the percent ever in school, the percent completing four years, and the percent completing primary education. The researchers found only six countries—Botswana, Kenya, Namibia, South Africa, Zambia, and Zimbabwe—in which at least 90 percent of fifteen- to nineteen-year-olds have ever attended school.

In eight of the seventeen countries—all former British colonies where early tradition placed greater emphasis on broad-based access to basic schooling—at least 75 percent of the fifteen- to nineteen-year-olds had attended school for four years. At least 60 percent of fifteen- to nineteen-year-olds in Botswana, Ghana, Kenya, South Africa, Tanzania, and Zimbabwe completed primary school. A few countries, including Burkina Faso and Senegal, registered very little change in the prevalence of schooling since gaining independence.

The researchers noted that, while gender gaps are closing everywhere, the enrollment rates for boys have begun to decline in some countries. "In economically difficult times, boys may leave school earlier than girls because of their relatively better opportunities for work," says Kaufman.

Because census–DHS comparisons suggest that DHS estimates could provide overestimates of current schooling levels, "the situation we portray is a best-case scenario," says Lloyd. "It may actually be worse than this, and it's certainly not better."

The researchers looked at two indicators of fertility transition in the seventeen countries: the percent decline in fertility from 1960 or 1965 to the present and the percent of currently married women practicing contraception. Seven of the seventeen countries have had fertility declines of less than 10 percent; only three countries, however, also had a contraceptive prevalence of less than 10 percent: Burkina Faso, Mali, and Nigeria. The rest of the countries are considered to have begun the transition from high to low fertility.

In comparing the fertility data with the schooling data, the investigators found a strong statistical relationship between the percent of fifteen- to nineteen-year-olds completing four years of schooling and the phase of the fertility transition. However, certain countries—among them, Cameroon, Tanzania, and Zambia—had fairly high levels of mass schooling, yet lagged in terms of fertility decline. The researchers speculated that poor school quality and linguistic diversity might play a role in this phenomenon.

Conversely, among those countries that had begun the fertility decline, Côte d'Ivoire and Senegal were exceptional in that the decline had begun despite a lack of widespread schooling. An increase in age at marriage and growing urbanization in these countries probably play a role in these fertility declines. "It's also possible that radio and television could serve some functions of mass schooling," speculates Lloyd.

Universal schooling for the young, nevertheless, would most likely speed the pace of fertility decline, the researchers argue. And, "education itself is an important goal, irrespective of fertility," says Kaufman. However, given the dire economic situation in most sub-Saharan countries as well as the rapid rates of population growth, improving the prevalence of primary education will pose major challenges. According to the investigators, governments might increase school enrollment and attainment through information campaigns on education—directed at parents—that use billboards, radio, and television, an approach similar to the one taken by many successful family planning campaigns launched in the past.

FIGURE 4.1.   Women's Education and Family Size in Selected Countries

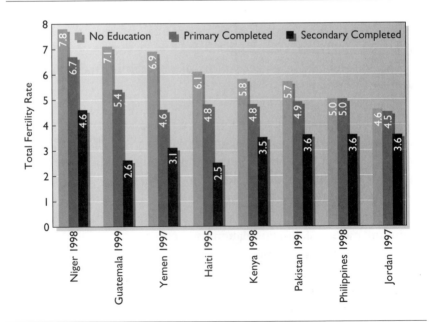

Source: Population Reference Bureau. Demographic and Health Services, 1991–1999. Website: www.prb.org (August 14, 2003).

Poverty

Demographic Dimensions of Poverty

This selection was excerpted from "Poverty," United Nations Population Fund (New York: United Nations Population Fund, August 2002).

There are close correlations between persistent poverty and rapid population growth. Fertility rates are highest in the poorest countries. And rapid population growth constrains economic progress by creating an age structure weighted heavily with dependent young. Population pressures and environmental degradation cause the rural poor to migrate to urban areas, overwhelming the infrastructure and creating new economic and environmental challenges.

Abundant evidence shows that slowing population growth helps nations achieve economic growth. Since the 1970s, developing countries with slower population growth have achieved greater gains in productivity, more savings, and enhanced development. Countries that invest in basic health, education, and social progress are the ones achieving major economic progress.

Poverty's face is feminine. Women account for as much as 70 percent of the world's poor. Traditional women's work—caring for children, cooking, household chores, and tending to livestock and subsistence crops—goes unpaid. And women are particularly affected when poverty and resource degradation combine, making basic resources like wood and water scarcer and more difficult to collect.

Women are also denied many opportunities that might help them contribute more to economic progress. The gender gap in education, for example, means that 60 percent of children out of school are girls. Women often lack certain rights—to own and inherit land, to acquire credit—essential for conservation and opportunity. Women also bear particular health burdens, especially related to childbearing. Pregnancy is the greatest threat to the health of reproductive-age women in developing countries.

SNAPSHOT: Hunger

Grim Facts on Global Poverty

Jeff Madrick

This selection originally appeared in the *New York Times* (New York: The New York Times Company, August 7, 2003).

The fierce arguments over whether income inequality and poverty rates in the world have risen or fallen somewhat in recent decades dominate international economic policy discussions. But for many poor nations, they are almost beside the point.

Even if the optimists are right, a little less inequality and modest poverty reduction hardly matter in a world where 1.2 billion people live on less than what one dollar a day will buy in America. And 2.8 billion live on less than two dollars a day.

Now comes more bad news. While some nations made considerable progress in the last decade or so—and there is no gainsaying that globalization was often a help—matters are actually worse for many nations and have more or less stagnated for a great swath of them.

For many countries, the 1990s were years of despair, the recently released Human Development Report 2003 of the United Nations Development Program concludes. The report's value is that the United Nations agency takes a broader perspective than do other international groups, like the World Bank and the International Monetary Fund.

Its finest achievement has been the Human Development Index, which has steered the analysis of a nation's standard of living away from sole reliance on per capita gross domestic product to include measures of education and health. The agency has added other formal indexes to measure gender equality, gender empowerment, and poverty.

The latest report emphasizes goals established by the United Nations in its Millennium Declaration of 2000, which ideally are to be met by 2015. They include halving poverty and hunger rates and reducing child mortality by two-thirds.

It's easy to scoff at this seeming idealism. But many similar goals have been met in the past, like eliminating smallpox and polio and immunizing most infants against major diseases.

So how has the world done since 1990?

Fifty-four countries are poorer, as measured by per capita gross domestic product (GDP). Sub-Saharan Africa is worst off, with per capita GDP falling in twenty nations. It fell in seventeen nations in eastern Europe, six in Latin America, and six in east Asia and the Pacific.

The rate of hunger has increased in twenty-one nations. The proportion of children who die under the age of five has risen in fourteen nations. The development index itself, which almost always rises over time, fell in twenty-one nations. In the 1980s, it declined in only four nations.

Still, some countries, even poor ones, have done well by many measures. China and India stand out, of course. Ghana reduced its hunger rates greatly in the 1990s, and Vietnam's index rose significantly.

And some take solace in the fact that only 23 percent of the global population lives on less than one dollar a day, compared with 30 percent in 1990. But most of this improvement has to do with the stunning economic progress in China, a nation that conspicuously did not follow Western economic policies. In absolute numbers, more people are now extremely poor than in 1990 if China is excluded.

Even in countries that have made significant progress on average, including China, the report notes that there are often large pockets of deprivation, especially in inland or rural areas. For example, only three nations with adequate statistics narrowed the gap in child mortality between the rich and the poor in the 1990s.

The bottom line is that at this rate, some crucial goals set for 2015 will not be met by many regions for several decades, and in some cases not until the next century.

What has gone wrong? Aside from generally slow growth, the spread of AIDS has been a tragic setback, reducing longevity significantly in many African nations. The collapse of Soviet-style economies is still extracting a heavy price. In general, more open markets and deregulation did not turn out to be cure-alls.

But much aid also seems to have gone to waste. In recent years, critics assert that good governance among recipients has been neglected too often. Corruption, lack of follow-through, and cookie-cutter policies afflicted development projects. But surely the call for good governance is no panacea, either. For example, did dictatorial China have good governance and dictatorial Russia poor governance? How can one tell before the fact? How do you enforce good governance even if you can define it?

More important, in my view, the West is beginning to recognize, if slowly, that it too bears some responsibility for the inferior performance of poor nations. For one thing, trade barriers keep out exports of agricultural goods, processed foods and beverages, and apparel and textiles from poor nations trying to climb higher.

But what is becoming increasingly clear is that advanced nations with highly educated populations and sophisticated technologies have an inherent advantage because they can exploit still more educated workers and newer technologies in ways that poorer nations cannot. And the gap between rich and poor keeps widening.

This gives advanced nations some responsibility in helping developing nations that are trapped because they cannot afford the public investment in transportation, education, health, and agricultural techniques that would enable them to benefit from new capital, technologies, and skilled labor. Spending what is needed on public investment by these governments often runs the risk of undermining market incentives for business with high taxes and inflationary deficit spending.

In fact, the story of the West's own development is one of significant public investment in health, transportation, and education. Fortunately, Western leaders are now promising more money. President Bush announced an increase in annual aid to 0.15 percent of national income by 2006. Belgium pledged 0.4 percent a year by 2010, France 0.5 percent by 2007, and Sweden 1 percent by 2006.

FIGURE 4.2. People Living in Extreme Poverty

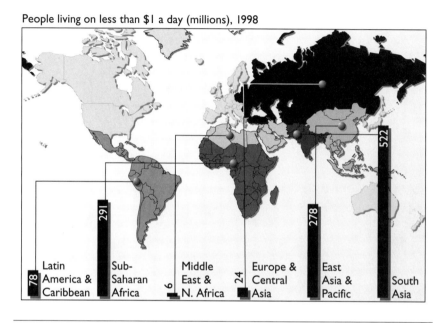

People living on less than $1 a day (millions), 1998

Latin America & Caribbean **78** — Sub-Saharan Africa **291** — Middle East & N. Africa **6** — Europe & Central Asia **24** — East Asia & Pacific **278** — South Asia **522**

Source: A Better World for All 2000, United Nations and World Bank.

TABLE 4.1. Estimated Educational Attainment by Sex: Population Age 15 and Over

		Average Number of School Years	
		Females	Males
World	1960	4.31	4.98
	1970	4.74	5.59
	1980	5.42	6.94
	1990	5.93	6.94
	2000	6.13	7.19
All Developing Countries	1960	1.46	2.63
	1970	1.94	3.38
	1980	2.74	4.37
	1990	3.61	5.21
	2000	4.33	5.92

Source: Robert J. Barro and Jong-Wha Lee, *International Data on Education Attainment Updates and Implications*, CID Working Paper No. 42, Harvard University (April 2000).

As the money available increases, none of the other lessons about international aid should be lost. Money is never the only solution. But if Western nations find the will, the odds are much higher they will find the way.

Chapter Thirteen

PROSPERITY LAISSEZ FAIRE STYLE

*Is a laissez faire approach to population a luxury
we can no longer afford?*

Institutions

Population Growth, Economic Freedom, and the Rule of Law

Seth W. Norton

This selection was excerpted from "Population Growth, Economic Freedom, and the Rule of Law," in You Have to Admit It's Getting Better: From Economic Prosperity to Environmental Quality *(Stanford, Calif.: Hoover Press, 2004).*

> **M**ore than two hundred years ago, the Reverend Thomas Malthus argued that people's tendency to have children would inevitably strain food supplies and limit the standard of living attainable by the mass of humanity. His pessimistic argument has proved remarkably durable, its influence ebbing and flowing through the ensuing centuries. In contemporary form, this contention has been expressed as a "Malthusian population trap."
>
> Michael P. Todaro, *Economic Development*

Malthus's idea was that the growth of human population keeps most people in society at a subsistence level of income. As income starts to go up, people produce more children, so the average (or per capita) income declines or stays at a low level. In the original Malthusian view, there were positive checks on population growth, but these were starvation, disease, and wars. Population growth was limited by an attendant mortality.

In today's neo-Malthusian perspective, preventive checks on population growth—persuasive and even coercive measures to lower fertility rates—are required if people are to escape from mere subsistence living.

Not everyone shares a dread of population growth. In many books and articles, the late Julian Simon has documented benefits associated with population growth and has also shown that many apocalyptic nightmares are without foundation. In addition, Ester Boserup took a favorable view of population growth when she said that in comparatively underdeveloped economies it induces technological change and stimulates innovation (*The Conditions of Agricultural Growth* [London: Earthscan, 1998]).

More recently, Bjørn Lomborg (*The Skeptical Environmentalist: Measuring the Real State of the World* [Cambridge: Cambridge University Press, 2001]) has provided a remarkable array of data showing that human well-being is improving. It is true that population growth is continuing worldwide, largely because of the lag in adjustments in birthrates that follow decreases in death rates. However, the striking fact is that death rates are declining, and decreased fertility rates characteristically follow decreased mortality rates. While population growth rates may appear unusually high by long-run standards, the data merely reflect a demographic transition with dramatic decreases in fertility rates already evident in many countries. Most important, Lomborg shows that the potentially adverse effects of population growth are swamped by the ubiquitous progress in many avenues of life, including science, technology, and human productivity. Despite these contributions, most popular literature on the subject still echoes Malthusian concerns.

I address the topic of population somewhat differently. My analysis emphasizes the importance of economic institutions, which so far has been much ignored in discussions of population growth. By economic institutions, I mean the formal and informal customs, laws, and traditions that guide behavior. A burgeoning body of research shows that several important institutions—economic freedom, protection of property rights, and the rule of law—are closely linked to human well-being. Consequently, it is reasonable to expect that such institutions can ameliorate population problems.

ECONOMIC INSTITUTIONS AND HUMAN WELL-BEING

There is growing evidence that many of the differences in well-being across countries are directly attributable to the quality of economic institutions—the existence of property rights, the quality of government, the rule of law, and economic freedom. The evidence is closely linked to the development in recent years of standard measures of institutional quality, so that countries can be compared based on these measures and on measures such as income or mortality. Two of the more prominent measures are the rule of law and economic freedom.

Countries with a strong legal framework are typically distinguished from countries where the law reflects political struggles for power. According to Robert Barro and Xavier Sala-i-Martin, countries with a well-established tradition of the rule of law have greater ability to carry out business transactions and correspondingly greater incentive for investment. Stephen Knack and Philip Keefer say that the rule of law "reflects the degree to which the citizens of a country are willing to accept the established institutions to make and implement laws and adjudicate disputes" ("Institutions and Economic Performance: Cross Country Tests Using Alternative International Measures," *Economics and Politics* [November 1995]).

A company called Political Risk Services ranks countries as part of its *International Country Risk Guide*. Customers use the guide to make decisions about investment and production in foreign countries. In the rule of law rankings, higher scores indicate sound political institutions, a strong court system, and provisions for orderly succession of power. Lower scores indicate a tradition of depending on physical force or illegal means to settle claims. Using this database, research by Knack and Keefer and by Barro and Sala-i-Martin shows that the rule of law enhances economic growth and human well-being (*Economic Growth* [New York: McGraw-Hill, 1995]).

Economic freedom, too, enhances growth. The *Index of Economic Freedom* is a comprehensive measure of citizens' rights to own and trade property unfettered by intrusive public policies. The Fraser Institute compiles this index with the assistance of numerous organizations throughout the world. Essentially, the project measures economic freedom as distinguished from political freedom. It emphasizes the ability of people to use and exchange property relatively free of the governmental interference of perverse monetary, fiscal, and trade policies.

A recent compilation by James Gwartney and Robert Lawson (*Economic Freedom of the World* [Vancouver, British Columbia: Fraser Institute, 2001]) ranks countries based on seven broad categories of economic freedom: the size of government, economic structure and role of markets, monetary policy and price stability, freedom to use alternative currencies, legal structure and security of private ownership, freedom to trade with foreigners, and freedom of exchange in capital markets. These measures, which are composed of twenty-one narrower yardsticks, are used to compile a summary measure of economic freedom for each country.

The role of economic institutions on human well-being can be examined by dividing the sample of countries into groups with low, medium, and high economic freedom and the same categories for the rule of law (see table 4.2). In all cases except water pollution, countries with low economic freedom are worse off than those in countries with moderate economic freedom, while countries with high economic freedom are better off in all cases than countries with medium economic freedom. By these measures, the quality of life is strongly linked to economic freedom.

For the rule of law measure, a similar pattern is evident. Well-being is better for citizens in countries with moderate rule of law as opposed to weak rule of law, except for the overall poverty index, adult illiteracy, and agricultural productivity. For citizens in countries with strong rule of law, well-being is uniformly better than in countries with medium rule of law. Thus, the relationship for rule of law is not as strong as that for economic freedom, but by many measures of the quality of life, life is better when the rule of law is stronger.

TABLE 4.2.   Economic Institutions and Human Well-Being

Measure of Well-Being	Economic Freedom			Rule of Law		
	Low	*Medium*	*High*	*Weak*	*Medium*	*Strong*
Poverty Index	38.1	30.5	14.5	31.8	33.0	16.4
Death by 40	29.1	19.4	7.7	19.6	21.7	10.8
Adult Illiteracy	39.2	34.7	12.5	32.1	37.8	17.0
Safe Water	43.3	34.7	19.5	34.8	36.2	20.1
Health Service	40.5	28.5	16.8	41.3	28.0	15.2
Undernourished Children	29.1	21.7	13.9	25.0	23.1	14.0
Deforestation Rates	0.429	1.351	−0.230	1.336	0.732	0.282
Water Pollution	0.200	0.214	0.196	0.202	0.221	0.194
Net Savings Rates	3.96	7.12	14.78	2.61	6.30	15.96
Agricultural Productivity	620.3	1,011.2	6,001.6	1,178.2	1,083.6	4,552.7

Sources: Gwartney and Lawson (2001); Political Risk Services (1997); United Nations Development Program (1997); World Bank (2001).

THE EFFECT OF INSTITUTIONS ON FERTILITY

Economic institutions are dramatically more important than population growth in affecting human poverty and environmental conditions. However, those conclusions still understate the importance of economic institutions with respect to population growth because economic institutions actually affect fertility rates, and thus population growth rates.

There are ample grounds to believe people will adjust their fertility, that is, increase or decrease the number of children born, in the light of their endowments and opportunities. Economists Gary Becker and Robert Barro ("A Reformulation of the Economic Theory of Fertility," *Quarterly Journal of Economics* 103 [1988]) have developed a model of human fertility indicating that people choose the number of their children in response to changing mortality rates, while taking into account the forgone opportunities associated with raising children. If people anticipate that many of their children will die before reaching adulthood, they will have more children. If they are confident that their children, or most of them, will reach adulthood, they will have fewer children. In both cases, they will also consider the costs of lost income and lost free time that occur when raising children. Becker and Barro argue that as the education and work experience of females increase and open up more productive opportunities for women, the costs of raising children will also increase.

By encouraging economic growth, economic institutions indirectly affect fertility, but there is also evidence that these institutions affect fertility for other reasons. Many poor countries have poorly specified or poorly enforced property rights. When fuel wood and fodder are not owned and formal laws of possession do not govern their harvest and use, people do not bear the full cost of their consumption. They have an incentive to appropriate resources at the fastest rate possible, often leading to excessive harvesting. The condition is generally labeled the "tragedy of the commons." What better way to capture open-access resources than to have as many gatherers as possible? Higher fertility is a way to do this. Theodore Panayotou observes that "most contributions by children consist of capturing and appropriating open access natural resources such as water, fodder, pastures, fish, fuel wood, and other forest products, and clearing open access land for cultivation" ("The Population, Environment, and Development Nexus," in *Population and Development: Old Debates, New Conclusions*, ed. Robert Cassen [New Brunswick, N.J.: Transactions Publishers, 1994]). This, he continues, makes "the number of children the decisive instrument in the hands of the household: the household's share of open access property depends on the number of hands it employs to convert open access resources into private property." Yet this could "become devastating for the resources, the community, and eventually the individual household."

The absence of economic freedom encourages fertility in another way, too. Arthur De Vany and Nicolas Sanchez ("Land Tenure Structures and Fertility in Mexico," *Review of Economics and Statistics* 61 [1979]) examined fertility patterns in Mexico based on the proportion of private farms and ejido farms—communally owned farms organized under the laws enacted following the Revolution of 1910. In addition to incentives to have children in order to appropriate resources, they assert there are incentives to have children in order to transfer property. Because of restrictions on sales of land, many people have the right to use but not sell the land. They can obtain some benefits of selling the land by transferring it to their progeny. More children increase the ability to make such transfers. On farms without clear ownership, the parents with more children will have a greater chance of at least some children taking over the farm and providing for the parents in their old age.

Finally, there may be a simple pronatalist bias to obtain "free" family farm labor. Not surprisingly, De Vany and Sanchez found that the higher the proportion of ejidatarios (workers on communal farms) relative to women or to total farm workers, the higher the fertility. In short, fertility and favorable economic institutions are inversely related. Where property rights are poorly defined and enforced, the incentive to have children is greater than where property rights are well-specified and enforced.

Fertility rates are notably lower in the countries that have a tradition of honoring contracts and not expropriating property (see table 4.3). These numbers are remarkable because they show that even among the poorer countries of the world, the security of contractual relations and protection of private property tend to lower fertility rates.

TABLE 4.3.   Economic Institutions and Fertility Rates: Poor Countries

	Total Fertility Rate	
	Weak Institutions	Strong Institutions
Institutional Measure		
Honoring Contracts	4.88	3.68
Expropriation Risk	4.62	3.22

Note: Total fertility rate is the number of children that would be born to a woman if she were to live to the end of her childbearing years and bear children at each age in accordance with the prevailing age-specific fertility rates. The fertility rates are for 1999.
Sources: Political Risk Services (1997); World Bank (2001).

When the capture of open-access resources is rendered unnecessary by a system of laws that assigns full ownership and the ability to transfer property, families do not need so many children.

INSTITUTIONAL REFORM AND POPULATION GROWTH

There are two reasons to advocate institutional reform. First, nations that adopt growth-enhancing reforms such as better protection of property rights and acceptance of the rule of law improve people's lives. Favorable economic institutions directly decrease human poverty and environmental degradation and enhance the environment, improving conditions even in realms where population growth has little effect.

Second, economic freedom, the rule of law, and related market-enhancing institutions also reduce fertility rates. By lowering population growth, they decrease any adverse consequences of population growth.

CONCLUSION

There is no population apocalypse. Institutional reform can largely offset population problems, both directly by improving well-being and indirectly by leading to lower fertility rates. Moreover, the findings understate the potential benefits of institutional reform because the sample excludes countries where economic institutions are substantially more supportive of human well-being. Reforming economic freedom to Hong Kong's level or the rule of law to Switzerland's level would surely have substantially greater impact on human well-being. In short, there is considerable basis for optimism.

Yet, despite these findings, there is also considerable room for pessimism. Institutional reform is not free. Many nation-states, for various reasons, resist the kind of reform that would ameliorate population problems specifically and human problems generally. This state of affairs is perplexing and troubling. Perhaps the evidence documented here will be used in the debates to help policymakers take action to reform the institutional environment and thus the most basic building blocks of human well-being—markets and growth-enhancing institutions.

Technology

Population Size and Technological Development

This selection was excerpted from "Population Size and Technological Development," in *Population and Technological Change: A Study of Long-Term Trends* (Chicago: University of Chicago, 1981).

Human history can be viewed as a long series of technological changes. Just a few of the crucial ones are the discovery of the usefulness of fire at least 350 millennia ago, the appearance of food production more than 10 millennia ago, the construction of urban centers more than 5 millennia ago, the invention of mechanized large-scale industry a few centuries ago, and the invention of nuclear power a few decades ago.

Some inventions were made by chance, others after centuries of speculation and experiments aimed at solving particular problems. Except for the inventions of recent centuries, the circumstances in which they were made are seldom known; nor, often, do we know even the approximate time of the invention or the region in which it occurred.

Many of the inventions had important effects on the size and distribution of world population. The use of fire reduced mortality by providing better protection against wild animals and permitted settlement in areas with temperate and cold climates. Many later inventions also helped reduce mortality rates and promoted either decentralization or centralization of population. World population grew from very small numbers at the time when human beings began to use fire to more than 4 billion today; and the rate of growth accelerated as well, especially in recent centuries. This multiplication of world population would not have been possible without successive technological changes.

It is generally agreed that successive changes in technology had an important influence on population size, but opinions are divided concerning the type of technological change that had the greatest influence in different periods and in different regions. The opposite side of the interrelationship, the influence of population size on technology, has attracted less attention. The focus in historical research has been on original inventions rather than on the transmission of techniques from region to region, and the influence of demographic factors on the invention of techniques is less obvious than is the influence of such factors on the transmission of techniques.

Yet societies have most often advanced technologically by introducing technologies already in use in other societies. If we want to study the causes of changing technology in various periods and parts of the world, it is more important to focus on the conditions for transmission of techniques than on the conditions for the appearance of inventions. It is, of course, a matter of choice where the line is drawn between a new invention and a technological adaptation of an existing technique to a new environment. The distinction between invention and transmission of technology becomes blurred if we use a definition of inventions broad enough to include minor adaptations of known technologies.

The speed with which major inventions have been transmitted from place to place varies enormously. During early stages of human history, some inventions seem to have been transmitted relatively quickly over huge distances. By contrast, other major inventions never moved from one people to its nearest neighbors, although contacts were frequent during many millennia. There are still some groups of people who have never introduced food production, and many more who have never constructed urban centers of their own. Much of the world population lives in areas still at early stages of the industrial revolution. It is more important to study the obstacles that prevent the transmission of technologies than to compare the number of inventions that have been made in different societies.

Demographic factors help to explain why some technologies fail to be transmitted in the wake of human contacts. Certain technologies are uneconomic or inapplicable in areas with a small and sparse population, others in areas where population density exceeds a certain level. A technology could be inapplicable for a small population because its use requires a large collective effort. Other technologies require the use of more space than is available in areas with a high population density. Large differences in population density between various areas have existed for many millennia, and the links between population size and the use of particular technologies must have significantly limited the possibilities for transmission. Thus, a technological invention might spread to distant areas with similar population size or density, but not to those areas in between with a different size or density.

Although demographic factors seem to have played a larger role in the transmission than in the invention of technology, they no doubt also provided some motivation for invention. In the twentieth century, nearly all invention is the result of demand-induced or cost-induced organized research, and there is usually correlation between the resources devoted to research in a given field and the speed of technological progress within that field. Thus, there is a link between the motivation for innovation and the amount of invention.

Such a link existed even before the time of organized scientific research. Most of the inventions in the early stages of the industrial revolution were not made by scientists but by people with little or no education, who experimented to find new and better solutions to urgent problems. Sometimes they succeeded after many years of vain effort, which they would not have made had the problem confronting them been less urgent. Experiments to find new solutions to urgent problems no doubt have been made at all periods of human history, since the time of primitive hunters, but in early periods the chance of success was much smaller, and the period of trial before positive results were obtained much longer, than today. Even today, when large resources are invested in scientific research, the attempts at innovation within some fields continue to be unsuccessful. In other fields the time lag between discovery and practical application is often many decades. In past ages, when inventions were made by trial and error, few experiments were likely to succeed, and in case of success, this time lag may have been centuries rather than decades. Even so, it would seem that motivation had a strong influence on invention.

If it is agreed that many inventions—today as well as in the past—have been demand-induced, it becomes pertinent to ask to what extent this demand pull was in turn determined by demographic changes. Radical changes in the relation between human and natural resources occur in areas in which population multiplies. Shrinking supplies of land and other natural resources would provide motivation to invent better means of using scarce resources or to discover substitutes for them. Moreover, population increase would make it possible to use methods that are inapplicable when population is smaller. Once these motivations led to invention or importation of technologies, the technological changes would then result in further population change, which in turn would induce still further technological change. In this, an interlinked process of demographic and technological change would occur. Other areas would have little or no technological change because of stagnant population and would continue to have stagnant population because of no technological change.

The interrelationship between population and technological change is a complicated one. Increasing population size may make life easier because there will be more people to share the burden of collective investments, but it may also make life more difficult because the ratio of natural resources to population decreases. At different periods and places, one or the other tendency may prevail. In some periods, a society with a growing population may be motivated to import new technologies by the desire to draw benefit from large collective investments. In other periods, the transmission of important new technologies may be a means to reduce or eliminate the disadvantages of a declining ratio of natural resources to population.

A growing population gradually exhausts certain types of natural resources, such as timber, virgin land, game, and freshwater supplies, and is forced to reduce its numbers by emigration or change its traditional use of resources and way of life. Increasing populations must substitute resources such as labor for the natural resources that have become scarce. They must invest labor in the creation of amenities or equipment for which there was no need so long as the population was smaller. Thus, the increase of population within an area provides an incentive to replace natural resources by labor and capital.

SNAPSHOT: Technology

Technology and Economic Growth in the Information Age

W. Michael Cox and Richard Alm

This selection originally appeared in the *NCPA Policy Backgrounder*, no. 147 (Dallas, Tex.: National Center for Policy Analysis, 1998).

A fundamental problem is that our economy is not simply mismeasured, it is misunderstood.

The economy has never tried to produce gross domestic product (GDP): it tries to produce happiness, or satisfaction. And there's a lot more to life than GDP.

In the information age, our economy is providing benefits beyond those easily captured by GDP. When making a list of needs and wants, most people start with food, clothing, and shelter. After that, they move on to safety and security and leisure time, then perhaps to some of the "fun" aspects of life, such as entertainment, travel, and cultural enrichment. Beyond that, most of us seek personal fulfillment, such as the satisfaction that comes from a worthwhile or enjoyable job. This hierarchy of needs and wants reflects the influential work of the American psychologist Abraham Maslow (1908–1970). Maslow's pyramid, a staple of psychology, consists of a hierarchy of needs that motivate human behavior. At the most basic level are the physiological needs. With those met, we move up to safety, social needs, self-esteem, and at the pinnacle of the pyramid, self-actualization.

Increased Leisure. As Americans grow wealthier, our physiological needs are being increasingly met, and there's a shift in wants from basic products to ever more intangible outputs. There are plenty of examples—from personal physical fitness gurus and Internet chat rooms to ecotourism and early retirement. For example, Austrian economist Joseph Schumpeter said, "The reduction of working hours is one of the most significant 'products' of economic evolution" (*Business Cycles: A Theoretical, Historical, and Statistical Analysis of the Capitalist Process* [New York: McGraw-Hill, 1939]). Hours at work have fallen for decades. The average workweek fell from 36.9 hours in 1973 to 34.5 hours in 1990. An equal percentage decline over the next twenty-five years would yield a 31.4-hour workweek in 2020. Many workers have flexible schedules, including regular breaks. Yet GDP gives the economy no credit for gains in leisure.

Better Working Conditions. Another of the biggest yet most overlooked examples of gains in living standards missed by GDP figures is improvement in our working conditions. For most of us, work is a major part of life. And better working conditions have routinely been a product of progress, right along with more GDP. This is evident not just from the steady decline in worker death rates but also from a comparison of our work concerns today versus yesterday. In the early 1900s, our work worries centered on safety, fatigue, long hours, excessive heat, poor ventilation, high humidity, bad lighting, exposure, disease, lack of adequate toilet facilities, and rigid schedules. Today, we seek interesting and fun jobs with meaningful work, nice offices, employee activities, flexible hours, empowerment, wellness classes, communication, employee counseling, and the ability to telecommute. Americans have progressed from narrow productivity concerns to "have a nice day."

Work-Time Leisure. Although measures of productivity—output per hour at work—credit time off, they generally miss leisure time taken at work. Time-diary surveys show that Americans today take up to six hours per week of leisure on the job, as compared with only one hour in 1965.

The point is not that American workers are cheating their companies. On the contrary, it's all a part of progress. We're not automatons, enslaved to productivity as if we were still in the fields or on an assembly line. One way we take the gains of technological progress is simply to enjoy life in an economy that, more and more, transcends measurement.

And what about work is fun? Most folks these days seek work they enjoy. Yet the standard statistics are apt to register economic regression if we quit a job we're good at but don't like in order to take one that's more enjoyable. It just doesn't make good sense. We take our progress in ways other than GDP.

The economy today reflects our wealthier society's preferences for harder-to-measure consumption. As we grow richer still in the future, we can expect society to spend more of its time, energy, and income addressing needs that are farther and farther from the physiological. Pity the poor statistician with the job of tracking our increasingly elusive economy.

The very notion of economic progress is an artifact of the modern, technology-rich era. Until the advent of capitalism in the eighteenth century, the world's living standards changed only slowly. The French farmer of the seventeenth century lived, worked, and died pretty much like the Roman farmer of the first century B.C. The same cannot be said for our world: living standards rise from generation to generation. We are in the throes of one of history's great bursts of technology, put to use quickly and effectively by a vibrant market economy.

It would, of course, be good to have statistics that capture all the nuances of the economy as it evolves to meet our needs. That's probably too much to expect. Expense and complexity make a daunting task of tracking an American economy centered less and less on tangible output. Our measurement technology cannot keep pace with the rest of our technological progress. Relying on our existing measures, we're going to miss a lot of what happens in the economy as it moves into the twenty-first century.

We are fast departing a time when progress can be measured by GDP or any other simple tally of what the economy produces. If we become fixated on the numbers and fail to imagine the possibilities, we may miss one of the greatest periods of economic advancement in history. Worse yet, if we judge twenty-first century progress by twentieth century measures, we may infer that our system is failing and in need of repair by government.

That is the bad news.

Free enterprise is America's greatest welfare program. For more than two centuries, the system has worked to make our lives better. Whatever we've wanted—new and improved products, more leisure, better jobs, easier lives—it has provided in abundance.

The pessimists fret that our best days are behind us. They are wrong. We stand poised on the brink of a new era, one endowed with technology and teeming with opportunities. The future offers even faster economic progress.

That is the good news.

FIGURE 4.3. World Gross Domestic Product and Population Since 1750

During the twentieth century, both output and population growth increased. However, as a result of accelerating technical progress, output growth increasingly exceeded population growth.

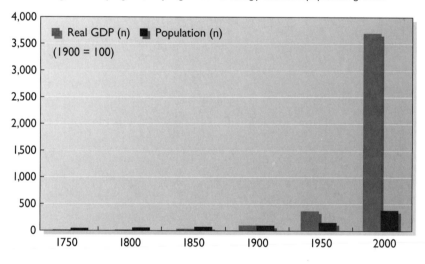

Source: Bradford J. Delong, "Estimating World GDP, One Million B.C.–Present." Available over the Internet at www.j-bradford-delong.net.

Globalization

Trade Openness, Sound Policies, and Prosperity

James Gwartney and Robert Lawson

This selection originally appeared in *Fraser Forum* (Vancouver, British Columbia: The Fraser Institute, May 2002).

Globalization means different things to different people. Critics often argue that globalization is responsible for most of the world's ills, including poverty, low wages, and political corruption. No doubt many of them are idealists motivated by good intentions. But they are also uninformed and misguided. Tragically, to the extent they are able to restrain trade, their actions will undermine the best hope of billions of people for a better life.

When economists speak of globalization they are typically referring to recent increases in the volume of trade as the result of both lower trade barriers and reductions in transport and communication costs. Since Adam Smith's time, economists of almost all persuasions have supported free trade. Trade makes it possible for people to produce more because of specialization, division of labor, and adoption of large-scale production processes. Trade also promotes the rapid dissemination of technological improvements and innovative breakthroughs that are the driving force of modern economic progress. With international trade, the residents of each country are able to concentrate more of their resources on activities they do relatively well and, as a result, they are able to produce and consume at a higher level.

In addition to these direct economic effects, there is an indirect benefit that is often overlooked: in an open economy, it is more difficult for political officials to pursue counterproductive policies. When economies are more open, governments with corrupt legal systems, unstable monetary policies, and costly regulations will find it difficult to attract either the capital or the entrepreneurial talent that propels modern growth. With openness, capital will flow toward those economies providing institutional environments more attractive for wealth creation. Thomas Friedman, in his book *The Lexus and the Olive Tree* (New York: Knopf Publishing Group, 2000), refers to this indirect effect as a "golden straitjacket" because it restrains the counterproductive actions of politicians around the world.

The new edition of *Economic Freedom of the World* rates 116 countries with regard to the presence of freedom of exchange across national boundaries. In order to receive a high rating, a country must have low tariffs, a freely convertible currency, a large trade sector given its size and location, and no capital market controls. Table 4.4 lists the fifteen economies that were most open in 2000, as well as the fifteen that imposed the most severe restrictions on international exchange. Hong Kong, Singapore, Ireland, Belgium, and the Netherlands head the list of the world's most open economies. The United States ranked twenty-third, Canada twenty-fourth, and Mexico twenty-fifth among the 116 countries. At the other end of the spectrum, the openness index indicates that

TABLE 4.4. Restrictions on International Exchange

Most Open		Least Open	
Rank	*Country*	*Rank*	*Country*
1	Hong Kong	102	Niger
2	Singapore	103	Algeria
3	Ireland	104	Belize
4	Belgium	105	Barbados
5	Netherlands	106	Benin
6	Estonia	107	Albania
7	Germany	108	Central African Republic
8	Luxembourg	109	India
9	United Kingdom	110	Bangladesh
10	Switzerland	111	Rwanda
11	Austria	112	Burundi
12	New Zealand	113	Pakistan
13	Finland	114	Sierra Leone
14	Sweden	115	Iran
15	Spain	116	Myanmar

Myanmar, Iran, Sierra Leone, Pakistan, and Burundi were the world's least open economies in 2000.

Table 4.5 shows that there is a strong positive relationship between trade openness and various indicators of economic welfare. The 116 countries were arrayed from most open to least open and divided into five groups (quintiles). The mean values for various indicators of economic welfare were then derived for each of the quintiles. The more open economies achieved substantially higher levels of per capita GDP. The average per capita GDP for the most open quintile of countries was $23,401, more than twice the level of the second quintile and more than six times the figure for the least open quintile. The more open economies also grew more rapidly during 1990–2000. The mean growth rate of the most open quintile of countries was 2.0 percent during the 1990s compared with 0.2 for the least open quintile.

Predictably, higher income levels and more rapid growth affect quality of life. Life expectancy figures highlight this point. The mean life expectancy at birth for the residents of the most open quintile of countries was 75.7 years, compared with 57.3 years for the least open quintile (see column 3 of table 4.5). Thus, people in the more open quintile of countries live more than eighteen years longer than those in the most closed quintile.

As table 4.5 shows, the data are highly consistent with the economic view of trade. The data illustrate that when a country's residents are freer to engage in economic activity across national boundaries, higher income levels and living standards emerge. Undoubtedly, some of the positive

TABLE 4.5.   Openness and Economic Indicators

Trade Area Rating	Gross National Income Per Capita, US$, 2000	GDP Per Capita, Percent of Growth, 1990–2000	Life Expectancy at Birth, in Years, 1999
Top Quintile	$23,401	2.0	75.7
Second Quintile	$9,852	1.7	69.8
Third Quintile	$8,065	1.2	67.4
Fourth Quintile	$5,007	1.3	63.8
Bottom Quintile	$3,621	0.2	57.3

TABLE 4.6.   Openness and Quality of Monetary and Legal Arrangements

Trade Area Rating	Sound Money	Legal System and Property Rights	Civil Liberties
Top Quintile	9.2	8.4	6.3
Second Quintile	8.3	6.2	5.2
Third Quintile	7.3	5.4	4.7
Fourth Quintile	6.3	5.2	4.4
Bottom Quintile	6.4	4.8	3.9

economic effects of trade reflect the indirect impact of openness on policies in other areas, such as legal structure and monetary arrangements. *The Economic Freedom of the World* index also rates countries in the legal and monetary areas. In order to get a high rating for its legal structure, a country must protect property rights, enforce contracts, and settle disputes even-handedly. High ratings in the monetary area depend on consistent price stability and the freedom to use alternative currencies.

As table 4.6 shows, openness is positively related to sound legal and monetary institutions. More open economies achieved higher legal and monetary area ratings than the more closed economies.

The civil liberties ratings of Freedom House also provide information about the quality and even-handedness of a country's legal institutions. As the right column in table 4.6 shows, openness is also closely linked with the protection of civil liberties. Measured on a 7-point scale, the mean civil liberties rating of the most open quintile was 6.3 compared with 3.9 for the least open quintile.

CONCLUSION

The economic record of more open economies is far superior to that of those that are more closed. To a degree, this superior performance reflects the standard textbook view of trade—expansion in output as the result of gains from specialization, trade, and the adoption of innovative approaches that have worked elsewhere. But the prosperity of the more open economies also reflects indirect factors. Compared with those that are more closed, open economies have a stronger incentive to improve their policies in other areas such as the even-handedness of their legal system and stability of their monetary arrangements. Spurred by openness, better policies in these areas will also enhance prosperity.

Taken together, the direct and indirect effects of trade openness are a powerful force for economic progress. If the critics of trade openness and globalization are really interested in reducing poverty and improving living conditions around the world, the best thing they could do is to switch sides in the ongoing policy debate about trade.

SNAPSHOT: Trade

When Globalization Suffers, the Poor Take the Heat

Gary S. Becker

This selection originally appeared in *BusinessWeek Online* (April 2003), www.businessweek.com/magazine/content/03_16/b3829031_mz007.htm.

The war on terrorism—and the rupture in the Western alliance produced by the Iraqi war—might sharply slow down the international movement of capital and people for an extended period. This will please the more extreme critics of globalization and immigration, but it will greatly reduce the opportunities for poor nations to grow out of poverty.

The expansion in trade and the movements of people among nations were unusually rapid during the past half-century. World trade in goods and services grew by more than 5 percent a year, the international flow of capital also accelerated, and the number of students from poor nations studying in the United States, Europe, and Japan grew remarkably.

As a result of this movement toward an integrated world economy, global income grew at its fastest rate in recorded history. World population more than doubled from 1950 to the end of the twentieth century. Yet real per capita income grew, on average, by about 2 percent a year around the world.

Not all poor nations had much growth during this fifty-year period; many of the African nations, the former Communist bloc, and some Asian nations lagged far behind. But on the whole, the per capita gross domestic product of poorer nations grew about as fast as that of richer nations, whereas populations in the less developed world grew much more rapidly.

Economist Xavier Sala-i-Martin of Columbia University has shown that inequality in world incomes has declined sharply since the mid-1970s. The decline in income inequality among individuals was much faster than among countries, in part because China and, to a lesser extent, India—two nations with about a third of the world's population—grew very rapidly. But there was also a narrowing of world inequality beyond the impressive performances of these huge nations.

Without carefully examining the statistics, some critics of the effects of globalization on the world's poor claim that the number of families living on less than one or two dollars a day basically remained the same during the past fifty years. Yet it is hard to measure the well-being of the world's poorest since most of them live on farms and get much of their income from the food they grow, the clothing they make, and the houses they build themselves. Still, using official data from the World Bank and the United Nations, Sala-i-Martin's study shows that the fraction of the world's population living on less than two dollars a day fell by about 20 percentage points during the past three decades.

Income measures do not do full justice to the extent of the improvement in the world's poor, for they take no account of advances in life expectancy and general health. Populations in the less developed world grew fast mainly because they used knowledge gained from the West to produce rapid declines in mortality. As a consequence, the world gap in life expectancy has narrowed considerably, despite the raging AIDS epidemic in Africa. My study with two colleagues shows that world inequality declined even more rapidly after national income accounts were adjusted for the greater declines in mortality rates in poorer nations.

It is telling evidence of the benefits of globalization that not a single poorer nation that was isolated from the global economic community, including the Soviet Union and China while they had rigid Communist regimes, raised their per capita incomes very much during that time. The poor nations that benefited from the world division of labor initially concentrated production on a few simple goods, which they traded for the high-quality goods produced by advanced nations.

These undeveloped nations also imported large amounts of capital to help their agriculture and their expansion of industrial production. Many of these nations also sent large numbers of students to the United States and elsewhere to study science, engineering, medicine, and other technical subjects. Some of these students stayed abroad to work and often to prosper, but many came back with the knowledge they had gained in the advanced nations.

It is the international movement of people and of capital that is put in greatest jeopardy by the events of the past few years. Owners of capital are reluctant to invest in developing nations when there is great uncertainty caused by war and terrorism. Rich countries are less willing to admit young male students and immigrants to study and work, especially those from Muslim nations or other countries with known hostility and resentment toward the United States and other Western nations.

The anti-globalization movement may get its wish for a breakdown in the world economic order because of sharp reductions in the international movement of capital and people due to terrorism and a more divided West. But the biggest losers will be not the relatively rich members of the G7 countries but rather the nations that want to extricate the mass of their populations from extreme poverty and disease.

WHO DECIDES

PART V: QUICK FACTS

"We must now act decisively and bring down the birth rate speedily. We should not hesitate to take steps which might be described as drastic. Some personal rights have to be kept in abeyance for the human rights of the nation."

Indira Gandhi, *Shah Commission Report* (1978)

"The things that make family planning acceptable are the very things that make it ineffective for population control. By stressing the rights of parents to have the number of children they want, it evades the basic question of population policy, which is how to give societies the number of children they need."

Kingsley Davis, *Population Policy: Will Current Programs Succeed?* (1967)

"The children who are born are generally desired. Children at any rate are unavoidable. To deny this is to suggest that parents in less developed countries procreate without an understanding of the consequences or without the will or the sense of responsibility to prevent them. This view treats people of the less developed world with altogether unwarranted condescension or contempt."

Lord Peter T. Bauer, *Equality, the Third World, and Economic Delusion* (1981)

- Eighty percent of the American public favors U.S. economic assistance for voluntary family planning programs overseas.

    RAND, *Beyond the Numbers: How Americans View Global Population Issues* (2002)

- Fifty-eight percent of Americans agree with the statement: "The federal government should provide free sterilizations for low-income men and women of child bearing age who voluntarily choose it."

    The Roper Center for Public Opinion Research, *Roper Poll on Population* (1998)

- Seventy-one percent of Americans believe that "too much population growth in developing countries is holding back their economic development" (as opposed to 55 percent in 1994).

    Washington Post, April 5, 2000

- A vast majority of the American public (92 percent) believe that individuals and families should have the right both to determine the number of children they will have and to have access to the necessary means and information for accomplishing this.

    RAND, *How Americans View World Population Issues: A Survey of Public Opinion* (2000)

- Forty-eight percent of Americans said, in a recent Gallup poll, that they were worried about population growth, down from 68 percent in 1992.

The Gallup Organization, *Gallup Poll* (1999)

INTRODUCTION

Who Decides

One of the most intensely argued issues surrounding the population conundrum is "who decides." The mind-sets of the population optimist and the population pessimist are based on suppositions about who decides what is best—the individual, an agent of the government, or some combination of the two—regarding the population issues at hand. These suppositions are often rooted in conflicting views of humankind and our ability to self-govern. Part 5 provides an overview of the broad spectrum of opinions surrounding the highly charged question of who decides.

The basic jurisdictional query of who decides is a springboard for many other questions. For example: Is it more important to protect the rights and freedoms of individuals or safeguard and ensure the general welfare of all the inhabitants of the earth? Should the wealth of the world be distributed using egalitarian, libertarian, or utilitarian principles and values? And, more pointed, do couples have the basic human right to decide freely and responsibly on the number and spacing of their children? And, if so, are there exceptions to this right? Does the government ever have a right, duty, or ethical obligation to interfere in reproductive decisions? Is coercion appropriate or necessary in some cases? And is there a distinction to be made between family planning and population control? As in most policy debates, one can boil the "who decides" dilemma down to a single question: where should we draw the line between individual and government rights and responsibilities?

Does freedom beget freedom or is it ultimately a license for destruction? The spectrum of articles in part 5 gives readers the opportunity to explore their views of humankind and their own relationship to freedom, rights, and responsibilities.

Chapter Fourteen

THE SPECTRUM

Who should decide what is best when it comes to population size and related issues?

Whose Choice?

Robert Whalen

This selection originally appeared in *Whose Choice: Population Controllers' or Yours?* (Front Royal, Va.: Human Life International, 1992).

> "Family planning begins and ends with individual couples choosing when to have children."
>
> Malcolm Potts, Family Health International

The assumption that the world is overpopulated is one of those things that "everyone knows." There has been such widespread agreement, in the media and among public policymakers, that the planet is threatened by a "population explosion" and that we in the West should do something about it, that any expression of doubt on the issue is akin to claiming membership in the flat earth society.

It comes as a surprise to most people to learn that much of the serious academic research carried out in the last twenty-five years into the effects of population growth has called into question the "population explosion" hypothesis. Economists, social scientists, and statisticians like Simon Kuznets, Julian Simon, Jacqueline Kasun, Colin Clark, and Lord Peter Bauer have questioned the supposed link between population growth and poverty, famine, unemployment, and other problems.

However, since Western governments were persuaded in the mid-1960s to start putting money into population control programs, a great industry has grown up. Tens of thousands of people are now employed worldwide in devising and administering programs to reduce population growth. The funding runs into hundreds of millions of dollars annually. Chairs of population studies have been endowed at leading universities where professors are paid to do nothing except argue for population control.

In such a situation it will be easily understood that attempts to broaden the population debate will be fiercely and effectively resisted. For many people, there is too much at stake. As a result, this volume of research, which contradicts the popular assumptions, is seldom referred to in "official" population publications.

However, there is an even more effective way of silencing debate on the issue. The population lobbyists claim that they only want to provide family planning services that will enable women around the world to control their fertility. The stated intention is to increase freedom of choice for women and to improve the state of women's health.

Those who oppose population programs are therefore cast in the unenviable role of being against women's rights. This is not a mantle that many people are rushing to assume. The population lobbyists have been so successful in deflecting criticism in this way that most debates concerning opposition to population control have been confined to the discussion of the Catholic Church's teaching on artificial contraception and perhaps the role of women in Islam.

The public has been misled concerning the nature and impact of population control programs on parents, particularly women, in developing countries. This has been achieved by distorting the use of the term "family planning" until it ceases to represent what we would understand by it in the rich nations of the West.

Family planning, in its true sense, is a fundamentally different concept from that of population control.

Family planning is the decision taken by couples, in the light of their own beliefs and circumstances, as to the number and spacing of their own children.

Population control is the decision taken by governments or other agencies that couples should have no more than a certain number of children, followed by measures to enforce this.

Family planning and population control are not, as some like to make out, only different in degree. They are fundamentally opposed to each other, because family planning increases freedom of choice for the individual, while population control restricts it.

Family planning, in its true sense, is not controversial. No one—not even the Catholic Church—disputes that it is the right of parents to plan their own families. There may be disputes about the methods to be used—for example, whether abortion should be regarded as a method of family planning—but the principle is unchallenged.

Handing decisions about fertility to government planners is another matter. There is now no doubt that population control programs have resulted in the widespread coercion of couples, sometimes involving the use of physical force, to ensure that they have fewer children than they would have wished.

How can this coercion have come about in the name of freedom of choice? When looking at population programs we have to ask ourselves, who is making the choices? The parents? The governments of the countries they live in? The governments of other countries? Or supranational bodies like the World Bank and the United Nations?

The study of the way in which population programs actually work should raise the most profound concern among those who care about human rights and, in particular, the welfare of women.

The Failure of Leadership

Lindsey Grant

This selection was excerpted from "The Failure of Leadership," in *Juggernaut: Growth on a Finite Planet* (Santa Ana, Calif.: Seven Locks Press, 1996).

Our government was far more forthright in addressing the issue of population growth a generation ago than it is now. Meanwhile, we have grown by 60 million people.

In 1969, President Nixon raised the issue of U.S. population growth. Let me quote him at some length, even though readers may have seen this quotation before. His was a prophetic vision from, perhaps, a surprising source.

> In 1917 the total number of Americans passed 100 million, after three full centuries of steady growth. In 1967—just half a century later—the 200 million mark was passed. If the present rate of growth continues, the third hundred million persons will be added in roughly a thirty-year period. This means that by the year 2000, or shortly thereafter, there will be more than 300 million Americans.
>
> The growth will produce serious challenges for our society. I believe that many of our present social problems may be related to the fact that we have had only fifty years in which to accommodate the second hundred million Americans. . . . Where, for example, will the next hundred million Americans live? . . . Other questions confront us. How, for example, will we house the next hundred million Americans? . . .
>
> How will we educate and employ such a large number of people? Will our transportation systems move them about as quickly and economically as necessary? How will we provide adequate health care when our population reaches 300 million? Will our political structures have to be reordered, too, when our society grows to such proportions?
>
> We should establish as a national goal the provision of adequate family planning services within the next five years to all those who want them but cannot afford them ("Special Message to the U.S. Congress on Problems of Population Growth," July 18, 1969).

The current president might well be urged to repeat that final rec-
ommendation as the first plank in any program to address welfare reform
and the exploding problem of pregnancy among unmarried teenage girls.
Here we have Richard Nixon and Joycelyn Elders hand in hand. Quite a
surprise. President Nixon proposed, and Congress later created, a distinguished National Commission on Population Growth and the American
Future, chaired by John D. Rockefeller III. In 1972, the Commission
concluded that the country would benefit if population growth stopped. It
made many explicit recommendations. Among them:

- That the government establish a permanent long-term strategic planning capability to monitor demographic, resource, and environmental trends, serve as a "lobby for the future," and recommend policies
  to deal with looming problems.
- That preparations be made to deal with the anticipated growth of met-
  ropolitan areas by reforming the governmental arrangements it has
  characterized as "archaic."
- That there be a national, publicly funded "voluntary program to reduce unwanted fertility, to improve the outcome of pregnancy, and to
  improve the health of children." (This was to include education, contraceptive information, and—delicate as the subject was even then—
  abortion.)
- That immigration levels not be increased, that those levels be periodically reviewed to see if they are too high, that there be civil and crim-
  inal penalties for employers of illegal aliens, and that the enforcement
  program be strengthened.

The Rockefeller Commission recommendations were quickly swept
under the rug. They were controversial and it was an election year. Let us
not forget that blunt, honest population study. The recommendations
would be a good starting place even now for organizations seeking to make
realistic proposals about how to address the United States's future.

Eight years later, the *Global 2000 Report* to President Carter described some of the connections between U.S. population growth and resource and environmental problems. It offered no recommendations, but

it was followed up by a booklet of action proposals from the U.S. Department of State and the Council on Environmental Quality, which included eight broad recommendations concerning U.S. population growth.

The United States should develop a national population policy, which addresses the issues of

- population stabilization
- the availability of family planning programs
- rural and urban migration issues
- public education on population concerns
- just, consistent, and workable immigration laws
- the role of the private sector—nonprofit, academic, and business
- improved information and capacity to analyze impacts of population growth within the United States
- institutional arrangements to ensure continued federal attention to domestic population issues

These proposals were less specific than those of 1972, but they reiterated the same themes.

We have been slipping backward since then. Business wants cheap labor. Would-be ethnic leaders want to enlarge their constituency. They play on others' guilt and the mystique of "a nation of immigrants" so that immigration policy is paralyzed. Politicians are intimidated by the ferocity of right-to-lifers who confuse family planning with abortion and who have promoted their view to an absolute—demanding the right to impose it on others. Immobilized on these two issues, Washington is unable to address population change. This is a particularly dangerous abdication of the government's oft-abdicated responsibility to serve the people.

FROM HOSTILITY TO AMBIVALENCE

The Reagan administration was openly hostile to the population movement. It tried at first to discontinue all foreign population assistance, and when Congress resisted, the funding was provided by a continuing resolution. It suspended assistance to the U.N. Fund for Population (UNFPA). At the U.N. Mexico City conference on population, the U.S. representative astonished world leaders by declaring that population growth was "neutral" in development. Only the Vatican representative agreed.

The Bush administration insofar as possible simply avoided the issue as too hot to handle, though Bush in earlier years had been openly supportive of world efforts to stop population growth. The Clinton administration has supported increased family planning assistance to poor countries, but it has avoided the issue of U.S. population growth.

Even those politicians who abstractly recognize the population problem instinctively revert to growth as a solution to the problems facing them. President Clinton has said some of the right words about population growth. On Earth Day 1993, the president observed that there may be 9 billion people on the planet in the future and that "its capacity to support and sustain our lives will be very much diminished."

When faced with current problems such as unemployment, however, he reverts to the thoroughly American and romantic idea of growing out of them. His March 14, 1994, address to the G7 was particularly revealing of his mind-set: "There is no rich country on earth that can expand its own job base and its incomes unless there is global economic growth. In the absence of that growth, poorer countries doing the same thing we do for wages our people can't live on will chip away at our position. When there is a lot of growth, you can be developing new technologies, new activities and new markets. That is our only option."

President Clinton gave a speech on population on June 29, 1994, to the National Academy of Sciences. He emphasized the need to invest in women. He added that "reducing population growth without providing economic opportunities won't work" and that the population problem would be pursued "as part of the larger issue of sustainable development." He said that "Our population policy is rooted in the idea that the family should be at the center of all our objectives," but he did not elaborate how that relates to population growth. In short, to be unkind: bromides.

The speech reflected the president's internal dichotomy, a mind-set that has not yet absorbed the lessons of a finite earth under environmental onslaught. He would solve every problem by encouraging growth.

"We're going to talk about what we can do within the G7 to promote not just growth, but more jobs—because a lot of the wealthy countries are finding they can't create jobs even when they grow their economy."

On world population, he said variously that "you must reduce the rate of population growth" or (ambiguously) "stabilize population growth." Few people in the population movement would consider those to be sufficient goals. If the *rate* were halved, third world population would still double every three generations. The earth could not sustain it.

Somebody should tell the president that perpetual growth is impossible on a finite planet. We must find other solutions.

PASSIVITY

Passivity is a broader and more general problem that paralyzes any effort to avert population growth. Politicians and planners, like scientists, regularly treat population as an "independent variable" that must be accommodated but cannot be changed.

This attitude can be seen at all levels of government. The planners accept a projection of population growth for the next few years and then calculate how many roads, schools, and sewage lines are needed. They do not ask where that leads us. What will our prospect look like then? Will we simply have to build more of everything, forever? They do not explore how that population growth might be avoided. This mind-set endures, even where the voters have elected city and county officials on "no-growth" tickets. When I chided a planner for that perspective, the retort was "planners lose their jobs when they begin to talk like that."

It does indeed require a change of thinking habits, particularly for a local government to recognize how it can influence population growth, but the change can be made. Any county, for instance, is entitled to develop zoning that would offer the hope of keeping population and water supplies in balance. Beyond that, county representatives should tell the state's elected representatives in Washington about the effect of national policies such as immigration laws on their own situation. They would, in a wiser world, also ask what fertility in their own county was doing to growth.

So far as I know, the only argument that interested the states and counties in the recent congressional debate over the immigration bills was the potential effect on their welfare and public health costs. They do not see the underlying population argument: immigration drives up population and creates an endless need for more services and more growth.

THE FAILURE OF LEADERSHIP

The United States needs leadership if we are to neutralize or convince the advocates of growth and do something about population. The two best candidates to provide it are environmental groups and our political leaders. Some leaders in both categories see the population problem, but almost none of them have dared to take on the forces that drive it.

THE TIMID CRUSADE

The big environmental organizations, which should be leading the crusade to bring U.S. population growth to a halt, see the dangers and say they believe population growth should stop. During the 1988 presidential campaign, a coalition of eighteen environmental organizations prepared a "Blueprint for the Environment" for the guidance of the incoming U.S. administration. The document included the statement that "U.S. population pressures threaten the environment all across our nation" and gave some examples. It said that family planning and the availability of contraceptives must be expanded worldwide. It recommended "an official population policy for the United States" and said that "We must assure that federal policies and programs promote a balance between population, resources, and environmental quality."

So far, so good, but they do not say how that goal might be pursued. I repeat: the only two variables available to influence population growth are fertility and migration. That proposition seems self-evident, but it poses an apparently insuperable stumbling block to the major environmental organizations. None of them has been willing to endorse specific policies on immigration or fertility, and only one—the Wilderness Society—has recently called for lower immigration and fertility.

Population Policy: Will Current Programs Succeed?

Kingsley Davis

This selection was excerpted from *Science* 158, no. 3802 (November 10, 1967).

Throughout history the growth of population has been identified with prosperity and strength. If today an increasing number of nations are seeking to curb rapid population growth by reducing their birthrates, they must be driven to do so by an urgent crisis. My purpose here is not to discuss the crisis itself but rather to assess the present and prospective measures used to meet it. Most observers are surprised by the swiftness with which concern over the population problem has turned from intellectual analysis and debate to policy and action. Such action is a welcome relief from the long opposition—or the timidity—which seemed to block forever any governmental attempt to restrain population growth, but relief that "at last something is being done" is no guarantee that what is being done is adequate. On the face of it, one could hardly expect such a fundamental reorientation to be quickly and successfully implemented. I therefore propose to review the nature and (as I see them) limitations of the present policies and to suggest lines of possible improvement.

THE NATURE OF CURRENT POLICIES

With more than thirty nations now trying or planning to reduce population growth and with numerous private and international organizations helping, the degree of unanimity as to the kind of measures needed is impressive. The consensus can be summed up in the phrase "family planning." President Johnson declared in 1965 that the United States would "assist family planning programs in nations which request such help." The Prime Minister of India said a year later, "We must press forward with family planning. This is a programme of the highest importance." The

Republic of Singapore created in 1966 the Singapore Family Planning and Population Board "to initiate and undertake population control programmes."

As is well known, "family planning" is a euphemism for contraception. The family-planning approach to population limitation, therefore, concentrates on providing new and efficient contraceptives on a national basis through mass programs under public health auspices. The nature of these programs is shown by the following enthusiastic report from the Population Council:

> No single year has seen so many forward steps in population control as 1965. Effective national programs have at last emerged, international organizations have decided to become engaged, a new contraceptive has proved its value in mass application, . . . and surveys have confirmed a popular desire for family limitation. . . . An accounting of notable events must begin with Korea and Taiwan. . . . Taiwan's program is not yet two years old, and already it has inserted one IUD [intrauterine device] for every 4–6 target women (those who are not pregnant, lactating, already sterile, already using contraceptives effectively, or desirous of more children). Korea has done almost as well . . . has put 2,200 full-time workers into the field, . . . has reached operational levels for a network of IUD quotas, supply lines, local manufacture of contraceptives, training of hundreds of M.D.'s and nurses, and mass propaganda. ("Studies in Family Planning," no. 9 [1966])

Here one can see the implication that "population control" is being achieved through the dissemination of new contraceptives, and the fact that the "target women" exclude those who want more children. One can also note the technological emphasis and the medical orientation.

What is wrong with such programs? The answer is, "Nothing at all if they work." Whether or not they work depends on what they are expected to do as well as on how they try to do it. Let us discuss the goal first, then the means.

GOALS

The promised goal—to limit population growth in order to solve population problems—is a large order. One would expect it to be carefully analyzed, but it is left imprecise and taken for granted, as is the way in which family planning will achieve it.

When the terms *population control* and *population planning* are used, as they frequently are, as synonyms for current family-planning programs, they are misleading. Technically, they would mean deliberate influence over all attributes of a population, including its age-sex structure, geographical distribution, racial composition, genetic quality, and total size. No government attempts such full control. By tacit understanding, current population policies are concerned with only the *growth* and *size* of populations. These attributes, however, result from the death rate and migration as well as from the birthrate; their control would require deliberate influence over the factors giving rise to all three determinants. Actually, current policies labeled population control do not deal with mortality and migration but only with birth input. This is why another term, *fertility control*, is frequently used to describe current policies. But, as I show below, family planning (and hence current policy) does not undertake to influence most of the determinants of human reproduction. Thus these programs should not be referred to as population control or planning, because they do not attempt to influence the factors responsible for the attributes of human populations, taken generally; nor should they be called fertility control, because they do not try to affect most of the determinants of reproductive performance.

The ambiguity does not stop here, however. When one speaks of controlling population size, any inquiring person naturally asks, What is "control"? Who is to control whom? Precisely what population size or what rate of population growth is to be achieved? Do the policies aim to produce a growth rate that is nil, one that is very slight, or one that is like that of industrial nations? Unless such questions are dealt with and clarified, it is impossible to evaluate current population policies.

Logically, it does not make sense to use *family* planning to provide *national* population control or planning. The "planning" in family planning is that of each separate couple. The only control they exercise is control over the size of *their* family. Obviously, couples do not plan the size of the nation's population, any more than they plan the growth of the national income or the form of the highway network. *There is no reason to expect that the millions of decisions about family size made by couples in their own interest will automatically control population for the benefit of society. On the contrary, there are good reasons to think they will not do so.* At most, family planning can reduce reproduction to the extent that unwanted births exceed wanted births. In industrial countries the balance is often negative—that is, people have fewer children as a rule than they would like to have. In underdeveloped countries the reverse is normally true, but the elimination of unwanted births would still leave an extremely high rate of multiplication.

IS FAMILY PLANNING THE "FIRST STEP" IN POPULATION CONTROL?

To acknowledge that family planning does not achieve population control is not to impugn its value for other purposes. Freeing women from the need to have more children than they want is of great benefit to them and their children and to society at large. My argument is therefore directed not against family-planning programs as such but against the assumption that they are an effective means of controlling population growth.

But what difference does it make? Why not go along for awhile with family planning as an initial approach to the problem of population control? The answer is that any policy on which millions of dollars are being spent should be designed to achieve the goal it purports to achieve. If it is only a first step, it should be so labeled, and its connection with the next step (and the nature of that next step) should be carefully examined. In the present case, since no "next step" seems ever to be mentioned, the question arises, Is reliance on family planning in fact a basis for the dangerous postponement of effective steps? To continue to offer a remedy as a cure long after it has been shown merely to ameliorate the disease is either quackery or wishful thinking, and it thrives most where the need is greatest. Today the desire to solve the population problem is so intense that we are all ready to embrace any "action program" that promises relief. But the postponement of effective measures allows the situation to worsen.

Unfortunately, the issue is confused by a matter of semantics. "Family *planning*" and "fertility *control*" suggest that reproduction is being regulated according to some rational plan. And so it is, but only from the standpoint of the individual couple, not from that of the community.

What is rational in the light of a couple's situation may be totally irrational from the standpoint of society's welfare.

The need for societal regulation of individual behavior is readily recognized in other spheres—those of explosives, dangerous drugs, public property, natural resources. But in the sphere of reproduction, complete individual initiative is generally favored even by those liberal intellectuals who, in other spheres, most favor economic and social planning. Social reformers who would not hesitate to force all owners of rental property to rent to anyone who can pay, or to force all workers in an industry to join a union, balk at any suggestion that couples be permitted to have only a certain number of offspring. Invariably they interpret societal control of reproduction as meaning direct police supervision of individual behavior. Put the word *compulsory* in front of any term describing a means of limiting births—*compulsory sterilization*, *compulsory abortion*, *compulsory contraception*—and you guarantee violent opposition. Fortunately, such direct controls need not be invoked, but conservatives and radicals alike overlook this in their blind opposition to the idea of collective determination of a society's birthrate.

That the exclusive emphasis on family planning in current population policies is not a "first step" but an escape from the real issues is suggested by two facts. (1) No country has taken the "next step." The industrialized countries have had family planning for half a century without acquiring control over either the birthrate or population increase. (2) The support and encouragement of research on population policy other than family planning is negligible. It is precisely this blocking of alternative thinking and experimentation that makes the emphasis on family planning a major obstacle to population control. The need is not to abandon family-planning programs but to put equal or greater resources into other approaches.

ENCOURAGING LIMITATION OF BIRTHS WITHIN MARRIAGE

In any deliberate effort to control the birthrate, a government has two powerful instruments—its command over economic planning and its authority (real or potential) over education. The first determines (as far as policy can) the economic conditions and circumstances affecting the lives of all citizens; the second provides the knowledge and attitudes necessary to implement the plans. The economic system largely determines who will work, what can be bought, what rearing children will cost, how much individuals can spend. The schools define family roles and develop vocational and recreational interests; they could, if it were desired, redefine the sex roles, develop interests that transcend the home, and transmit realistic (as opposed to moralistic) knowledge concerning marriage, sexual behavior, and population problems. *When the problem is viewed in this light, it is clear that the ministries of economics and education, not the ministry of health, should be the source of population policy.*

THE DILEMMA OF POPULATION POLICY

It should now be apparent why, despite strong anxiety over runaway population growth, the actual programs purporting to control it are limited to family planning and are therefore ineffective. (1) The goal of zero, or even slight, population growth is one that nations and groups find difficult to accept. (2) The measures that would be required to implement such a goal, though not so revolutionary as a Brave New World or a communist utopia, nevertheless tend to offend most people reared in existing societies. As a consequence, the goal of so-called population control is implicit and vague; the method is only family planning. This method, far from de-emphasizing the family, is familistic. One of its stated goals is that of helping sterile couples to *have* children. It stresses parental aspirations and responsibilities. It goes along with most aspects of conventional morality, such as the condemnation of abortion, disapproval of premarital intercourse, respect for religious teachings and cultural taboos, and obeisance to medical and clerical authority. It deflects hostility by refusing to recommend any change other than the one it stands for: the availability of contraceptives.

The things that make family planning acceptable are the very things that make it ineffective for population control. By stressing the right of parents to have the number of children they want, it evades the basic question of population policy, which is how to give societies the number of children they need. By offering only the means for *couples* to control fertility, it neglects the means for societies to do so.

Because of the predominantly pro-family character of existing societies, individual interest ordinarily leads to the production of enough offspring to constitute rapid population growth under conditions of low mortality. Childless or single-child homes are considered indicative of personal failure, whereas having three to five living children gives a family a sense of continuity and substantiality.

In short, the world's population problem cannot be solved by pretense and wishful thinking. The unthinking identification of family planning with population control is an ostrich-like approach in that it permits people to hide from themselves the enormousness and unconventionality of the task. There is no reason to abandon family-planning programs; contraception is a valuable technological instrument. But such programs must be supplemented with equal or greater investment in research and experimentation to determine the required socioeconomic measures.

There Is No Global Population Problem: Can Humanists Escape the "Catch-22" of Population Control?

Garrett Hardin

This selection originally appeared in *The Humanist* (Chicago: The American Humanist Association, July–August 1989).

Almost two hundred years have passed since Malthus disturbed the world's slumber with his celebrated *Essay on Population*. Today, the world has more than five times as many people in it, and the rate of population increase is nearly four times as great as it was in Malthus's day. Each year, the globe must support 90 million more people. Population control is needed.

Many plans have been proposed, and some have been half-heartedly tried. Out of these trials has come the realization that we are caught in what novelist Joseph Heller called a "Catch-22" situation: *if the proposal might work, it isn't acceptable; if it is acceptable it won't work.*

Unacceptable schemes to control numbers are easy to find. We could elect a dictator and let him shoot the excess population. But we won't. Such a solution would "work" only in a theoretical, beyond-politics sense. (*Homo sapiens*, the political animal, as Aristotle called the human, does not live "beyond politics.") Or we might take no action while waiting for gross overpopulation to produce its own cure in the form of starvation and mass disease. But who is willing to call such inaction a "solution"?

Looking at the other fork of the population Catch-22 is more productive. When we understand exactly why acceptable proposals fail, we may be able to correct them. Humanists, committed to the rational analysis of problems, are in a favorable position to ferret out workable solutions. But a real solution to overpopulation may be as painful to humanists as to others. An effective solution will not be obvious, for, as Freud taught us, the preconscious mind protects its peace by blocking off painful avenues of thought.

The simplest defense against dangerous thinking is to presume a natural self-correcting mechanism. Such a presumption worked pretty well in economics in Malthus's day. Before then, some governments had fixed prices to keep greedy merchants from fleecing their customers. Unfortunately, price-fixing caused more harm than good. Leaving prices free to fluctuate—"laissez faire economics"—worked better. Merchants who were too greedy got less business; some of them went broke. Overall, laissez faire benefited the consumer by producing low prices.

Reasoning by analogy, some optimists in the twentieth century have argued for a laissez faire approach toward population growth. They postulate a "demographic transition" process that automatically stops population growth before it hurts. Since European fertility fell as Europeans became richer, it was argued that all we need to do to help today's poor countries is to try to make them rich. The past half-century has shown that a laissez faire approach toward population growth fails. The needy poor greatly outnumber the charitable rich, and the poor breed faster. Africa's numbers are increasing more than ten times as fast as Europe's.

The argument that greater prosperity produces lower fertility has some support in rich countries, where the industrialized, urbanized way of life leads many couples to prefer a better automobile to another child. In poorly industrialized, rural nations, an increase in income translates into more medicine, less infant mortality, and a faster rate of population growth. The ancient saying, "The rich get richer, and the poor get children," has more wisdom in it than does the demographic transition theory.

That numbers play a role in shaping human behavior we know from the experiences of the Hutterites on our own continent. This hardworking religious group lives by the Christian-Marxist ideal expressed so well by Karl Marx in 1875: "From each according to his ability, to each according to his needs." Two centuries of experience have taught the Hutterites that this ideal works only within small groups—of about 100 to 150 at the most. When the number of the operating community is small, backsliders can be shamed into behaving better. When the number goes beyond 150, noncooperators destroy social unity. Hutterites respond to this threat by constant, amoebalike fissioning of their communities. The experiences of the Hutterites tell us that a voluntary system of population control, when it is *not* backed by legal sanctions, can work only with small groups of people who are intimately involved with one another daily. Shame works when everybody lives in everybody else's pocket.

So what are the chances that American society as a whole can achieve population control by voluntary means? Essentially zero, at present. We have nothing like the Chinese production groups to build on. If we cannot or do not want to evolve in the Chinese direction, we will have to find a means of population control that builds on the traditions of our own society.

Let's look again at the Chinese system. I don't know whether the Chinese language has any equivalent for the word *coercion*, but if it does I see a way the Chinese could acknowledge the propriety of their population control without cringing at the word coercion as we westerners do. Each woman in a production group must realize that the others need to be controlled by the coercion of shame and that she herself can be no exception. The control of all is achieved by *mutual coercion, mutually agreed upon*. Mutuality removes the sting that would come from being singled out of the group. Can such coercion be generated in our society? Of course it can. In fact, it has been from time immemorial. Mutual coercion, mutually agreed upon, is an apt description of *any* restrictive law passed by a democracy. *I* might want to rob banks, but I certainly don't want you to do it. So since I know of no way to keep all others voluntarily from robbing banks, I will help pass a law that keeps everyone—including myself— from doing so. Does mutual agreement have to be unanimous? Certainly not. Only a majority is required to pass a coercive law.

In some cases, however—remember Prohibition—a very large majority may be required. But to demand unanimity would be to abandon all hope of a workable democracy.

By what means will Americans achieve real population control? We don't know yet. Americans are too comfortable to try hard to find an answer; poor countries that are more strongly motivated may beat us to it. Whatever methods prove effective must be grounded in human nature, as China's method is. Individuals must be rewarded for actions that benefit mainly the group (which includes all individuals). In China, freedom from shame is an effective reward. In America, we will probably have to offer monetary rewards for relative sterility. For instance, we might limit the dependency deduction on income tax to two children, or maybe only one. Or the government might give an allowance to every female between the ages of twelve and twenty so long as she does not get pregnant. Ingenuity is called for.

In the meantime, one large step toward population control is already necessary and may be possible: *we must bring immigration virtually to an end and do so soon.* In the absence of immigration, present trends in fertility, if continued unchanged, would bring America to zero population growth in about fifty years. If needed then, the government could offer incentives to parenthood, thus producing population stability. But all that is so far in the future that there is no profit in trying to spell out the details.

Someone asks, "But is not variety a necessary component of a healthy nation?" Before we answer hastily, we should note that Japan admits essentially zero immigrants per year — and what American would be so bold as to say that the Japanese are not doing very well in the modern world? They don't admit new bodies, but they do admit new ideas from everywhere. With modern methods of communication, ideas no longer have to be brought into a country wrapped in human bodies. A wise nation admits just the ideas, leaving the bodies to be taken care of by the nations that produced them. This is the way of survival. Patriotism is rather unfashionable in our time, but can a conscientious humanist be contemptuous of the survival of the people with whom he or she associates daily?

Lastly, someone cries, "But the population problem is a *global* problem. We need global solutions!" Before panicking, let us look at the word *global.* Some problems are certainly global. Take acid rain. Take the greenhouse effect. Both cases involve the atmosphere, which is forever distributed and redistributed over the entire globe. Admittedly, it will be difficult to produce the global cooperation that is needed to solve such global problems, but no lesser solutions will work.

Now, let's look at the potholes in the streets. There are potholes all over the civilized world, but is that any reason for setting up a global pothole authority to fix our potholes? Would the pothole in your street be filled sooner if we globalized the problem?

NO GLOBAL POPULATION PROBLEM

The moral is surely obvious: *never globalize a problem if it can possibly be solved locally*. It may be chic but it is not wise to tack the adjective *global* onto the names of problems that are *merely widespread*—for example, "global hunger," "global poverty," and "the global population problem." We will make no progress with population problems, which are a root cause of both hunger and poverty, until we deglobalize them. Populations, like potholes, are produced locally, and, unlike atmospheric pollution, remain local—unless some people are so unwise as to globalize them by permitting population excesses to migrate into the better-endowed countries. Marx's formula, "to each according to his needs," is a recipe for national suicide. We are not faced with a *single* global population problem but with about 180 separate national population problems. All population controls must be applied locally; local governments are the agents best prepared to choose local means. Means must fit local traditions. For one nation to attempt to impose its ethical principles on another is to violate national sovereignty and endanger international peace. The only legitimate demand that nations can make on one another is this: don't try to solve your population problem by exporting your excess people to us. All nations should take this position, and most do. Unfortunately, many Americans seem to believe that our nation can solve everyone else's population problems. I have presented no more than a sketch of the population problem, but this is surely enough to show that humanists have some hard thinking to do in the near future. Humanism, like science, is a self-correcting system. Humanists should not cling to error merely because it is traditional. With deeper insight into the nature of the world, humanists must reexamine their past attitudes toward rights in general, universal human rights, the primacy of the individual, coercion, the imperatives of the environment, human needs, generosity, and our duty toward posterity. The inquiry will be painful, but faith in the power of reason can give us strength to do what has to be done.

Population Growth: Disaster or Blessing?

Lord Peter T. Bauer

This selection was excerpted from *The Independent Review: A Journal of Political Economy*, vol. III, no. 2 (Oakland, Calif.: The Independent Institute, 1998).

The twenty-third General Population Conference of the International Union for the Scientific Study of Population, which met in Beijing in October 1997, focused on overpopulation as a serious threat to human survival and a major cause of poverty. Warren Buffet, Bill Gates, corporations, governments, and international organizations are dedicating and promising to dedicate enormous resources to reverse the threat of overpopulation. But population density and poverty are not actually correlated.

Poverty in the third world is not caused by population growth or pressure. Economic achievement and progress depend on people's conduct, not on their numbers. Population growth in the third world is not a major threat to prosperity. The crisis is invented. *The central policy issue is whether the number of children should be determined by the parents or by agents of the state.*

Since World War II it has been widely argued that population growth is a major, perhaps decisive, obstacle to the economic progress and social betterment of the underdeveloped world, where the majority of mankind lives. Thus Robert S. McNamara, former president of the World Bank, wrote: "To put it simply: the greatest single obstacle to the economic and social advancement of the majority of peoples in the underdeveloped world is rampant population growth. . . . The threat of unmanageable population pressures is very much like the threat of nuclear war." And many others have made similar statements.

THE APPREHENSIONS REST ON FALSE ASSUMPTIONS

These apprehensions rest primarily on three assumptions. First, national income per person measures economic well-being. Second, economic performance and progress depend critically on land and capital per person. Third, people in the third world are ignorant of birth control or careless about family size; they procreate regardless of consequences. A subsidiary assumption is that population trends in the third world can be forecast with accuracy for decades ahead.

Behind these assumptions and, indeed, behind the debates on population are conflicting views of mankind. One view envisages people as deliberate decision-makers in matters of family size. The other view treats people as being under the sway of uncontrollable sexual urges, their numbers limited only by forces outside themselves, either by Malthusian checks of nature or by the power of superior authority. Proponents of both views agree that the governments of less developed countries (LDCs), urged by the West, should encourage or, if necessary, force people to have smaller families.

National income per person is usually regarded as an index of economic welfare, even of welfare as such. However, the use of this index raises major problems, such as the demarcation between inputs and outputs in both production and consumption. Even if an increase in population reduced income per person, a matter to which I will return later, such a reduction would not necessarily mean that the well-being either of families or of the wider community had been reduced.

In the economics of population, national income per person founders completely as a measure of welfare. It ignores the satisfaction people derive from having children or from living longer. The birth of a child immediately reduces income per person for the family and for the country as a whole. The death of the same child has the opposite effect. Yet for most people, the first event is a blessing, the second a tragedy. Ironically, the birth of a child is registered as a reduction in national income per person, while the birth of a calf shows up as an improvement.

The wish of the great majority of humankind to have children has extended across centuries, cultures, and classes. The survival of the human race evinces that most people have been willing to bear the cost of rearing two or more children to the age of puberty. Widely held ideas and common attitudes reflect and recognize the benefits parents expect from having children. The biblical injunction is to be fruitful and multiply. Less well known in the West is the traditional greeting addressed to brides in

India, "May you be the mother of eight sons." The uniformly unfavorable connotation of the term *barren* reflects the same sentiment. The practice of adoption in some countries also indicates the desire for children. All this refutes the notion that children are simply a cost or burden.

Some have argued that high birthrates in the LDCs, especially among the poorest people, result in lives so wretched that they are not worth living, that over a person's lifetime, suffering or disutility may exceed utility; thus, fewer such lives would increase the sum total of happiness. The implication is that external observers are qualified to assess the joys and sorrows of others; that life and survival have no value to the people involved. This outlook raises far-reaching ethical issues and is unlikely to be morally acceptable to most people, least of all as a basis for forcible action to restrict people's reproductive behavior, especially when one recalls how widely it was applied to the poor in the West only a few generations ago.

Nor is this opinion consistent with simple observation, which suggests that even very poor people prefer to continue living, as shown, for instance, by their seeking medical treatment for injuries and illnesses. Clearly, the much-deplored population explosion of recent decades should be seen as a blessing rather than a disaster, because it stems from a fall in mortality, a prima facie improvement in people's welfare, not a deterioration.

Much of the advocacy of state-sponsored birth control is predicated on the implicit assumption that people in high-fertility third world countries do not know about contraceptives and that, in any case, they do not take into account the long-term consequences of their actions. But most people in the third world do know about birth control and practice it. In the third world, fertility is well below fecundity; that is, the number of actual births is well below the biologically possible number. Traditional methods of birth control have been widely practiced in societies much more backward than contemporary third world countries. Throughout most of the third world, cheap Western-style consumer goods have been conspicuous for decades, whereas condoms, intrauterine devices, and the Pill have so far spread only very slowly. This disparity suggests that the demand for modern contraceptives has been small, either because people do not want to restrict their family size or because they prefer other ways of doing so.

It follows that children are generally wanted by their parents. Of course, a woman who does not want many children may have to bow to the wishes of her husband, especially in Catholic or Muslim societies. Attempting to enforce changes in mores in such societies raises issues that I cannot pursue here. In any event, this matter does not affect my argument. Children are certainly avoidable.

Nor are people in LDCs generally ignorant of the long-term consequences of their actions. Indeed, young women often say that they want more children and grandchildren to provide for them in their old age. The readiness to take the long view is evident also in other decisions, such as planting slow-maturing trees or embarking on long-distance migration.

CONCLUSION

The central issue of population policy is whether individuals and families or politicians and national and international civil servants should decide how many children people may have.

Advocates of officially sponsored population policies often argue that they do not propose compulsion but intend only to extend people's options by assisting the spread of knowledge about contraceptive methods. But people in LDCs usually know about both traditional and more modern methods of birth control. Moreover, in many third world countries, especially in Asia and Africa, official information, advice, and persuasion in practice often shade into coercion. In most of these societies, people are more subject to authority than in the West. And especially in recent years, the income and prospects of many people have come to depend heavily on official favors. In India, for example, promotion in the civil service, allocation of driving and vehicle licenses, and access to subsidized credit, official housing, and other facilities have all been linked at times to the restriction of family size. Forcible mass sterilization, which took place in India in the 1970s, and extensive coercion in the People's Republic of China are only extreme cases in a spectrum of measures extending from publicity to compulsion.

Policies and measures pressing people to have fewer children can provoke acute anxiety and conflict, and they raise serious moral and political problems. The implementation of such policies may leave people dejected and inert, uninterested in social and economic advance or incapable of achieving it. Such outcomes have often been observed when people have been forced to change their mores and conduct. It is widely agreed that the West should not impose its standards, mores, and attitudes on third world governments and peoples. Yet, ironically, the most influential voices call for the exact opposite with regard to population control.

Trust the Parents

Robert Whalen

This selection originally appeared in *Whose Choice: Population Controllers' or Yours?* (Front Royal, Va.: Human Life International, 1992).

> "The children who are born are generally desired. Children at any rate are avoidable. To deny this is to suggest that parents in less developed countries procreate without an understanding of the consequences or without the will or the sense of responsiblity to prevent them. This view treats people of the less developed world with altogether unwarranted condescension or contempt."
>
> Lord Peter T. Bauer, *Equality, the Third World, and Economic Delusion*

> "The birth of every unwanted child is a tragedy, for itself and for the unwilling parents, but in spite of all the attention we have given to the matter, more unwanted children are born to us, the rich, than to them, the poor."
>
> Germaine Greer, *Sex and Destiny*

The population control movement is fired by a strange witches' brew of idealism, selfishness, and fear.

There is no doubt that many of its key activists, together with a large section of grass roots supporters, are motivated by a genuine desire to improve the health of third world women by giving them access to Western contraceptive technology.

There is also the selfishness of those who, consciously or subconsciously, feel that the growing numbers of people in developing countries may represent a challenge to the supremacy of the West.

Finally there is the fear that population growth may be one of the factors propelling us toward an environmental holocaust that will leave the earth uncomfortable for us and perhaps uninhabitable for future generations.

It is clearly impossible, in a monograph of this size, to deal with all the serious issues with which population growth has been connected. It is enough to say here that we must acknowledge these fears to be real enough to the people who express them. Many, no doubt, would say that they deplore the fact that third world parents have to be denied the sort of freedom of choice in matters of family size, which we in the West take for granted, but that this is the lesser of two evils. They regard third world parents as some parents regard their children—well-meaning but so irresponsible that they have to be restrained from behaving in a way that damages themselves and others.

Fundamental to this view is the assumption that third world parents are unable to control their own fertility and that government planners would make a better job of doing it for them. Both of these assumptions are fundamentally flawed.

There is a considerable body of anthropological evidence to suggest that people in different cultures at different times have always regulated their fertility, using a variety of traditional means such as breastfeeding, post-partum abstinence, and *coitus interruptus*. It does not all depend on having access to the latest Western contraceptive technology. Moreover, as Germaine Greer argues in her book *Sex and Destiny* (London: Harper-Collins, 1984), by rushing Western contraception, which is the product of Western culture, onto what she calls traditional societies, we may be disrupting or even destroying the cultural mechanisms that regulate fertility in third world countries. This could result in unwanted pregnancies, the elimination of which is the very aim of family planning.

Parents take into account a variety of factors when deciding how many children they wish to have. They consider their own circumstances, of course, as well as the sort of society in which they are living. Factors such as educational and employment opportunities for their offspring are usually included in these calculations.

The reason that women in India have more children than women in Islington is not that they do not have access to contraception. They do. The reason is that they live in cultures that carry different assumptions about marriage, the family, and childbearing. A traditional greeting for an Indian bride is "May you be the mother of eight sons." This is a contingency against which most Western wives would wish to insure themselves!

The British population group Marie Stopes International (MSI) operates from a house in Whitfield Street that was bequeathed by Marie Stopes herself to the Eugenics Society. Its Georgian door and fanlight, characteristic of London townhouses of the period, are reproduced on the front of MSI clinics around the world to symbolize the way in which, in the view of the clinics' promoters, "the familiar MSI door opens onto life."

It would appear that no one at MSI has considered the possibility that, to an Indian slum-dweller, a Georgian door and fanlight might also symbolize a foreign culture with alien values.

PARENTS OR PLANNERS?

Those who advocate population control do not trust parents. They prefer to put their trust in government planners or in international bureaucrats at the United Nations or the World Bank. These people are supposed to be able to decide how many children parents in third world countries should have, more wisely than third world parents can decide themselves.

Of all the foolish confidences which have been placed in the wisdom of central planning, this must be one of the most absurd. How can a politician or a U.N. official believe that he (or she) comprehends the peasant woman's needs better than she does herself? The politicians would no doubt answer that they have the best interests of the country at heart and that they must plan for a nation, whereas parents work with the more limited horizons of family needs.

In the real world we now have ample evidence that centrally planned economics are wasteful, corrupt, and inefficient. With the collapse of communism in the Eastern bloc and the almost universal acceptance of market economics, it hardly seems necessary to argue this point.

Why should the planners think they know more about other people's reproductive needs than they knew about their economic behavior? Their failure in the one sphere is likely to be every bit as complete as their failure in the other has been shown to have been. It is a failure that carries greater penalties for those who pay the costs, however, because family life and the rearing of children constitute, for most people, their main chance of happiness. Better to be poor than childless—particularly in the under-developed economies of the third world, with no pension funds and no financial institutions to allow people to invest for the future. In those circumstances, children are your pension—your guarantee against an old age of poverty and loneliness.

As the developing countries modernize, or westernize (the terms are interchangeable), it is quite likely that parents will begin to imitate first world norms in family size, as they obtain access to universal health care and education, unemployment benefit and pension funds, and the whole rainbow spectrum of exciting choices and opportunities that science and technology offer us.

To coerce third world parents into taking only one part of the package—the preference for small families or no children at all—without getting the rest is to force them to pay the bill before they have taken delivery of the goods.

THE ROLE OF THE STATE

Perhaps the fundamental question, with regard to population programs, is the relationship between the state and its citizens. This is a core issue, one that underlies any discussion on population, whether it concerns food output, scarcity of resources, energy policy, or the environment.

Do you think that governments and other outside bodies should have the power to coerce people in the most private areas of their lives?

Those who believe in the wisdom and beneficence of planners and politicians may say yes. Those who take a more sceptical view, and regard those in the public sector as every bit as self-interested as private citizens, will say no.

Those with reservations about population control programs view the institutions of the state as existing to serve their families—not the other way around. Given the choice between trusting parents and trusting government planners, they would choose parents every time. Of course parents may make mistakes, but they will bear the cost of those mistakes, because in every culture parents shoulder the main burden of bringing up their children. They are unlikely to make the same mistake twice.

Government planners, on the other hand, need never face the consequences of their failed programs. On the contrary, when they fail—as they must, because population control will never solve the problems it purports to tackle—this failure will provide the justification for strengthening their own powers and increasing the severity of the policies.

THE NEED TO SPEAK PLAINLY

Finally, it would be of the greatest assistance in the public discussion of population policies if those promoting them would observe a more exact use of terminology.

The term *family planning* should not be used to describe schemes that are designed to pressure people into having fewer children than they wish to have. These are more properly designated by the term *population control.*

If Western governments are determined to use their taxpayers' money to finance programs that do not respect the freedom of choice of individual couples, then they should, at least, make clear the nature of the programs to the people who are paying for them.

PREDICTIONS

PART VI: QUICK FACTS

"It is a good deal easier to utter warnings against prophecy than to abstain from it. . . . The real question is not whether we shall abstain altogether from estimating the future growth of population, but whether we shall be content with estimates which have been formed without adequate consideration of all the data available, and can be shown to be founded on a wrong principle."

> Edwin Cannan, "The Probability of a Cessation of the Growth of Population
> in England and Wales during the Next Century" (1895)

- The population of the world is expected to increase by 2.6 billion during the next forty-seven years, from 6.3 billion today to 8.9 billion in 2050.

> United Nations Population Division, *World Population Prospects* (2002 revision)
> (See figure 6.1.)

- The United States is projected to add nearly 140 million people by 2050, bringing the population total to 420 million.

> U.S. Census Bureau (2002)

- One out of every ten persons is now sixty years or older; by 2050, one out of five will be sixty years or older; and by 2150, one out of three persons will be sixty years or older.

> Population Reference Bureau, *Quick Facts* (2002)

- Because fertility levels for most developed countries are expected to remain below replacement level from 2000 to 2050, the population of thirty-three countries is projected to be smaller by midcentury than today (e.g., 14 percent smaller in Japan, 22 percent smaller in Italy, and between 30 and 50 percent smaller in Bulgaria, Estonia, Georgia, Latvia, the Russian Federation, and Ukraine).

> United Nations, *World Population Prospects* (2002 Revision)

- According to the International Institute for Applied Analysis, there is an 85 percent probability that the world's population will have stopped growing by the year 2100, and a 60 percent probability that it will not have exceeded 10 billion before then.

> *National Geographic*, August 6, 2001
> (See figure 6.2 for the United Nations's projected annual population
> growth rate for the world.)

INTRODUCTION

Predictions

For at least two centuries a tremendous battle has been fought over questions associated with future population scenarios. Will world population outweigh our supply of resources? Or is rapid population growth coming to an end? If so, will this limit economic opportunity? And what are the implications for immigration rates and programs such as social security? Future trends in population size are of interest to policymakers, scientists, planners, and other analysts. Many projections have been produced by agencies such as the United Nations, the World Bank, the United States Census Bureau, the United States Social Security Administration, and the International Institute for Applied Systems Analysis in order to get a better handle on what's in store for the future. The purpose of part 6 is to explore how accurate population projections really are. What are the projections claiming, can they be trusted, and can they be improved?

Before looking into the future, it may be useful to take a look at past predictions. In 1798 reverend Thomas Malthus declared, "The power of population is indefinitely greater than the power of the earth to produce subsistence for man." Great advances in agriculture and technology have rendered his prophecy obsolete. Other projections have proved fallible as well. In 1972, Paul Ehrlich warned that 65 million Americans would die of starvation by 1985. This has not been the case. In reality, according to the U.S. Surgeon General, 61 percent of American adults are overweight or obese, and one out of every eight children in the United States is now overweight. In "World Population Prospects: The 1994 Revisions," the United Nations projected that by the year 2050 there would be 9.8 billion people in the world. In 1996 that projection was dropped to 9.4 billion. And in 1998 the projection was down to 8.9 billion people. Almost 1 billion people disappeared in just four years.

These types of predictions can breed unnecessary fear and paralyze reasoned judgment. Thus, it is imperative that we acknowledge the pitfalls of predictions before we can look to the future. The articles in chapter 15 seek to clarify the uncertainty about the demographic future and address new thinking on ways to deal with this uncertainty in order to improve population forecasts. Although the actual outcome of future population levels will never be known, improved forecasting could help humanity better meet the needs of world population in the decades ahead. In chapter 16, the book concludes by exploring recent changes in academic arguments—changes that offer hope for the future wellfare of people around the world.

Chapter Fifteen

FORECASTS

Population forecasts: fact, fiction, or somewhere in between?

Projection Methods: The Hazy Crystal Ball

Joel E. Cohen

This selection was excerpted from "Projection Methods: The Hazy Crystal Ball," in *How Many People Can the Earth Support?* (New York: WW Norton & Company, Inc., 1995).

THE FUTURE IS UNLIKE THE PAST BECAUSE IT HAS NOT HAPPENED YET

Population and professional accounts of population matters often fail to make clear the real uncertainty about the demographic future. For example, in 1990, the *Economist* magazine, a distinguished British source of generally reliable information, published a graph of global population growth rates for the period from 1950 to 2025. The graph made no distinction between the past and the future. It showed the world population growth rate flat for the decade and a half prior to 1990, and then declining after 1990. The graph gave the misleading impression that the future decline in the rate is just as factual as the past estimates were. While a future decline is plausible, it is anything but certain. The *Economist* should have distinguished the future from the past graphically—for example, by using a solid line to draw past data and a dotted line to draw projections of the future. Still better would have been a pair of diverging dotted lines from 1990 into the future to indicate a range of uncertainty about the future population growth rate.

In 1991, the United Nations published a similar figure for the period 1950–2025 in its official *World Population Prospects 1990*, with the identical shortcoming. Neither the caption nor the graphic content of that figure gave any hint that the future of population growth is a matter of surmise, not of fact.

Here is one of the best-kept secrets of demography: most professional demographers no longer believe they can predict precisely the future growth rate, size, composition, and spatial distribution of populations. In 1979, in an official United Nations publication on the methods of population forecasting, the eminent British demographer William Brass, a former president of the International Union for the Scientific Study of Population (the worldwide organization of population scientists), stated flatly: "The science of demography has not yet reached a stage of development where the future growth of population and its subgroups can be predicted."

This uncertainty derives from the way demographers try to develop knowledge about the future of populations. The "how" and the "what" of demographic knowledge about the future are inseparable, for methods shape what people know as much as what people know shapes methods. Demographic knowledge of the future of a population focuses on its internal dynamics. Other views of the future of a population emphasize how ecological, economic, cultural, and other factors may affect a population's internal dynamics.

All approaches to population prediction assume that some mechanism (whether deterministic or partially random) that has operated in the past will continue to operate in the future. (Even divination assumes that the oracle still functions effectively.) Approaches differ, sometimes radically, in the details of the supposed mechanism, including the number and kind of quantities that are assumed to matter. To keep life simple, I will concentrate on predicting total population size.

Attempts to predict total population size have followed three main paths. Mathematical extrapolation assumes that future population sizes are determined by present and past population sizes, and nothing more. A mathematical curve is fitted to the total sizes of a population at past times; then the curve is continued, by using the same mathematical formula, into the future. In most instances, the mathematical formula has no visible connection to the observable mechanisms of human population growth. A second approach, called the cohort-component method, assumes that the composition or distribution of the population according to age and sex plus past age-specific and sex-specific rates of birth, death, and migration are enough to predict the future size of each subgroup of the population and hence the population's growth and size. Various methods are used to extrapolate from past age-specific and sex-specific rates of birth, death, and migration to those of the future. Finally, system models, while typically ignoring the detailed age and sex composition of the population, posit quantitative interactions of population growth and size with nondemographic factors such as industrialization, agriculture, pollution, and natural resources.

While it is desirable to embed population projections in models that represent the economic, political, environmental, and cultural factors that interact with populations, the most ambitious efforts so far show that present knowledge is not up to the task. This book assumes that population size and growth are not independent of the world's economies, environments, and cultures. But for quantitative projections of population, given present limited knowledge, we probably learn as much from the cohort-component method as from the largely untested assumptions of system models.

Examples of the failures of past population forecasts abound. Reciting them seems to be one of demographers' favorite forms of self-flagellation, another being, of course, reading each other's academic publications. When enough examples are collected, patterns begin to emerge. First, the farther in the future the target year of a population forecast lies, the lower the forecast's accuracy, measured either in absolute numbers or as a percentage of error. Second, simple projection methods are at least as good as complicated ones for short-term forecasts. Third, forecasters are generally overconfident of the forecasts they produce and of the central assumptions underlying them.

Predictions based on system models are too recent to evaluate in terms of their success, but the twenty years of experience with the World3 model give grounds for serious doubt.

Population forecasts are prone to error. That is bad news for the demographers who make population forecasts and for the people who use them. The good news for demographers is that they are not the only forecasting professionals without a crystal ball. Political, economic, technological, and cultural forecasts are also prone to error, not to mention forecasts of epidemics, volcanoes, and the weather. Nathan Keyfitz, a mathematical demographer at Harvard, observed: "Demographers can no more be held responsible for inaccuracy in forecasting population twenty years ahead than geologists, meteorologists, or economists who fail to announce earthquakes, cold winters, or depressions twenty years ahead. What we are responsible for is warning one another and our public what the error of our estimates is likely to be" (*Population Change and Social*

Policy [Cambridge, Mass.: Abt Books, 1982]). Even that is difficult, because demographic projection techniques omit important factors that influence population change.

CONFIDENCE: THE LAW OF PREDICTION

I offer a simple proposition about predictions by experts and others. Here is my Law of Prediction: The more confidence someone places in an unconditional prediction of what will happen in human affairs, the less confidence you should place in that prediction. If a prediction comes with an estimated range of error, then the narrower that range, the less you should believe it.

Beyond Six Billion: Forecasting the World's Population

John Bongaarts and Rodolfo A. Bulatao

This selection was excerpted from "Executive Summary" and "Introduction," in *Beyond Six Billion: Forecasting the World's Population*, edited by John Bongaarts and Rodolfo A. Bulatao (Washington, D.C.: The National Academies Press, 2000).

Future trends in population size, age structure, births, and other demographic variables are of interest to a wide range of analysts, including policymakers, scientists, and planners in industry and government. For example, global and national trends in population size are needed to project the future demand for food, water, and energy and the environmental effect of the rising consumption of natural resources. Subnational projections help planners decide where to build new schools and where investments in roads and other infrastructure are required. Reliable estimates of the number of retired people in need of pensions and health care are essential to the optimal design of social security systems.

To address the needs of such a variety of potential users, global as well as national population projections for all countries have been produced in recent decades by various agencies, such as the U.N. Population Division, the World Bank, and the U.S. Census Bureau. (The International Institute for Applied Systems Analysis has also made world and regional but not country projections.) The Panel on Population Projections was asked (by the National Academy of Sciences) to examine these projections: to assess their assumptions, estimate their accuracy and uncertainty, evaluate the implications of current demographic research for projection procedures, and recommend changes where appropriate as well as research that might improve projections. Generally, the panel finds current world projections up to 2050 to be plausible, although they could indeed be improved in some ways, and their uncertainty deserves more precise quantification.

We expand on this broad conclusion below, summarizing, in order, what current projections say about future population trends and how their conclusions were arrived at; how accurate such projections have been in the past; how the projected components of population growth—fertility, mortality, and migration—compare with historical trends; and what degree of uncertainty should be attached to these forecasts. Then we detail our conclusions and suggest how research might improve population projections.

CURRENT WORLD PROJECTIONS

From the 6 billion that had been reached by the end of 1999, world population is now projected to approach 9 billion by 2050. This increase of 3 billion in the next fifty years will be only slightly smaller than the increase of 3.5 billion in world population in the past fifty years. Beyond 2050, forecasts involve so much uncertainty that we do not examine them.

Nearly all world growth to 2050 is projected to occur in developing regions, that is, in Africa, Asia, and Latin America. The population of the industrial (or more developed) world is expected to remain close to its current size, and in some countries, population is likely to decline. Thus the distribution of world population will shift significantly. Over the next fifty years, the share of world population in sub-Saharan Africa, in particular, will rise from 10 to 17 percent of the world total, while the share in Europe will decline from 13 to 7 percent. The population in industrial regions as a whole, now outnumbered almost four to one by the population in developing countries, will be outnumbered by about seven to one by the year 2050.

The projections also indicate a rise in the proportion of people age sixty-five and older in every major region of the world. In the next half-century, the proportion of the population age sixty-five and older is expected to rise from 5 to 15 percent in developing regions, and from 14 to 26 percent in industrial regions.

Fertility, mortality, and migration constitute the components of population growth. The United Nations and other forecasters determine levels and the likely future path of each component, combine these with information on the existing distribution of the population by sex and age (or birth cohort), and then, through extensive though straightforward calculations called the cohort-component method, project future populations.

Projections are inevitably uncertain. The present demographic situation is not known perfectly, and future trends in births, deaths, and net migrants are subject to unpredictable influences. At the start of the twentieth century, forecasters would have had difficulty foreseeing such technological achievements as the development of antibiotics or such social trends as women's increased participation in the labor force. Many other social, economic, political, technological, and scientific developments have influenced population growth by affecting birth, death, or migration rates. Growth has also been influenced by deliberate social policy, such as decisions about public health services, policies affecting the availability of family planning methods, and regulations on immigration. Policies themselves may result from the consideration of population projections, which complicates the attempt to make accurate forecasts.

ACCURACY OF PAST PROJECTIONS

The accuracy of current projections cannot be directly evaluated, but older global and country-level projections can be assessed against current estimates. For instance, the United Nations has been making projections since the 1950s of world population size for the year 2000. These projections have almost all been off by less than 4 percent.

Errors in past projections of the population for specific countries have typically been larger. Across several sets of U.N. and World Bank forecasts, absolute error in projected country populations averaged 4.8 percent in five-year projections but 17 percent in thirty-year projections. As these figures suggest, projection error increases systematically as the projection interval lengthens. Other factors affecting projection accuracy include level of development and size. Errors have been larger for developing countries than for industrial countries, and for smaller countries (especially those under 1 million) than for larger countries.

Country projections became progressively more accurate during the 1950s and 1960s, as demographic data for developing countries improved. Since then, no significant further improvements can be demonstrated. Better data quality played a large role in the earlier improvements. Erroneous estimates of initial population, fertility, mortality, and migration are the dominant cause of error in projections up to ten years long, although longer projections are more sensitive to misspecified trends in population growth components.

Error in projecting a country's total population is generally accompanied by errors in regard to the sizes of particular age groups. Projections of the youngest and the oldest age groups tend to be the least reliable. In the past, these errors have been the result of too high projections of fertility (resulting in too many infants and young children) and too high projections of mortality (resulting in too few elderly).

Current projections are not necessarily subject to the same errors as past projections. Past forecasts, for instance, produced slightly too high world projections for 2000, due mainly to larger than expected fertility declines in a few major countries. Such unexpected fertility declines will never be exactly replicated, and future demographic conditions generally are likely to diverge from conditions that prevailed during the periods covered by past forecasts.

Recognizing this limitation on the conclusions that can be drawn from reviewing past forecasts, the panel also reviewed historical trends and current levels for each component of population growth — fertility, mortality, and migration — in order to determine what inferences might be drawn about likely future trends.

THE UNCERTAINTY OF PROJECTIONS

While broad trends in fertility, mortality, and migration can be discerned and projected into the future with reasonable confidence, substantial uncertainty is attached to the specific trend for any particular country or region. Quantifying this uncertainty is helpful to users of projection results, such as social security actuaries or environmental modelers, because it focuses their attention on alternative population futures that may have different implications and requires them to decide what forecast horizon to take seriously.

In current forecasts, uncertainty is typically expressed by providing alternative scenarios, varying the trajectory for fertility (and, rarely, for mortality and migration). "High" and "low" scenarios are used to indicate a range of possible futures. However, no specific probability is attached to the range, and what it means is therefore unclear.

Probability distributions for projection error can be estimated using an ex post approach. We analyze the distribution of past errors in U.N. forecasts over two decades and use this information, by way of stochastic simulations, to define predictive intervals for the current medium U.N. projection. The approach assumes that the accuracy of current forecasts will be closely related to that of past forecasts.

We estimate that a 95 percent prediction interval for world population in 2030 would extend from 7.5 to 8.9 billion, and a similar interval for world population in 2050 would extend from 7.9 to 10.9 billion. The intervals are asymmetric around the U.N. medium projection of 8.9 billion in 2050. This indicates that, based on the record of previous projections, a greater risk exists of a large understatement of future world growth than of a large overstatement. The intervals suggest that world population decline between 2000 and 2050 is quite unlikely.

Because many country errors cancel each other after aggregation, these prediction intervals for world population are proportionally much narrower than those for individual countries. Across thirteen large countries, the median prediction interval for population in fifty years runs from 30 percent below the point forecast to 43 percent above it, for a total width of 73 percent. This width is more than three times the width of the corresponding projection interval for world population. The width of intervals for regional projections is intermediate, reflecting an intermediate degree of aggregation. The width of prediction intervals does vary greatly across countries — in line with the errors in past projections — and tends to be larger for smaller countries, especially in developing regions.

The historical record on which these prediction intervals are based includes some major unanticipated influences on demographic behavior, such as the HIV/AIDS epidemic, civil wars, and other disturbances that have produced crisis migration and mortality in several countries. To some extent, therefore, these predictive intervals allow for unexpected events. But it is always possible that the future will see developments different in kind from those in the past few decades. These probability distributions do not and cannot allow for such unprecedented catastrophes as nuclear war. If such events occurred, the planning that projections are intended to inform would be of little relevance.

IMPLICATIONS

Current world population projections from the United Nations and the World Bank incorporate the major expected trends in population growth components: continuing decline in fertility in developing countries to low levels; persistence of fertility at these levels in demographically advanced countries; continued rise in life expectancy, although at a slower pace globally than in previous decades; and the persistence of migration into the major receiving countries. The panel's review finds that the projection assumptions regarding future trends in fertility, mortality, and migration are generally supported by available scientific evidence.

SNAPSHOT: Prediction

Forecast Sees Halt to Population Growth by End of Century

John Roach

This selection originally appeared in *National Geographic News* (Washington, D.C.: National Geographic Holdings, Inc., August 6, 2001).

The foreboding threat of world disaster from explosive population growth could turn out to be overly alarmist, say the authors of a new demographic study.

Their forecast shows there's a high chance that the world's population will stop growing before the end of the twenty-first century. It suggests that the total number of people may peak in seventy years or so at about 9 billion people, compared with 6.1 billion today.

The scientists say their prediction is more reliable than other population forecasts because they employed nontraditional but more rigorous methods of analysis. The study was conducted by the International Institute for Applied Systems Analysis (IIASA) in Laxenburg, Austria.

In their report, published in the August 2 issue of *Nature*, the authors attribute the rosier-than-usual outlook to successful efforts in the last few decades to curb fertility rates.

Now, they say, the time has come for society to think seriously about how to meet the needs of a stable but considerably larger world population in the decades ahead.

"We are going to have a stable population. So we have to make sure we have a sustainable environment and a sustainable economy to go with the sustainable population," said Warren Sanderson of IIASA, a co-author of the report.

The figures obtained in the new study are roughly in line with future population scenarios released by the United Nations in 1998.

But some population experts are at odds with IIASA's conclusions, arguing there is no guarantee that population growth will stabilize before the end of the twenty-first century.

"In the 1960s we were panicked about population growth and did something about it," said Carl Haub of the Population Reference Bureau in Washington, D.C. "We find ourselves about halfway to this point of stable population growth. We will get there, but to call the game over in the fifth inning isn't quite right."

CALCULATING PROBABLE OUTCOMES

Determining accurately what the world's population will be in the distant future is impossible because fertility, mortality, and migration rates are highly uncertain. Because of this, some demographers who do population forecasting have adopted an approach — called probabilistic analysis — that helps account for uncertainty. "We don't know what future fertility will be, we don't know future life expectancy, but we can gather information about the ranges [of possible outcomes] they might be in," said Sanderson. From this, demographers calculate the probability, or likelihood, of certain trends or events occurring.

According to IIASA's forecast, there is an 85 percent probability that the world's population will have stopped growing by the year 2100, and a 60 percent probability that it will not have exceeded 10 billion before then.

The study also shows that the world population is likely to be much older in the future, with 34 percent of the population over the age of sixty by the end of the century. Addressing the needs of an older population will require a rethinking of programs providing social security, health, and education, said Sanderson.

Before the world stabilizes, however, there will be a growing demographic divide, the IIASA study warns. On one side will be countries with shrinking populations, such as the European states that were formerly part of the Soviet Union; on the other side, countries with growing populations, such as Nigeria.

This demographic divide is likely to result in enormous stresses both within countries and between countries over immigration and other issues, said Sanderson.

LOTS OF UNCERTAINTY

Although probability-based forecasting is an improvement over population scenarios that do not take uncertainty into account, probability analysis itself is uncertain to some extent, Nico Keilman, an economist at the University of Oslo in Norway, points out in an accompanying article in *Nature*.

Critics of the IIASA study say that no mathematical model can accurately measure the socioeconomic factors that affect population growth. Fertility decline, for example, which is the major factor in a slowdown of population growth, can happen in a variety of settings for unpredictable reasons, Haub explained.

Eastern Europe has always had a higher fertility rate than western Europe, he noted. But when the former Soviet Union broke up, fertility rates in those former Soviet countries plummeted unexpectedly. "The actual outcome of world population growth will depend on how people's social behavior changes," said Haub. "That is really very difficult to predict using any kind of mathematical method."

FIGURE 6.1. Estimated and Projected Population of the World by Projection Variant

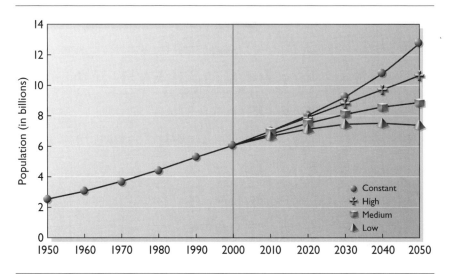

Source: Population Division of the Department of Economic and Social Affairs of the United Nations Secretariat (2003). *World Population Prospects: The 2002 Revision. Highlights.* New York: United Nations. Available via the Internet at http://esa.un.org/unpp/p2k0data.asp.

FIGURE 6.2. Projected Annual Population Growth Rate for the World (Medium Variant)

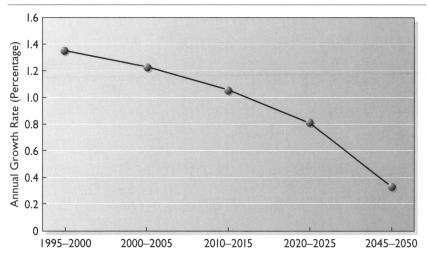

Source: Population Division of the Department of Economic and Social Affairs of the United Nations Secretariat (2003). *World Population Prospects: The 2002 Revision. Highlights.* New York: United Nations. Available via the Internet at http://esa.un.org/unpp/p2k0data.asp.

Chapter Sixteen

A SHIFT IN THINKING

Will a new view of population growth lead to changes in population policy?

A Further Word on the New, Calmer Thinking

Karl Zinsmeister

This selection originally appeared in *The 9 Lives of Population Control*, edited by Michael Cromartie (Washington, D.C.: Ethics and Public Policy Center and Wm. B. Eerdmans Publishing Co., 1995).

In recent years there has been some retreat from population alarmism, and three factors are behind the shift. One is the influence of new statistical data on population growth and its effects, data that have directly contradicted the claims and predictions of "population bomb" theorists. A second factor is reaction against the gross human rights abuses committed in the 1970s and 1980s in the name of population control. A third is important new theoretical research recently carried out by a group of talented and iconoclastic scholars. The new, calmer view of population growth may not be well reflected in popular and mass-media discussions, but it has brought major changes in the academic argument, in U.S. policy, and in U.N. programs. So let us consider the three causative factors in more detail.

THE NEW DATA

The dire predictions of the population explosionists utterly failed to come true. There were no population wars in the 1970s or 1980s. There were no mass die-offs. There were famines, but they were not population famines. The loudly predicted calamities just didn't take place. And indeed there were many pleasant surprises. For instance, Paul Ehrlich wrote in *The Population Bomb* in 1968 that it was a "fantasy" to think that India, which he cited as a paradigm of overpopulation, could feed itself any time in the near future, "if ever." A participant in the Second International Conference on the War on Hunger (also 1968) argued that "the trend of India's annual grain production over the past eighteen years leads me to the conclusion that the present output of about 95 million tons is a maximum level." The prevailing wisdom then was that we had entered a new era of limits, we had reached the end of the line economically in advancing the quality of life, and we were going to have to learn to live with less.

Well, India's annual grain production now totals, not 95 million tons as in 1968, but over 150 million tons, and India is now actually a net exporter of food. The fact that even a country that used to be referred to as a basket case could produce this sort of a gain suggests that those who argue that food production can never keep up with population growth fail to appreciate how quickly new technology and improved economic practices (in this case Green Revolution agricultural products and new market incentives for farmers) can convert formerly redundant people into useful producers.

Another fact that the traditional population theorists did not fully appreciate was how fast the world was changing demographically. As mentioned earlier in this chapter, between 1970 and 1990, the average number of children borne by women in the less developed world declined from 6 to about 3.5. This is a tremendous drop, and I think it's fair to say that it took most demographers by surprise. In just two decades, the birthrate declined about three-fifths of the way toward 2.2, or "zero population growth." The problem of high fertility now seems to be in the process of solving itself in most places.

Still another fundamental fact often overlooked by population alarmists is that, contrary to popular claims, the quality of life in most of the third world has been rapidly *improving*, not declining, during the last few decades. Those were, of course, the very decades when population was growing the fastest. Over the last thirty years, the third world infant-mortality rate has been almost cut in half. Life expectancy at birth has risen by about twenty years. Adult literacy rates in the less developed world have more than doubled since 1960. The claim that rapid population growth vetoes social progress and economic progress runs head on into some very strong countervailing evidence.

REACTION AGAINST ABUSES

The second factor that has produced some skepticism about the international population-control movement is its record of human-rights violations over the last two decades. In 1976 the Indian government declared,

"Where a state legislature . . . decides that the time is ripe and it is necessary to pass legislation for compulsory sterilization, it may do so." In the six months following that ruling, more than 6 million Indians were sterilized, many thousands forcibly so. That episode inspired such fierce grassroots resistance that the government of Indira Gandhi was eventually brought down.

Even before the government issued its public justification, coercion in the name of population control had been rife in India. The distinguished American demographer Richard Easterlin reports that when he was a member of a United Nations Family Planning Mission to India in 1969, program administrators in Bombay told him how strong-arm tactics were used in the slum districts to ensure that government vasectomy targets were met. When Easterlin expressed concern at this, the surprised official answered that "surely the end justifies the means." And high international officials supported these injustices. In November 1976, after the forced sterilization program had been unveiled, World Bank president Robert McNamara paid a personal visit to the Indian family-planning minister to "congratulate him for the Indian Government's political will and determination in popularizing family planning" (quoted in "Population Scares," *Commentary* 84, no. 5 [1987]).

An even more extensive campaign of intimidation and violence in the name of population control has been and continues to be conducted in China. In the early 1980s reports began to reach the West—through, for instance, the work of Stanford anthropologist Stephen Mosher—that the Chinese government was exerting enormous and often brutal pressure on couples to limit their family size to one child. What made this accumulating evidence unignorable in official Washington was a graphic series of three articles in the *Washington Post* in January 1985. After returning from a four-year assignment in China, *Post* reporter Michael Weisskopf was finally free to publish his findings about population-control practices without risking expulsion from the country. I will quote at some length from his report:

> China's family-planning work is backed by the full organizational might of the Communist Party, which extends its influence to every factory, neighborhood, and village. Every Chinese belongs to a . . . workplace or rural gov-

erning [unit], and every unit has a birth control committee headed by party officials. These officials . . . carefully plan new births for their unit, requiring written applications from any couple wanting to have a child, and matching requests with quotas that trickle down from Peking.

[One campaign in northern China], described by a participating doctor, began in November 1983, when officials from every commune in the county searched their records for women under the age of 45 with two or more children. Then they broadcast their names over public loudspeakers and set dates by which each had to report to the clinic for [sterilization]. There was a warning to potential evaders: the loss of half of their state land allotment, a fine of $200—equal to about a year's income—and a late fee of $10 for every day they failed to report. . . . [Such a campaign often sends] whole villages of eligible women into hiding. To head off a mass exodus last year in coastal Fujian province, officials reportedly organized late-night surprise attacks, hustling sleeping women from their beds to twenty-four-hour sterilization clinics. . . .

[Women are] required by national regulation to have IUDs [intrauterine devices] inserted after their first child is born and are strictly forbidden to remove the stainless steel loops. . . . In some city hospitals, doctors automatically implant the devices immediately after a woman gives birth, often without informing the woman or seeking prior consent, according to a Peking gynecologist. . . .

Up to six times a year . . . [Chinese women] are stood before decades-old equipment to endure the kind of fluoroscopic examination discouraged in the West for fear of causing radiation damage to ovaries or fetuses. Frequent X-ray exams are considered necessary because of the high failure rate of IUDs, which are often inserted in a factory-line fashion without concern for sizing. . . . Few unauthorized pregnancies can elude the tight supervision of birth control activists, a phalanx of female members of the party . . . who are deputized by local officials to monitor the reproductive lives of Chinese couples. . . . They know everyone's contraceptive method and make daily house calls to remind birth control pill users to use their pills. . . . The activists closely watch for signs of pregnancy—morning sickness, craving for sour food, or swollen breasts—and cultivate informers to report on their neighbors or co-workers. They keep detailed records of every woman's menstrual cycle, checking to make sure of regularity. . . . [In some cases they post them, very often in workplaces so that if a woman is late everyone knows about it and can begin to exert pressure.]

First come the tactics of persuasion. . . . Several activists visit the pregnant woman's home to explain the need for population control. She is urged to have an abortion for the good of her nation, her community, her family. . . . If she holds her ground, the talks intensify. [Heavy fines and loss of state benefits are threatened.] The meetings go on, often all the way up to the point of delivery. Where talking fails, force often prevails. Sometimes officials use collective coercion in operations like that in Dongguan, where thousands of pregnant women were picked up in trucks and Jeeps, taken to commune headquarters for lectures, then driven to abortion clinics, some reportedly under police escort. (Michael Weisskopf, "Abortion Policy Tears Fabric of China's Society," *Washington Post*, January 7, 1985)

This coercive family planning extends even to Chinese nationals living overseas. We know of Chinese couples studying in the United States in the late 1980s, for instance, who got letters from government officials back home ordering them to have an abortion when the wife got pregnant. They were told that if they did not do so, the entire factory or village from which they had come would be harshly punished.

The Indian and Chinese programs are the leading examples of human-rights abuses that have occurred in a number of different countries in the name of population control. And scandalously, family planners and leaders of the population-control movement in the West have defended and rationalized harsh measures of these sorts. In 1983 the United Nations awarded its first U.N. medal for family-planning achievement. The joint winners were—you guessed it—the directors of the Indian and Chinese programs. The Chinese minister, Qian Zin-Chong, explained a few months later that "the size of a family is too important to be left to the personal decision of a couple. Births are a matter of state planning."

Again, the sad fact is that it isn't merely officials of totalitarian nations that are willing to see this delicate family decision made by government fiat. In 1978, more than half the members of the Population Association of America, which is this country's professional association for demographers, endorsed the opinion that "if world population continues to grow at its present rate, coercive birth control will have to be initiated." Fully a third of these professionals wanted some coercive birth control to begin immediately.

In the mid to late 1980s, a number of prominent Western demographers developed arguments in favor of "beyond voluntary family planning" measures. A major 1984 World Bank report asserted that "ensuring that people have only as many children as they want . . . might not be enough." A 1986 study by leading U.S. academicians favorably entertained the idea of financial and legal penalties to manipulate a couple's childbearing decisions. In other words, important parts of the official international family-planning apparatus have begun to veer toward something much stronger than voluntary family planning. As John Aird wrote in his authoritative 1990 book, *Slaughter of the Innocents* (Washington, D.C.: American Enterprise Press, 1990), "The international family planning movement has crossed the line from humanitarianism into zealotry. It needs desperately to be called back before it does itself further damage." Richard Easterlin, one of the most honored deans of demography, has written,

> We have had sufficient experience now with population programs to realize that they can easily become a vehicle for elite pressure on the poor. I fear that the elevation to legitimacy of "beyond voluntary family planning" measures lends itself to precisely such pressure. . . . Of course one might claim that such measures are in the "ultimate" interest of the poor, but this view leaves one in the uncomfortable position of having to define the person, group, or institution that is better able to judge the interests of the poor than the poor themselves ("World Development Report 1984 Review Symposium," *Population and Development Review* [1985]: 119).

Beyond this obvious potential for the abuse of power, there is a deeper philosophical issue in this debate. The argument is sometimes made that the lives of certain Asian or African or Latin American peasants are miserable and that "we who understand" cannot allow them to perpetuate their misery. But there is another point of view, which starts with the fundamental belief that there is dignity and potential in every human life and that even extraordinarily simple lives, even an existence that is deprived by modern standards, nonetheless can carry great meaning and pleasure. Those of us on the opposite side of the fence from the alarmists believe it is very dangerous to construct a generalized, systematic argument whose bottom line is that human beings are economic, social, and ecological nuisances—that, in short, people are a kind of pollution. That is a road to perilous territory.

THE NEW RESEARCH

The third factor behind the calmer thinking on population is the new theoretical and empirical research on the *actual* results of population growth. Over the last decade, the prevailing arguments about the economic and social ill effects of population growth have been examined, one by one, and most have been found wanting. These arguments—about resource shortages, capital dilution, unemployment and schooling problems, and the like—were taken up earlier in this chapter. Suffice it to say here that the predictions of the population-bombers haven't worked out very impressively.

One of the insights of the new demographic thinking is that the number of people a given area can "support" is subject to constant change and is related to how the people are organized economically and socially. There are 125 million people jammed onto the rocky islands of Japan. Yet, because of their well-structured and highly productive social system, they are among the richest and longest living people in the world.

Table 6.1 makes it apparent that there is no predictable relationship between population density and economic success. The number of people is not the critical variable in determining a society's success. In most places where there is squalor, hunger, and high unemployment, the problem is not *overpopulation* but *underproduction*. People do not only consume, they also produce—food, capital, even resources. More precisely, they produce the ideas that transform a useless resource—say, bauxite sixty years ago—into a useful resource.

The vital requirement for every nation and its leaders is to organize the society economically and politically so that each person will be an asset rather than a burden. In a country whose economy is a mess, each additional baby can be an economic problem; but if the country is structured in such a way as to allow that child to labor and think creatively, he becomes an asset.

What prevents almost all developing countries from providing for their growing populations is not a lack of family-planning programs, nor a shortage of natural resources, nor a lack of Western aid. Rather, it is a *defective economy and government*. Those concerned for the welfare of people in poor countries around the globe ought to focus not on raw numbers but on the institutions that prevent citizens from exercising their creative and productive potential.

TABLE 6.1.   Population Densities of Rich and Poor Nations (1992)

	People per Square Kilometer	*Per Capita Gross National Product*
Japan	329	$28,190
United States	27	23,240
Germany	226	23,030
Netherlands	373	20,480
Hong Kong	5,536	15,360*
South Korea	444	6,790
Brazil	18	2,770
Guatemala	91	980
Bolivia	7	680
China	124	470
Nigeria	113	320
India	272	310
Bangladesh	794	220
Ethiopia	47	110

* Gross domestic product

CONCLUSION

Population puzzle—boom or bust?

It is the duty of governments, and of individuals, to form the truest opinions they can; to form them carefully, and never impose them upon others unless they are quite sure of being right. But when they are sure, it is not conscientiousness but cowardice to shrink from acting on their opinions, and allow doctrines which they honestly think dangerous to the welfare of mankind, either in this life or another, to be scattered abroad without restraint. . . . Men and governments must act to the best of their ability. There is no such thing as absolute certainty, but there is assurance sufficient for the purposes of human life. . . . Complete liberty of contradicting and disproving our opinion, is the very condition which justifies us in assuming its truth for purposes of action; and on no other terms can a being with human faculties have any rational assurance of being right.

John Stuart Mill, *On Liberty*

This compendium of essays tells the story of the population debate—a debate about the race between human population and human ingenuity, about the very nature of the human experience. We have sought to provide an even-handed and thorough examination of the main issues concerning world population by looking at the history of the population debate, discussing the ethical underpinnings, highlighting important facts and trends, examining the major public policy controversies, acknowledging the pitfalls of predictions, and addressing recent changes in the debate.

By fostering the competition of ideas, we hope to encourage the reader to set aside preconceived conclusions and to think critically about the population conundrum. Population has inspired an intellectual battle of ideas, complete with contradictory data. The differences in the forecasts—prosperity or plight—are so extreme that one might consider dismissing the entire debate. If the experts can't make headway on the issue, then why should the average citizen try to sort it out? But after peering through the cloud of information, it is clear that population is an issue that affects everyone. Consequently, it is essential to obtain a true sense of what lies ahead for the state of humanity.

The population debate is an old one but not a tired one. Current headlines continue to acknowledge its importance and highlight the discourse on emerging trends and potential outcomes. The population puzzle of boom or bust remains to be solved.

APPENDIXES

A Brief History of Population

This selection was excerpted from *A Brief History of Population*, available online at www.popinfo.org (Seattle, WA: Facing the Future, 2003).

Through nearly all of human history, our ancestors lived as hunter-gatherers. They lived in small clans or tribes and followed the migration of animals and the seasonal growth of edible plants. But from about eight thousand to fifteen thousand years ago—in a variety of locations around the world—they began to take up a settled existence.

The reason for this fundamental change in the way people lived was quite simple—human numbers had grown to the point that it had become necessary. The population had outgrown the capacity of hunting and gathering to support it. (Depending on the productivity of local ecosystems, it may take as much as one to three square miles of land per person to support the hunter-gatherer lifestyle.)

Humans had already penetrated and colonized all the continents by then. They had begun to modify their environments, burning grasslands, clearing forests, and hunting many large species to extinction. Except in areas too cold, too hot, or too dry to support them, they had exploited local ecosystems to the best of their ability. And, apparently, in a variety of regions around the world, they had reached the limits of local resources.

The need to feed larger populations forced people to take up agriculture, because farming produces anywhere from ten to one hundred times as much food per unit of land as hunting and gathering. Human ingenuity and technology made this transition possible, because people had, by this time, learned how to sow crops and domesticate animals. The need to tend and defend their fields and pastures then required the founding of fixed settlements.

When this fundamental shift from hunting and gathering to farming, and from a nomadic to a settled existence, began, the earth's population was still quite small, perhaps 5 to 10 million. That number had increased only slowly over the previous 2 million years, because life was hazardous and short. People probably lived only twenty to twenty-five years on average, and almost as many people died each year from hunger, accidents, or disease as were born.

Beginning with the Age of Agriculture, however, humans began to prosper, and population began to grow dramatically. (One of the basic realities of biology is that when any organism has excess food and available habitat, its numbers increase.) Farming produced a lot more food than had ever been available in the past, and population grew in response. More people required more food, so production was increased, allowing population to grow even further.

From an anthropological perspective, this convergence of agriculture, a settled existence, and population growth made for a fascinating time. A number of significant changes occurred that we identify with the emergence of civilization.

One of the first changes was architectural. When societies had excess food, they typically built walls to protect it, and people began to live within those walls.

As food production expanded, certain members of society could be freed from producing food to do other things. Some became soldiers to guard the food. Some became administrators and collected taxes to support the soldiers. Some became priests. (This is the point at which formalized religions emerge, and at which the priesthood becomes a social class.) And some became artisans and inventors, pushing the technological envelope with creations such as pottery, bronze, and the wheel.

As food surpluses mounted, it became necessary to identify the ownership of stored food, and writing systems developed. As social complexity increased, the demand for writing grew. Scribes were needed, as were schools and teachers to train them.

As civilizations expanded, they developed legal systems, because once population reached a critical mass, the kind of social enforcement that served to keep order in tribal groups became ineffective. Some sort of justice system—police, courts, prisons, and executioners—had to be created.

The combination of all these factors led not only to flourishing cultures but also to unprecedented population growth. By the time of the First Dynasty in Egypt, circa 3000 B.C.E. (before the common era), global population had grown to an estimated 100 million—ten to twenty times the increase in human numbers over the preceding 2 million years. By the birth of Jesus Christ, that number was perhaps 250 million—almost the size of the United States today.

As productivity increased—fostered by inventions such as the plow, pottery, ironwork, and the water wheel, as well as a greater understanding of raising plants and animals—food supplies increased further. In response to available food supplies, human numbers increased again.

More people required more land for fields and towns, which in turn led to greater productivity and prosperity, and again to more people.

THE IMPACTS OF GROWTH

As human numbers increased, both positive and negative impacts of growth became apparent. Larger populations contributed to greater military power through larger armies. More people stimulated economic growth due to increased numbers of producers and consumers. They pushed technological development because some people could be freed from producing food to become craftsmen and inventors.

Larger populations also provided sufficient labor to construct public works projects, such as fortifications, roads, and irrigation systems, as well as administrative centers and monuments. But larger populations also caused environmental destruction, forced migration, and conflict.

Civilizations typically arose and flourished because of the availability of such resources as fertile soil, good water, minerals for metalwork, or forests for fuel and shipbuilding. In the prosperous times that followed the exploitation of those resources, population tended to increase. That larger population then exploited the resource base to a greater degree.

At some point a threshold was reached, beyond which the resource base could no longer support the population. The resulting disruption then caused problems similar to those we see today from severe population pressures—social and economic turmoil, hunger, migration, and war.

As civilizations faced extreme resource scarcity, typically one of three things happened: they overran and often assimilated another civilization to secure new resources; in their weakened condition, they were overrun by another culture; or they simply collapsed and their people dispersed. We can see this in our cultural birthplace in the Fertile Crescent, and the progression of civilizations that flourished and collapsed there—from Babylon, to the Hittites, to Assyria, and to Persia. All these societies committed what author Jared Diamond calls "ecological suicide" (*Guns, Germs, and Steel: The Fate of Human Societies* [New York: WW Norton and Co., 1997]).

The transition from nomadic lifestyles to agriculture and civilization as we know it began in three primary regions of the world—southwest Asia, China, and Mesoamerica. But none of those areas could sustain the intensive agriculture necessary to support large populations, and all became increasingly degraded. Because of food scarcity, large numbers of people lived on the edge of starvation.

Resource scarcity also caused other impacts. As historian Gwynne Dyer wrote, "The basis of civilization is agriculture, which transforms the land into a valuable possession that requires protection" (*War* [New York: Random House, 1987]). It is understandable then that the first recorded war in human history was fought between two cities in the Tigris-Euphrates Valley over the movement of a boundary stone marking fields. To threaten a society's farmland was to threaten its food supply, which was to threaten its very existence.

Since that time, countless wars have been fought over hunting grounds, farmland, forests, water, salt, minerals, or control of strategic areas or trade routes. Underlying all these conflicts have been the greater needs of greater numbers of people.

Viewed through a demographic lens, the rise and fall of civilizations fits a similar pattern. The Hyksos' conquest of Egypt around 1600 B.C.E., for example, is credited to their use of horses and chariots. But driving that conquest were population growth and resource scarcity, compounded by deforestation, desertification, and soil erosion in the Hyksos' original homelands in Syria and Palestine. When their traditional homeland could no longer support their population, the Hyksos seized Lower Egypt, the richest territory they knew of.

The expansion of the Greek Empire can be similarly linked to population pressures. By 650 B.C.E., population had increased significantly in response to the prosperity brought by trading. Unfortunately, environmental destruction—mainly deforestation and soil erosion—also increased. Plato, in his *Crititas*, wrote: "What now remains compared with what then existed is like the skeleton of a sick man, all the fat and soft earth having wasted away, and only the bare framework of the land being left. . . ."

The combination of population growth and environmental destruction meant that the supply of farmland—and therefore food—was insufficient to meet the needs of Greece. This stimulated the Greek colonization of the forest and farmlands around the Mediterranean and the Black Sea.

The rise of Rome was also profoundly affected by increasing human numbers. The fledgling civilization fought its first major wars against the Samnites of northern Italy, who were forced by population growth down into the Roman province of Campania in search of farmland. After three major wars, the Romans prevailed. They then employed their expanded and improved army to seize additional cropland, forests, and mineral resources all around the Mediterranean. With a larger population, a larger army, and a booming economy due to captured resources, Rome became the world's first great empire.

But population growth and the resulting environmental destruction also contributed to the fall of Rome. The constant need to feed more people, maintain armies, and support a growing economy forced the Romans to overexploit their resource base.

Rome had guaranteed every citizen a daily ration of bread since 58 B.C.E. to ensure political stability. To create fields to produce enough grain (and to provide construction and shipbuilding materials), forests were cleared around much of the Mediterranean. Deforestation and erosion worsened as fields were carved out on ever steeper slopes in an attempt to produce still more grain. Rome was forced to nearly abandon several major cities such as Leptis Magna, in what is now Libya, as erosion and climate change caused by deforestation destroyed their harbors and grain fields.

The empire began gradually to contract as environmental destruction, outside military pressure, and internal dissent mounted. By the time the Roman capital was overrun in the early fifth century C.E. (common era) by the Goths, the western empire was only a shadow of its former glory.

SETBACKS

Population growth was not always linear. Famine, war, or disease often decimated local or regional cultures. In fact, as population grew, another pattern of human history emerged—natural and human-induced disasters that killed large numbers of people.

Historically, human numbers were greatly limited by disease. This was especially true as growing populations became more concentrated in cities, where people were more easily exposed to infectious agents. (It takes a minimum population for diseases to sustain themselves. Measles, for example, requires about seven thousand susceptible individuals to ensure its survival. A regional population of three hundred thousand to four hundred thousand, with regular contact, is probably the minimum necessary to sustain that disease.)

Plague devastated Athens in 429 B.C.E. and large parts of China two hundred years later. It ravaged the Roman Empire from 160 to 184 C.E., killed a large percentage of the population of Constantinople in 542 C.E., and reached Britain by 547. By the end of that cycle, in 594, the population of Europe had been halved. Plague returned periodically, peaking in the fourteenth century, when it killed an estimated one-third of the population of Europe.

Other diseases were equally devastating, if more localized. When Spanish conquistadors invaded Mexico in 1517, the native population was perhaps 25 million. In less than a century, it had fallen to just over 1 million because of introduced diseases, such as measles. In South America, the introduction of smallpox by Europeans damaged the Inca Empire so badly that Pizarro's few soldiers, horses, and guns easily toppled it.

Famine also slowed population growth, appearing regularly around the world from the earliest times in recorded history. The Near Eastern and Mediterranean worlds were always susceptible to famine, as indicated by Biblical references.

Famine was an integral part of Roman history and closely linked to the final collapse of the empire. As its population grew, and environmental destruction limited local productivity, the empire became dependent on foreign sources of grain. As the empire contracted—and grain-producing lands in Germany, Egypt, and Britain were lost—Roman authorities were unable to provide the guaranteed distribution of food that had long maintained domestic stability. Between 400 and 800 C.E., the population of the city of Rome fell by more than 90 percent, largely because of famine.

Large-scale famine also occurred in the Byzantine Empire in 927, Japan in 1232, Germany and Italy in 1258, England in 1294 and 1555, all of Western Europe in 1315, Russia in 1603, Bengal in 1669 and 1769, Ireland in 1845–1849, and China and India in 1876 and 1879. Tens of millions died in these events, sometimes reducing local populations by as much as one-third or more.

Despite these setbacks, however, population continued to grow. By 1500, world population had reached an estimated 500 million. It was around this time that the era of western colonial expansion began in earnest, driven by the demands of more people for more resources.

THE AGE OF EUROPEAN EXPANSION

Historically, shortages of farmland, water for irrigation, timber for construction and fuel, or minerals for manufacturing all limited population size and economic opportunities. Lack of work, economic instability, local food scarcity, and lack of available land also drove migration and conflict, as people competed for resources.

But those effects tended, for the most part, to be localized. People migrated from country to city, and neighboring or regional civilizations clashed. So while the distribution of resources changed with the ebb and flow of cultures, the general availability of resources in any region did not increase. The Europeans broke out of this pattern, however, when they began to conquer and colonize distant areas of the world.

The first Europeans to actively colonize other regions were the Vikings. The forces behind their expansion were complex, but scarcity of farmland was a key element. As historian J. M. Roberts wrote, "These Scandinavians combined trade, piracy and colonization, stimulated by land hunger" (*A History of Europe* [New York: Allen Lane, 1997]).

The first known Viking raid occurred in 793 C.E., and over the next four hundred years they discovered and settled the Faroe Islands, Iceland, Greenland, and parts of Newfoundland.

Moving east and south, the Vikings penetrated the heartland of Russia (which is named for the Rus, as the Vikings were called there) and founded city-states such as Kiev and Novgorod. They raided as far south as Constantinople and Baghdad and threatened French cities to the point that they were given huge tracts of land in what is now Normandy ("land of the Northmen") in exchange for peace. And they conquered much of the richest farmland of northern England and Ireland.

By the early fifteenth century, Portugal had begun to explore and exploit the west coast of Africa. The wealth the Portuguese captured created an economic and population boom at home and stimulated further explorations. The Portuguese pushed down the coast of Africa, then eastward. They established trading colonies in India about the time Columbus reached the Caribbean and launched the era of Spanish exploration and colonization.

Although the early European colonies were seen primarily as sources of wealth, the flood of resources they returned to Europe caused a profound shift. As expected, increased prosperity stimulated local population growth in Portugal and Spain. But new protein sources increased the ability of northern European nations to produce food, and their populations began to expand rapidly.

Less than one hundred years after the introduction by the Spanish of the potato from South America and maize corn from Mexico, England and Holland had joined the scramble for overseas colonies.

This new burst of growth (world population grew as much between 1500 and 1750 as it had in the previous fifteen hundred years) created renewed scarcities, particularly of farmland. Because of this, smaller nations such as England and Holland began to see colonies not only as places to obtain resources from but also as places to send excess population to.

This trend continued through the nineteenth century, with nations such as Germany, Sweden, and Norway, as well as British-occupied Ireland, also reducing population pressure through emigration to North America.

Conflict between nations intensified throughout the Age of Expansion, as competing powers fought over trade routes and access to resources in North and South America, Asia, and Africa. But conflict also occurred on a more local scale, as the new arrivals clashed with indigenous populations.

As European settlers expanded across North America, for example, they displaced or dispossessed native inhabitants. These peoples were forced to migrate and subsequently displaced the tribes onto whose lands they were driven. If they failed to do so, they vanished as a culture.

As Americans pushed further west in search of more land and resources to supply a growing population, more clashes followed.

By the time the western edge of the continent was reached, the new immigrants controlled the majority of the land and resources, and most surviving indigenous populations were relegated to reservations.

THE INDUSTRIAL REVOLUTION AND THE AGE OF SCIENCE

World population growth continued through the nineteenth century at a high rate, spurred by the general economic expansion and increased food production as new lands were opened up. Around 1830, human numbers reached 1 billion for the first time.

The Industrial Revolution generated a tremendous economic boom, as machine power made mass manufacturing possible. Steam-powered transportation systems allowed people and goods to move easily from one place to another, while mechanization made it possible for fewer farmers to work more land. And the possibility of working for cash wages opened up opportunities to accumulate capital and to move it easily, whether for investment or migration.

Improved living conditions and an optimistic view of the future also contributed to increasing birthrates in many areas. People in the past had sometimes limited family size because of resource constraints (often through abortion or infanticide), but they now began to have more children.

Just as birthrates in the United States dropped during the Great Depression and rose after World War II (the "baby boom"), they peaked in Europe during times of peace and prosperity in the nineteenth century. French birthrates peaked after the Peace of Amiens in 1802. Russian birthrates peaked after the freeing of the serfs in 1861. And German birthrates peaked after the formation of the empire in 1871.

Despite a subsequent drop in birthrates in the late nineteenth and early twentieth centuries—as more people moved to cities and larger families were no longer needed to work the land—population growth continued. Advances in medicine and sanitation lowered mortality and increased life expectancy. During the Civil War, health care workers demonstrated that steps as simple as doctors washing their hands between operations and sterilizing instruments dramatically reduced infection. Development of safe water sources, sewer systems, and food preservation technologies also improved health.

The scientific advances of Koch, Lister, and Pasteur provided increased understanding of infectious agents, while the development of general anesthetics, X-rays, and corrective surgery saved countless lives. The invention of antibiotics, such as sulfonamides and penicillin, in the 1930s allowed treatment of many previously fatal infections, and vaccinations protected people against diseases such as smallpox, typhoid, and measles.

THE MODERN ERA

After World War II, relief workers from the United Nations and other organizations introduced these public health measures to the less developed regions of the world. Without the historical constraints of hunger and disease, population growth in those regions has been dramatic—so dramatic that the term "explosion" has sometimes been used to describe it. In some regions growth rates reached 3 to 4 percent annually, which equates to a doubling of population every seventeen to twenty-three years.

It took all of human history for population to reach 1 billion, but barely a century to reach 2 billion. The third billion was added in just thirty years and the fourth in only fifteen years. Today, we're adding another billion people roughly every twelve to thirteen years. If current rates of increase continue, world population will double again in just over forty years.

Population Timeline

Year	Event	World Population
10,000	End of the last Ice Age; humans lived as hunters and gatherers	4,000,000
8000	Agricultural Revolution; domestication of plants and animals	5,000,000
3000	Bronze Age begins; use of wagons and sailing vessels	
2000	Contraceptives in use in Egypt	
1500	Iron Age begins	
1100	Permanent roads in China	
800	Anatomical models used in medical training in India	
A.D. 550	Fall of Rome	250,000,000
615	Petroleum used in Japan	
700	Population explosion in China; first large urban developments	
750	Prime of medicine, pharmacology, optics, chemistry in Arab Spain	
900	Plague, consumption, smallpox, rabies identified by Rhases	
1000	Chinese develop gunpowder	
1200	Alcohol used for medical purposes	
1230	Leprosy imported to Europe by Crusaders	
1233	Coal mined in Newcastle, England	
1290	Invention of spectacles	
1347–1351	Black Death/Plague: 75 million people die	
1416	Dutch fishermen use drift nets	
1492	Europeans discover the Americas	
1495	Syphilis epidemic spreads through Europe	

Year	Event	World Population
1567	Two million South American Indians die of typhoid	450,000,000
1650	Extermination of American Indians begins	
1661	*Fumifugium*, John Evelyn's attack on air pollution, published	
1700	Unmarried women taxed in Berlin	
1750	Industrial Revolution begins in Europe	
1790	First U.S. Census; population, 3.9 million	
1796	Smallpox vaccination introduced	
1800	Beginning of Industrial Revolution in the United States	
1803	Steamboat invented	
1810	Food canning begins	
1824	Sperm essential to fertilization proved	
1825	Passenger railroad	1,000,000,000
1827	Water purification filter developed	
1836	Revolvers and rifles invented	
1846	Irish Potato Famine	
1859	Charles Darwin's *On the Origin of Species by Natural Selection* published	
1863	Hypodermic syringe created	
1866	Dynamite invented	
1883	Synthetic fiber created	
1893	Automobile built	
1903	First airplane flight	1,600,000,000
1915	Margaret Sanger jailed for writing *Family Limitation*, the first book on birth control	
1916	Food shortages and rationing in Europe	
1926	Scopes trial prohibited teaching theory of evolution; repealed in 1967	
1927	Airplanes used to dust crops with insecticide	

Year	Event	World Population
1928	First scheduled television broadcasts	
1936	Hoover Dam completed, creating largest reservoir in world	
1943	Penicillin used against infection	
1945	Atomic bomb detonated	
1946	Discovery of mutations caused by radiation exposure	
1952	Contraceptive pill produced	
1954	Vaccine for polio; U.S. has 6% of world's population, 60% of cars, 34% of railroads	3,000,000,000
1957	Great famine in China; 20 million die	
1966	Moon landing	
1967	Synthetic DNA	
1973	U.S. Supreme Court legalizes abortion in Roe *v.* Wade	
1975	Obstetrician found guilty of manslaughter in legal abortion case	
1977	U.S. tests neutron bomb designed to kill with massive radiation	
1978	Test-tube baby born	
1979	China implements government's one-child family program	
1984	3,300 die, 20,000 injured by industrial toxic fumes in Bhopal, India	5,000,000,000
1994	World population conference, Cairo	
1996	World population: 5.8 billion	5,800,000,000
1998	Kyoto Protocol	
1999	World population: 6 billion	6,000,000,000
2002	World Summit on Sustainable Development, Johannesburg	

Source: Public Broadcasting Service. Available over the Internet at www.pbs.org.

Population Vocabulary

Age Structure: The distribution of people in a population by age. A population is considered young if 35 percent or more of its people are under the age of fifteen, and considered old if 10 percent or more are age sixty-five and older.

Birth and Death Rate: The annual number of births and deaths per one thousand total population. These rates are often referred to as "crude rates" since they do not take a population's age structure into account.

Birth Control: Practices employed by couples that permit sexual intercourse with reduced likelihood of conception. The term is often synonymous with such terms as contraception, fertility control, and family planning.

Carrying Capacity: The maximum number of organisms that an ecosystem can support.

Contraceptive Prevalence: The percentage of couples currently using a contraceptive method.

Doubling Time: The number of years it will take for a population to double, assuming a constant rate of natural increase.

Exponential Growth: A constant rate of growth applied to a continuously growing base, for example, a savings account increasing at compounded interest or a population growing at 3 percent.

Family Planning: The conscious effort of couples to regulate the number and spacing of births. Family planning usually connotes the use of birth control to avoid pregnancy but also includes efforts of couples to induce pregnancy. (Note: U.S. law and the International Conference on Population and Development [ICPD] Program of Action state that "in no case should abortion be promoted as a method of family planning.")

Fertility Rate: The annual number of live births per one thousand women ages fifteen through forty-four.

Fertility: The actual reproductive performance of an individual, a group, or a population.

Growth Rate: The rate at which a population is increasing or decreasing in a given year because of natural increase and net migration, expressed as a percentage of the base population.

High-risk Pregnancies: Pregnancies occurring under the following conditions: too closely spaced, too frequent, mother too young or too old, or accompanied by such high-risk factors as high blood pressure or diabetes.

Immigration: The process of entering one country from another to take up permanent residence.

Infant Mortality Rate: The annual number of deaths of infants under the age of one per one thousand live births.

Maternal Morbidity: The frequency of disease and illness in women due to pregnancy and childbirth.

Maternal Mortality Rate: The annual number of deaths to women due to pregnancy and childbirth complications per one hundred thousand live births.

Natural Increase: The birthrate minus the death rate, implying annual rate of population growth without regard for migration.

Net Migration: The net effect of immigration and emigration on an area's population in a given time period, expressed as an increase or decrease.

Population Increase: The total population increase resulting from the interaction of births, deaths, and migration in a population in a given period.

Population Momentum: The tendency for population growth to continue beyond the time that replacement-level fertility has been achieved because of a relatively high concentration of people in the childbearing years.

Population Projection: Computation of future population numbers, given assumptions about future trends in the rates of fertility, mortality, and migration. Demographers often issue low, medium, and high projections of the same population based on different assumptions of how these rates will change in the future.

Replacement-level Fertility: The level of fertility at which a group of women on the average are having only enough daughters to replace themselves in the population. By definition, replacement level is equal to a net reproduction rate of 1.0. The total fertility rate is also used to indicate replacement-level fertility. In the United States and other industrialized countries, a total fertility rate of 2.1–2.2 is considered to be replacement level.

Reproductive Health: The state of complete physical, mental, and social well-being, and not merely the absence of disease or infirmity, in all matters relating to the reproductive system and to its functions and processes . . . the right of men and women to be informed and to have access to the safe, effective, affordable, and acceptable methods of family planning of their choice, as well as other methods of their choice for the regulation of fertility which are not against the law, and the right of access to appropriate health-care services that will enable women to go safely through pregnancy and childbirth and provide couples with the best chance of having a healthy infant . . . (ICPD Program of Action)

Reproductive Rights: Reproductive rights embrace certain human rights that are already recognized in national laws, international human rights documents, and other consensus documents. These rights include the basic right of all couples and individuals to decide freely and responsibly the number, spacing, and timing of their children and to have the information and means to do so, and the right to attain the highest standard of sexual and reproductive health. Other basic rights include the right to make decisions concerning reproduction free of discrimination, coercion, and violence, as expressed in human rights documents. In the exercise of this right, parents should take into account the needs of their living and future children and their responsibilities toward the community. (ICPD Program of Action)

Stable Population: A population with an unchanging rate of growth and an unchanging age composition, because age-specific birth and death rates have remained constant over a sufficient period.

Sustainable Development: Development that meets the needs of the present without compromising the ability of future generations to meet their own needs. (World Commission on Environment and Development)

Total Fertility Rate (TFR): The average number of children that would be born alive to a woman (or group of women) during her lifetime if she were to pass through her childbearing years conforming to the age-specific fertility rates of a given year.

Zero Population Growth: A population in equilibrium, with a growth rate of zero, achieved when births plus immigration equal deaths plus emigration.

Thanks to the Population Reference Bureau for many definitions.

Permissions

Allyn and Bacon: "Chapter Eight: Disease," by Richard H. Robbins, in *Global Problems and the Culture of Capitalism.* Boston: Allyn and Bacon, 2002. Copyright © 2002 by Pearson Education. Reprinted by permission of the publisher.

American Association for the Advancement of Science: "Population Policy: Will Current Programs Succeed?" by Kingsley Davis, *Science,* vol. 158, issue 3802 (Washington D.C.: 1967). Reprinted with permission from Marta Seoane, Kingsley Davis Estate.

Cambridge University Press: "Concern for Land" by Anthony Young, in *Land Resources: Now and for the Future.* London: Cambridge University Press, 2000, pp.1–24. Reprinted with the permission of Cambridge University Press.

Council on Foreign Relations, Inc.: "Grey Dawn: The Global Aging Process," by Peter G. Peterson, in *Foreign Affairs,* January/February 1999. Reprinted by permission of *Foreign Affairs.* Copyright ©1999 by the Council on Foreign Relations, Inc.

Foreign Policy: The Population Implosion ("Death Makes a Comeback") by Nicholas Eberstadt, in *Foreign Policy,* www.foreignpolicy.com.

Human Life International: "Introduction," and "Trust the Parents," by Robert Whalen, in *Whose Choice? Population Controllers or Yours?* published by Human Life International.

The Independent Institute: "The Scientific Case against the Global Climate Treaty," by S. Fred Singer, in *Hot Talk, Cold Science: Global Warming's Unfinished Debate,* copyright © 1999; "Population Growth: Disaster or Blessing?" by Lord Peter T. Bauer, in *The Independent Review: A Journal of Political Economy* (Summer 1998, vol. III, no. 2, pp. 165–206), copyright © 1998. The Independent Institute, 100 Swan Way, Oakland, CA 94621-1428 USA; info@independent.org; www.independent.org. Reprinted with permission.

McGraw-Hill Companies: "When Globalization Suffers, the Poor Take the Heat," by Gary S. Becker, in *BusinessWeek Online* (April 2003). Copyright © 2003 by The McGraw-Hill Companies, Inc.

National Academies Press: "Executive Summary" and "Introduction," edited by John Bongaarts and Rodolfo A. Bulatao, in *Beyond Six Billion: Forecasting the World's Population.* Reprinted with permission. Copyright © 2000 by the National Academy of Sciences. Courtesy of the National Academies Press, Washington, D.C.

Index

About the Author

KATHRYN E. HENNE is a senior research fellow at the Regulatory Institutions Network, a center housed at the Australian National University. She is the author of articles published in journals that cross a number of disciplines, including *International Journal of the History of Sport, PoLAR: Political and Legal Anthropology Review, Signs: A Journal of Women in Culture and Society,* and *Theoretical Criminology: An International Journal.* She is also the current associate editor of *PoLAR: Political and Legal Anthropology Review.*

CPSIA information can be obtained at www.ICGtesting.com
Printed in the USA
BVOW03s0341300315

393725BV00001B/6/P